TEACHING ADULTS
Third Edition

ALAN ROGERS

OPEN UNIVERSITY PRESS

Open University Press
McGraw-Hill Education
McGraw-Hill House
Shoppenhangers Road
Maidenhead
Berkshire
SL6 2QL
United Kingdom

email: enquiries@openup.co.uk
world wide web: www.openup.co.uk

and
Two Penn Plaza
New York, NY 10121-2289, USA

First edition published 1986
Reprinted 1988, 1989, 1991, 1992, 1993, 1994
Second edition published 1996
Reprinted 1998, 1999, 2000, 2001

First published in this third edition 2002
Reprinted 2003, 2004, 2005

Copyright © Alan Rogers 2002

A catalogue record for this book is available from the British Library.

ISBN 0 335 21099 6 (pbk)

Library of Congress Cataloging-in-Publication Data
Rogers, Alan.
    Teaching adults / Alan Rogers. – 3rd ed.
        p. cm.
    –Includes bibliographical references and index.
        ISBN 0-335-21099-6 (pbk.)
        1. Adult education.   2. Learning.   I. Title.
    LC5214 .R58 2002
    374–dc21   2002021401

Typeset by Graphicraft Limited, Hong Kong
Printed and bound in Great Britain by Biddles Ltd, King's Lynn, Norfolk

CONTENTS

PREFACE AND ACKNOWLEDGEMENTS

This book is about teaching adults in a wide variety of contexts. Most books on adults' learning have tended to concentrate on either non-vocational leisure-type programmes or on vocational, professional and other more formal training courses; rather fewer have addressed themselves to the different forms of community education groups. This book attempts to look at what is common to, and distinctive about, all forms of teaching adults, whether in advanced instructional courses in formal institutions or in informal learning situations, and whether taken by lecturers, teachers, tutors, instructors, supervisors, trainers, extension workers, facilitators or other people in the so-called 'developed' countries or the 'Third World'. It is not intended to be a theoretical work, however, or an academic textbook (although there is something of this in it). Nor is it a book of handy tips for teachers – a manual on how to cope (although again there is something of this in it). Instead it occupies the middle ground. It aims to explore some of the basic principles that I have come to believe teachers of adults will find it helpful to know.

The question is often asked whether there are differences between teaching adult students and teaching younger people. The answer to that question is not simple, because two different things tend to get mixed up: what is good teaching practice in any circumstances and what is special to the teaching of adults. It is not always easy to distinguish between these. What will concern us will be good teaching of adults and the criteria by which we can judge this.

Language

The book is intended for all those who find themselves teaching adults. In these circumstances, language is always a problem. I have throughout used the word 'teacher' (sometimes qualified as 'teacher-planner' or 'teacher-agent') for all these people, although I appreciate that many people prefer the term 'tutor' to indicate the informal relationship between teacher and adult student participants. The true role of the teacher – helping student learners to learn – is no different from that of the tutor. I have also used the form 'student participant' frequently, although it is rather clumsy, to indicate that I do not see the learner as a pupil but as participating in a range of activities that bring about learning.

The possibility of a further edition of this book has provided me with an opportunity to review what had been written more than ten years earlier in rather stressful conditions in Northern Ireland. I was and still am surprised at how much of this still seems to be valid today. The large amount of writing on adult education both in Europe and in North America over recent years has confirmed much of what was then thought. In particular, since 1995 when the second edition was drafted, much important work has appeared in print in relation to adult learning. And the whole scene in which those who teach adults are working has changed radically since the 1980s: the concept of lifelong learning has been taken up by the politicians, and the context of many learning programmes for adults has moved to work-related and institutional settings. The publishers therefore asked me to prepare a further edition taking into account this new material, especially that on lifelong learning.

I have revised the whole text, especially the two chapters which deal with learning and teaching, so that the implications of the distinction I made in the earlier editions between the natural learning processes we all use in our 'learning episodes' and the learning that goes on in assisted/guided/taught learning (a distinction which research into adult learning in specific areas is demonstrating, as Chapter 5 indicates) becomes clearer.

As with the earlier editions, I have tried to make the exercise as practical as possible. The book has been written in association with groups of teachers who have worked through every section of the material presented here. It will be of value not merely to teachers of adults but also to those engaged in tutor training. The material presented in box form represents some of the handouts I used in my training programmes.

Although this book is not about adult education as a sector of the educational scene but about the practical side of teaching adults in different sociocultural contexts, and although I have dealt with the way I see adult education making an impact on contemporary society in my study *Adults Learning for Development* (Rogers 1992), which deals with other areas of adult education, especially its social change objectives, I have added here a very short introduction which covers this field. But this is not the main aim of the book. Its aim is to help all those who teach adults in lifelong learning/education to develop their understandings and skills more fully.

I send it out as my contribution to the discussions about teaching adults and hope it will continue to generate both debate and enhanced practice in the field of helping adults to learn.

Acknowledgements

I must thank all those who have helped in the preparation of this book over many years. In a number of ways it is a product of the corporate experience built up at Nottingham University's Department of Adult Education, and it reflects the work of former colleagues such as Alan Champion, Gordon Douglas and Sam Lilley, and of Paula Allman, John Daines, David Jones and Karl Mackie, all of whom will see something of themselves in these pages. I wish particularly to thank John Fox and Brian Graham, both of whom read an early draft of the text and offered much encouragement. In later years, away from Nottingham, I have many to thank, especially Brian Street who drew my attention to a range of literature I would not normally have read. The book has also gained from the six months I spent at the University of Massachusetts Amherst campus in 1999. I am grateful to all those who have helped to make this a better book, not least the reviewers. Above all I must thank my students, who challenged everything and contributed so much.

Acknowledgement is gladly made for permission to print the extract on pages 183–5 from Clyde Reid's book *Groups Alive – Church Alive* (1969), the 'Poem for Everyman' by John Wood from his collection *How Do You Feel? A Guide to Your Emotions* (1974) on pages 73–4 and the poem by R. D. Laing from *Knots* (1972) on page 76.

Alan Rogers
Uppingham

INTRODUCTION

From certainty to uncertainty

In the 1980s, when the first edition of this book was being prepared on the basis of training programmes for mostly part-time tutors, we were all very certain about adult education. We knew that adult learning was different from the learning of children; and we asserted this difference strongly, perhaps because adult education was a marginal activity in both the educational world and the political world and we felt the need for reassurance. Today, now that adult education (in the form of 'lifelong learning') has moved centre stage in both of these arenas, now that more of those who teach adults are full-timers working in institutions of some sort or another, now that there is a vastly increased literature on adult learning, we are paradoxically much less certain about the distinction.

From deficit to diversity

There are several reasons for this change of mood. One is the growing strength of postmodernist thinking and/or the growing appreciation of the significance to education of anthropological concepts rather than the sociological concepts of the 1970s onwards. This change of climate has been outlined by several writers (e.g. Paulston 1996) in the following terms (for a fuller discussion, see Rogers, forthcoming):

- From the 1940s to the later 1960s, education was dominated by an *orthodox* set of ideologies – i.e., there is one right form of education, and the main aim is to provide this education for all persons as part of the modernisation project. The implication for adults was that adult education was seen as largely remedial, making up the *deficit* of education not received in earlier years, whether this was basic education or more advanced education. In the UK, much Workers Education Association

(WEA) and university extramural education was seen as providing a 'second chance' to adults who for one reason or another had not been able to take advantage of the 'normal' educational provision up to and including university-level education.

- From the later 1960s, education was dominated by a *heterodox* set of ideologies. Education was seen as one of the contributory factors creating rather than remedying inequality. Those who were excluded were seen to be oppressed, *disadvantaged*, not just in deficit. What was needed was a new kind of education, different from the schooling model. The implication for adults was that educational opportunities should be provided not just for personal gain but to address issues of inequality (racial, gender, religious etc.), to lead to individual empowerment and/or social transformation. Adult education was a different form of education specifically for adults, not just an adapted repetition of the schooling of earlier years.
- Since the later 1980s, however, education is becoming dominated by a *heterogeneous* set of ideologies. *Diversity* is the keynote, not deficit or disadvantage. And the aim of education is to promote difference and the understanding and acceptance of difference. The implication for adults is that education is not something which is confined to the early years and of one kind only. Rather, there are many different kinds of education needed by and available to people of all ages and kinds. Explorations of women's ways of knowing are one major part of this emphasis on difference. Thus, instead of trying to help our students to conform to the norm (the orthodox approach) or for all to be 'liberated' in our terms (the disadvantaged approach), some adult educators are seeking for every student to create their own learning in their own way, to 'celebrate the other' rather than to extinguish the other.

So, since I and my readers are all part of this changing scene, it is inevitable that the tone of this book is different from the tone of the first edition. There is (I hope) less certainty, more awareness that most that is said about teaching adults is highly contextualised, contested and contingent. The text stresses some of the differences to be found in the now very wide literature on adult learning and education.

Modes of adult education

I have been accused in some reviews of the earlier editions of omitting the sociopolitical dimensions of adult education. This was deliberate, for several reasons. First, I hoped that the readers would come from a variety of different contexts, and it would be an impossible task to try to sum up all of those contexts (this has in fact proved to be true; the book has been translated into several different languages and is used as far apart as China, India and Greece). Second, I was not sure that readers of the book were interested in my personal picture of what was happening in the field of adult education in the UK – for every history, every attempt to describe what has occurred over the past half a century or more is an individual construct, a personal painting of scenery for the stage on which actions are occurring. But more important than this, I was not writing a book about *adult education* as a sociocultural phenomenon (I did that later). Rather, I was (and still am) trying to help all those, in whatever ideological context they may be, to embark on *helping adults to learn* in their own context – put very simply, to encourage them to investigate that context and to design programmes appropriate to their own and their students' ideologies.

But I have elsewhere indicated my own views on such matters (Rogers 1992). In summary form, I see in Western societies three main forms of education for adults:

- what is often called vocational education (I prefer to use the word 'occupation', for the discourse of 'vocational' education is normally taken as applying to paid work, whereas many adults are engaged in occupations which may not be remunerated in the formal sense);
- social role and socially transformative education; and
- personal growth education.

I see these three strands forming something of a plait, so that over the past 100 years or more, different strands come out on top and the other strands are underneath. At some times and in some contexts, personal growth (e.g. the great liberal tradition) predominated in adult education, with social transformation next and occupational education as less important. At other times, social transformation predominated (e.g. access programmes; social exclusion etc.), with personal growth next, and occupational development again the least privileged. Clearly what happens in each context (e.g. Sweden and France) and what is provided by each agency, government and non-governmental organisation (commercial or welfare) will be different.

The same picture may be drawn another way. It can be argued that one form of adult education is designed to enrich the lives of 'the people', to make them more happy where they are. Another form of adult education is aimed at helping some persons to escape from their existing (marginal and/ or necessitous) way of life into what is seen as a more centrally located or richer one. While yet a third form of adult education seeks to help some people to change the society in which they find themselves. As I have put it elsewhere, we need to decide whether the education we provide for adults is to help them to reconcile themselves to their lot in the slums (make them happier), to help a few of them to escape from the slums, or to help those who live in the slums to change those slums in their own ways rather than in our ways. I know where I stand in this scenario.

Today, in the UK as in much of Western society, under the influence of what is often called post-welfare 'neo-liberalism' (Youngman 2000), occupational education is clearly privileged, although some elements of personal growth and some very minor elements of social transformation still survive. Contemporary adult education is dominated by instrumental concerns rather than empowerment, social transformation or personal fulfilment.

From adult education to lifelong learning

The discourse of adult education came to be replaced by continuing education which emerged as the major discourse in the 1980s. Continuing education was seen as opening formal education to wider groups and extending its range and validity into later life rather than cutting it off in the first two or three decades of life. Courses for adults became more institutionalised (more like 'education') while at the same time distance and open learning 'modes of delivery' took formalised courses off campus. There was an epistemological lurch into the discourses of formal education which took over much of adult education. A useful picture here is that of the athletics match against the marathon. In the marathon, anyone can enter (self-selection); it is collaborative (each entrant helps and encourages the other participants); and the goals are set by the individual entrant (to finish, or just to complete the first 13 miles or so, to race against another competitor or against one's own time in an earlier marathon, etc.), so that all can 'win' in their own terms. In an athletics match on the other hand, only a few who have pre-qualified can enter, selected by others; it is competitive, not collaborative; it is run on a special track, not on normal roads; and only the first three (hierarchically) can 'win' – the rest 'fail'. The main part of adult education up to the late 1980s was much like the marathon, but under the onslaught of continuing education it is fast disappearing today from our society, although its influence can still be felt in some parts of the educational world.

Lifelong learning came along to redress this formalised approach. The revolution in thinking cannot be overstressed: 'Within a generation we have moved from a world where most people could still expect to undertake little or no education or training after adolescence, to one where such education is a condition of economic survival for most if not all. [This has] overturned the notion that education and training are solely a preparation for, and separate from, life and work' (Jarvis 2001a: 25).

Lifelong learning sought to change the focus away from the competitive to the situated, away from institutionalised education to 'lifeworld learning'. It tried to refocus agency onto the individual learner rather than the providing institution – more of the control of one's own learning programme lies with the learner. Perhaps the most valuable element in lifelong learning is its emphasis that all learning is *embedded learning* – it takes place in and from a specific context and returns to affect and shape that context. And it sees 'adult education' (to use what is now something of an out-of-date terminology) as the encouragement and maximisation of learning more than the provision of courses.

But much of the current discourse of lifelong learning has moved away from these issues. For one thing, as we shall see, the concepts of education and learning (which are not the same thing) tend to get confused (see Chapter 5). Secondly, most of the discussions of lifelong learning are economic in nature, accredited vocational training of a new kind, and more of the adult learning settings are work related. There have been some attempts to reconcile lifelong learning with social transformation education but they find it hard to make their voices heard, except perhaps in the new social movements (Mayo 1997; Foley 1999). And the personal growth element in lifelong education seems at the moment to be mainly confined to what is somewhat patronisingly called 'third age learning' (Jarvis 2001b). But these elements are still there and I do not doubt that they will grow stronger over the years to come. The plait still exists and it is constantly changing as power changes.

For underlying all forms of education, including and perhaps especially adult education, lies the question of power. Discourses are created and perpetuated by special interest groups who seek to use them as an instrument of hegemony to control the value systems of other people. We need to ask, in all the teaching of adults we do, whose interests are being served? For lifelong education does not come without a price tag, and it serves the interests of particular sections of society. It has been shown that in any society some forms of knowledge are privileged above others (Barr 1999), and we need to ask ourselves whether the adult education we are engaged in reflects rather than challenges these dominant concepts.

Why lifelong learning now?

The question arises as to why the discourse of lifelong learning (something which adult education practitioners have been urging on power-brokers for many decades) has suddenly been taken up by governments, firms and educational institutions who previously had no sympathy with adult education *per se*. I do not believe it is related directly to the information and communication revolution which has created an entirely new environment for the education and training of adults. Rather, it would seem to me that in part the answer is money. Profits can be made from lifelong education, an inheritance from continuing education. The commercial elements in society have brought about the consumerisation of education; the participants are now customers or clients. This is the reason why the practice of lifelong education is largely confined to the vocational strand of the plait;

and why the personal and the socially transformative strands have become demeaned (that is, I think, largely the fault of those adult educators in the 1960s and 1970s like myself who signally failed to assert strongly enough the socially purposive nature of liberal adult education). Again, huge changes have come about in what is called 'civil society' (like lifelong learning, a term of many colours). The older social movements (e.g. trade unions) are being replaced with new social movements (e.g. environmental pressure groups); the role of government *vis-à-vis* both commercial interests and civil society has changed and is still changing.

But I suspect that the main reason for the predominance of the lifelong learning/education discourse today is that the formal systems of education, finding that various forms of adult education were growing in strength and social purposefulness, have co-opted adult education by redesignating it as lifelong education. They have expanded their empires. They are asserting their claim to be the standard by which the effectiveness of all educational activities (including what you and I do in teaching adults) may be judged. But then I have never had any great love for the arrogance of the learned – even though I have benefited personally from their institutions and programmes. Which is perhaps why, throughout this edition of the book, I have retained from time to time the term 'adult education' rather than the uncertainties of 'lifelong learning/education'.

What is the implication of all of this for the readers of this book? Is it just an interesting sideshow? I suggest that perhaps we all need to ask ourselves what we are doing when we seek to teach adults; how far our programmes are persuading our students into a norm set by ourselves or our institutions (reducing deficit); how far we are helping the students to reflect critically on their own situation and to overcome oppression leading to a more equitable society (challenging disadvantage); or how far we are encouraging our students to become different from each other and at the same time appreciative of these differences (increasing diversity). We teachers are, I feel, at the forefront of promoting uniformity, transforming society or increasing and welcoming diversity. These are questions which should really be posed at the end of this book, not at the beginning; but it is not easy to put an introduction at the end of anything.

Further reading

Aspin, D., Chapman, J., Hatton, M. and Sawano, Y. (eds) (2001) *International Handbook of Lifelong Learning*. London: Kluwer.

Barr, J. (1999) *Liberating Knowledge: Research, Feminism and Adult Education*. Leicester: NIACE.

Coben, D. (1998) *Radical Heroes: Gramsci, Freire and the Politics of Adult Education*. London: Garland.

Field, J. and Leicester, M. (2000) *Lifelong Learning: Education Across the Lifespan.* London: Taylor & Francis.

Fieldhouse, R. (1996) *A History of Modern British Adult Education.* Leicester: NIACE.

Jarvis, P. (ed.) (2001) *The Age of Learning.* London: Kogan Page.

Rogers, A. (1992) *Adults Learning for Development.* London: Cassell.

Welton, M. (ed.) (1995) *In Defense of the Lifeworld: Critical Perspectives on Adult Learning.* New York: SUNY.

Youngman, F. (2000) *The Political Economy of Adult Education.* London: Zed.

BEFORE YOU START

I am assuming that, as a reader of this book, you are a practising teacher of adults, or that you are responsible for organising programmes for adults, or that you hope at some time to teach adults. Whichever of these is true of you, you bring with you a good deal of experience and expectation. The best way of relating to the material that follows would be for you to make it concrete for yourself, to apply it to some immediate situation; for this book is not intended to be a theoretical discussion but a practical examination of some of the principles of teaching adults.

You may therefore find it helpful, before you go any further, to choose an example of a learning programme that you have taught, are going to teach or would like to teach to adults, for which you have been or are responsible, or have attended as a student participant – any situation, in fact, in which you can envisage yourself in a position of teacher in relation to a group of real or imaginary students. It will, I think, help if you write it out here before you start. You might care to answer the following questions briefly:

What is the subject of the learning programme?

How long is the programme and how often will the group meet?

Who and how many are the students?

Where and at what time will the group meet?

You can keep turning back to this case study as you read the rest of the book and fill it out in more detail.

Chapter 1

A CONTRACT TO LEARN

How do we come to be here . . . ?

It has on occasion been suggested that the most important factor which adults bring to their learning is their experience. In this chapter, I suggest that equally important are the expectations and the agendas which adult student learners bring and that these are in large part created by the information about the learning programme which we supply to the prospective participants.

Teaching adults: a world of difference

People engage in teaching adults in many different contexts and for many different purposes.

Sometimes the *context* is formal, within the walls of one of our educational institutions. At other times the teaching takes place through an organisation specifically set up to help adults learn like an industrial training agency or professional body. Or again it may be within one of a host of informal situations: community and voluntary associations, social movements and women's groups, sports agencies, churches, museums and libraries, or among members of the rescue and caring professions.

The *formats and settings* are many. People teach adults formally or informally in prisons and church halls, in colleges and private houses, in sports and leisure centres and in factories, in shops and offices, in community buildings and military bases, in schools and specialist adult education centres, in health clinics and on university campuses, in training centres and temporary caravans. They teach during the day, in the evening, at weekends and while on holiday. They can teach face to face or by distance learning methods.

Sometimes the *process* is a direct one – a structured course on management or computers, or retraining in new techniques of construction, an extension course for farmers, a woodwork class or church confirmation group, a diploma or degree programme. Sometimes it is less direct – a residents' group fighting a planning proposal, a choir rehearsing, a health group striving to use a controlled diet, a group of villagers setting up a cooperative, a drama group putting on a performance.

And it is undertaken for a variety of *purposes* – to lead to qualifications, or changed personal attitudes, or the development of the community, or new skills for work purposes or for hobbies, or the improvement of basic skills, or to open doors to further learning or the increase of confidence.

Activity

Write notes on your chosen learning programme as follows:

- setting: would you say that it is formal or informal?

- format and context:

- process: would you say that it is direct or indirect?

- purpose:

The field we operate in, the teaching of adults, is thus a vast one with a myriad of different expressions, confusing because unlike schooling and college education, it seems to lack structure and form. Anywhere where two or three people are gathered together to learn something on a systematic basis under supervision, someone is found teaching adults.

It may be helpful to distinguish between three main adult education sectors (Figure 1.1):

- *formal* – courses and classes run by schools, colleges, universities and other statutory and non-statutory agencies making up the educational system;
- *'extra-formal'* – courses and classes run by formal agencies *outside* the educational system, for example other government departments, industrial training agencies, trade unions and commercial concerns (what are sometimes called today 'learning providers');
- *informal* – educational activities engaged in by voluntary agencies and informal groups.

	Qualification courses	Vocational courses	Personal growth courses	Basic/access courses	Community development
Formal: statutory bodies, educational • general programmes open to adults, e.g. schools/colleges/universities • special provision for adults, e.g. extramural/Open University/advanced continuing education/industrial training bodies/adult literacy agencies/technical training and validating bodies	School-leaving certificates/diplomas/degrees/higher degrees	Short courses and conferences/management/information technology	Non-vocational 'liberal' adult education	New opportunities/return to study	
Extra-formal: courses provided by central or locally administered public bodies and other agencies outside the formal educational system • training agencies/government departments/army/prisons/sports bodies/arts and cultural agencies/museums and libraries • trade unions/firms and businesses/professional associations/mass media	Certificates and other awards	Shop stewards/shopfloor training/farmers' training schemes	Health (smoking)/alcohol/pregnancy/family planning/nutrition/sports and hobbies/cultural		
Informal: voluntary bodies • primarily educational, e.g. WEA/adult literacy agencies/private colleges/correspondence courses • primarily non-educational, e.g. aid and welfare organisations/churches/community groups/unemployed workers' groups/self-help groups	Some non-professional certificates		Leisure/crafts/do-it-yourself/art Residents' programmes/planning/weight-watchers	Basic education	Women's programmes/unemployed programmes/retirement courses/marriage guidance

Figure 1.1 A possible taxonomy of teaching adults, with examples

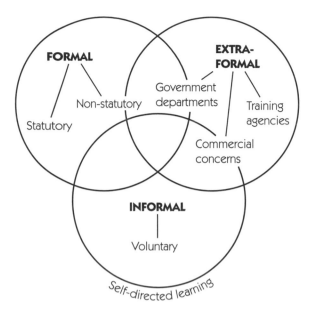

Figure 1.2 The sectors of education for adults (you may find it helpful to locate the learning programme(s) you are involved in on this figure, if you can)

The categories partly overlap, since informal programmes may be provided by formal agencies and many informal bodies run very formal learning programmes (Figure 1.2).

There are in addition non-taught *self-programming groups of adults*, study circles without a face-to-face teacher such as a natural history society. There is also the area of *self-directed learning*. The latter comprises educational opportunities for individuals provided by bodies like broadcasting organisations, correspondence agencies and publishers of books. Web-based and distance education are forms of self-directed learning. One of the most extensive modes of adult learning are those journals and magazines that mount programmes of study in subjects like cooking, dressmaking, do-it-yourself, woodworking, computing, health and beauty, and gardening, all of which attract large audiences. Self-directed learning opportunities are also provided by numerous cultural organisations offering musical and dramatic events, public lectures, art exhibitions, visits to places of environmental and historic interest and the like – activities that an adult may choose to take up on their own (or with their family) in order to follow a special interest and to achieve a particular accomplishment, whether related to their job or not (Brookfield 1985).

A number of different ideologies lie behind these various forms of teaching adults, and they affect the way we as teachers of adults react. The most important of these relate to the objectives of the learning programme, and the involvement or non-involvement of the student participants in the planning process. Some programmes are offered with clearly identified and specific pre-set objectives, especially those in the training field. Others are offered with more open-ended goals, such as personal growth (see Chapter 6). Most programmes lie somewhere between these two extremes. Equally, some programmes are organised with and some without consultation with the prospective participants; again, each teaching-learning activity lies somewhere along the continuum formed by these two opposites (Figure 1.3). The determination of both of these matters is a question of policy on the part of the providing agency.

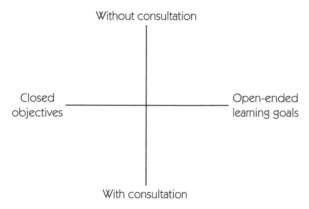

Figure 1.3 Organisation of adult learning programmes

Activity

You may wish to plot where on Figure 1.3 your own learning programme comes.

Such issues reflect the distinction that needs to be drawn in most cases between the *providers* (organisations, institutions or individuals who plan the programme and outline the various parts of it) and the *teachers*. There are today a number of intermediate agencies – bodies who act as a servicing intermediary between providers and student participants (and sometimes between providers and employers for their workforces – e.g. Learning Partnerships). Thus the relationship between teacher and provider in the many different forms of adult learning programmes is often a complex one and varies from context to context. In some parts of the non-formal sector (e.g. the churches), teachers and providers may be one and the same person; and in all cases, the teacher is a planner of the learning situation as much as an instructor (see Chapter 8). But the interests of provider/organiser and teacher are in many respects different, and it is well to bear this distinction in mind. The construction of the learning programme can then be a matter for negotiation between provider, intermediary agency, employer and teacher; but in the end it is the *student participant* who will respond to the learning opportunity on offer, who will determine whether to take up the programme or not.

Agreeing to learn together

It is factors like this which mark the education of adults off from other sectors of education. Apart from other matters, teaching adults is different from other educational programmes

* because the organisation of learning is different;
* because the relationship between the teacher and the student participants is different.

Adult participation is voluntary and purposeful

Two characteristics are common to virtually all forms of teaching adults. The first is that *the participants are voluntary learners*. Those who come as student participants to the programmes being offered come out of choice, and the teachers who come face to face with them are confronted by people who in most cases have selected their teachers rather than the other way about. There are, it is true, a number of forms of adult learning in which the freedom of the participant is somewhat circumscribed (see p. 71). Programmes of industrial training or staff development provided by firms, for example, are at times less than fully voluntary. Pressures may be exerted on some people to attend learning programmes when they would rather be somewhere else. So it is necessary to keep some qualification in mind when we speak of the voluntary nature of the adult student. Nevertheless the adult nature of the participants means that they are attending programmes of education because they have decided for one reason or another to be there and not to be elsewhere.

Second, *they have come with an agenda*, an intention, in most cases to achieve a learning goal. Again, we need to bear in mind some qualification to this general statement. Some will have come more for social reasons than for the immediate learning, while others may not always know clearly what they want, or may want one thing and in fact find achievement in something different. Those who are there because they have been told to come may have less clear intentions than the others. Nevertheless, they each come for a purpose – and if they don't get it, sooner or later they will stop coming. There are, it is true, cases of adults staying in learning programmes from which they are getting little for long periods out of politeness or a sense of loyalty, but in the end they will usually drop out.

Two conclusions follow:

- The provider and the teacher in programmes for adults need to *attract* participants into their programmes. The key word in all the many varied fields of adult learning programmes is 'offer'. The providing agency offers a learning opportunity, and the individual or organisation determines whether to accept the offer.
- This means that a *bargain* has been struck. A (usually unspoken) agreement is concluded between the provider/teacher and the learner: that the one will offer the learning opportunity and that the other will work to achieve some goal or other. This is true not only of those cases where the programme has been negotiated between the provider (and/or the teacher) and the potential participants, where the terms of the engagement may be set out in some detail. It is also true when the organisers devise the programme without such negotiation. The terms of the bargain may not be set out in full, but an agreement is there nonetheless.

A contract to learn

An agreement exists, then, in all forms of teaching adults. There are major differences among those who teach adults concerning the nature of adult education and its goals and objectives. Some providers and teachers see their main function as imparting skills or knowledge; they instruct their students. Some see their aim as the development of awareness, comprehension and understanding; they involve their students in discussion and other activities. Others see their purpose in more general terms as influencing attitudes (especially confidence building) and, through this, behaviour; they pursue a more active engagement with the participants in simulation and other exercises. Yet others see their role in a less directive fashion as providing opportunities for the participants to learn what they want to learn in their own way, to grow and develop, to explore for themselves, to engage in critical reflection, to come to their own conclusions, to finish up in a place determined not by the teacher but by the learner.

These differences do not negate the proposition that an agreement has been struck between teacher/provider and learner. It takes a different form for each type of teaching-learning programme. But what will not be in doubt is the willingness of the teacher-agent to set up the learning environment and programme, and the agreement of the participant to engage in a series of activities in order to achieve certain outcomes. A contract[1] between the student-learner on the one side and the provider and/or the teacher on the other side exists, however vague it may be.

The information provided

Such an agreement is based on a series of assumptions made by both teacher and adult participant even before the two have met. Neither teachers nor learners start with a blank sheet. The teachers begin with a set of ideas about who the students will be and what they will be teaching. The participants have some idea of what they want and what they are going to get.

Most of these assumptions are unspoken, even when a process of consultation with prospective student participants has been engaged in or when the learning programme is set out in detail. For on both sides there are hidden presuppositions about the process on which they are embarking. These presuppositions may not be true, but to a large extent they determine the effectiveness of the learning process.

The assumptions of the potential participant are created in part by calling into play views developed over many years and also, and particularly, by interpreting the information given about the programme on offer. This latter varies widely. In educational institutions such as universities, the information is usually included in the institutional brochure and conforms to the format dictated by that institution. In general adult education, at its minimum, the programme publicity gives some indication of the subject (usually a title), format (frequency of meeting and length of time involved), location and timing, and the institution or organisation under whose umbrella the programme is being provided. There is sometimes a 'blurb' containing information about the content of the programme of study. The following examples[2] reveal something of the range of information offered to potential student participants.

From a local authority leisure and learning programme consisting of four sectors (accredited courses, pathways to learning, leisure courses and sports):

---

1 The phrase 'learning contract' has been used to describe a particular form of educational encounter, but I am using the word 'contract' here in a more general sense as applying to all forms of teaching adults.

2 Most of the examples come from programmes on offer in the years 2000–2.

Monday					
Clarinet tuition	4 p.m. onwards	17.9.01. to 26.11.01.	10 weeks	Tutor FMcC	£100
Yoga	10–11.30 a.m.	17.9.01. to 26.11.01.	10 weeks	Tutor MT	£30
Still Life	2.15–4.15 p.m.	17.9.01. to 26.11.01.	10 weeks	Tutor MS	£40
An Introduction to Herbs and Health	7–9 p.m.	17.9.01. to 26.11.01.	10 weeks	Tutor FC	£40
Basic Photography	7–9 p.m.	17.9.01. to 26.11.01.	10 weeks	Tutor DB	£40

From a field studies centre (run by a commercial concern):

July 8/9th	Dry Stone Walling	[name of centre]	10 a.m.–4 p.m.	£30 per weekend
July 10/14th	Painting course with AO (watercolours)	[name of centre]	9.30 a.m.–4 p.m.	£125 per person for the week
July 28th	An Evening with the Moths	[name of centre]	Tutor JH 8.15 p.m.	£3 per person

Sometimes more detail is provided. From a university open studies programme:

Genetics: Modern Frankenstein

Genetics impinge on all aspects of life today – we clone pigs, modify soya and tomatoes and diagnose diseases in the unborn. In this course we will examine the science underpinning the modern genetic revolution and look at the possible consequences of genetic modification for society and ethics.

Tutors: RM BSc, PhD and PH BSc, PhD	7–9 p.m.	Starting date: 7 March
10 meetings	10 credits	Fee: £40.50

Meeting place: School of Continuing Education, University of . . . [site given].

From a commercial agency describing itself as The World Leader in Vendor-Independent Training for IT Professionals':

FrontPage 2000 Website Development: Hands-On

[*A whole page in an elaborate catalogue of courses, covering the following items:*]
You Will Learn To: (7 items)
Course Benefits
Who Should Attend
Course 207 Content
Hands-On: Throughout this course, extensive hands-on exercises guide you through the design and creation of a fully functional website. Exercises, performed under the guidance of an expert instructor [not named] include: (8 items)
Yours FREE To Take Home: a CD of Web-related software to aid site creation
4-Day Courses, Tuesday to Friday in LONDON [dates given]
This course helps you to prepare for Microsoft professional certification exam(s)
The fees are set out elsewhere in the brochure at £1495 for a standard 4-Day course (£473 for a 10-Course Passport and other tariffs)

Such information, even the briefest, immediately creates a set of expectations. For example, the implication of

---

Monday Still Life 2.15–4.15 p.m. 17.9.01. to 10 weeks Tutor MS £40
26.11.01.

---

in an adult and community education service programme is clear. A series of meetings will be held on each Monday afternoon for a set number of weeks in a suitable (designated) building, open to anyone of either sex who wishes to attend (however inexperienced they may be) and who pays the relevant fee. A series of activities will be undertaken, the intended outcome of which will be a person more able to create and/or appreciate still-life paintings. All this and more can be read into those few words viewed in the context of the rest of the brochure.

Balancing publicity against the contract to learn

As we can see, the information provided for potential participants about the contract on offer is often very limited. It is argued by some providers that this is due to the lack of resources available to many adult education agencies, but frequently it is because organisers do not see the necessity of giving more detail. In these cases, the material produced is primarily issued as publicity for the programme rather than as a description of the learning agreement. Its main aim is to persuade the readers to join the learning programme.

This desire to attract participants into our programmes often leads providers to feel that they dare not say too much about what is involved in their programmes in case they 'put people off'. The publicity aspect predominates, and the search for striking phrases sometimes outweighs the informative content ('Whose Afraid of Virgins and Wolves?' for a course on myths and legends, for example).

But some planners argue that there is no need for more than a list of titles with dates and times of meeting and cost:

Thursday	7.30 p.m.	Beehive Construction	Starting 21 September	£30

The potential learners do not need to know the name of the teacher. It is enough (so the argument goes) for them to know that if they turn up on Thursday evenings in the place and at the time specified, pay the stated fee and do the work (unspecified), they will be taught how to make a beehive.

But such a list will only appeal to those who already know a good deal about the subject – to those, for example, who know that 'still life' refers to paintings. It provides no indication of the level of work intended, of the demands to be made upon the learners, of the entry requirements for each course, and so on. The organiser tends to assume that all these pieces of information are already known by the reader. But they may not be. Is the beehive construction course intended for the expert-carpenter-but-novice-apiarist or for the expert-apiarist-but-novice-woodworker – or for both?

The omission of details reveals much about the assumptions of the organisers. Some tend to rely on the reputation of the providing agency for the credibility of what they offer. They base their constructed learning programmes on their experience of previous student participants. The fact that the programme is run by such-and-such university, local authority, college, voluntary body or training organisation is to them enough indication and guarantee of the kind and quality of the learning programmes offered.

But whether it is enough to persuade new participants to join in these programmes must be doubted. Potential student participants need to have enough information if they are to formulate in their own minds whether to accept the proffered contract of learning: what the learning programme is all about, what is expected of them and what they themselves might expect to gain from the experience. Simple lists of titles, unless backed up by other information, will frequently lead to a good deal of uncertainty even on the part of those participants who do come, and it will take some time once the learning programme has commenced to resolve this uncertainty.

Books and blurbs
We can illustrate all of this by looking at books. Books are often a form of adult learning opportunity; they offer the chance to their readers to pursue a course of activity (reading) that will lead to some more or less concrete result (greater understanding, satisfied interest or more developed skills etc). They thus make a bargain with their readers, a contract.

This book is itself an example of such a learning contract. It is intended for those who know or wish to know something about teaching adults. If you experiment on the basis of it, then you will have an opportunity to reassess your teaching of adults and to examine possible alternative approaches. You can use the book entirely as you please, reading some bits and skipping others; you can use it to achieve your own purposes. It is a tool of your self-directed learning. In fact this is its main aim, to become a resource for you to reflect critically on your teaching of adults. This is the contract this book offers and by which it should be judged.

The contracts offered by books are usually drawn up unilaterally by the publisher and/or the author. There can rarely be any process of consultation, and there is little the reader can do to change the terms of the contract. Sometimes the terms of the offer are expressed in the title and the name of the author without further detail. To take an example at random from my shelves, *Strategies for Lifelong Learning: A Symposium from Europe and the USA* (1981) has nothing other than the title to indicate what the book is all about. But this is very rare today; in almost all cases, a blurb on the dustjacket or cover serves as both publicity to sell the book and as an information sheet. In many cases, the contract is set out in more detail in the introduction, indicating what the book is about, who the author is, how it came to be written and who it is intended for. But however it is presented, the prospective purchasers in each case must make up their minds, on the basis of the information provided (including the appearance of the book, its illustrations, format, length and price), what sort of opportunity is being offered and whether to accept it or not.

A similar situation exists in teaching adults. The information needed to attract potential students into our programmes and to set out for them the terms of the learning contract is much the same: a title, a statement of the format of the programme, a note of the teacher and of the cost of the learning programme, and some description of the content of the learning programme – an indication of the market at which the programme is aimed and the intended outcomes of the experience.

The parts to the contract

The different parts of the statement we produce about our learning programmes need further discussion.

As with some books, the *title* is on occasion chosen more for its euphony or intended striking qualities than for the light it throws on the subject matter. This may be adequate for those student-learners who come back year after year to the same sort of programme and who have grown accustomed to the stylistic habits of the organiser, but it does not always help to draw new people into our programmes. 'Men under Masters', without any further elaboration, is not exactly indicative that a study of local history in a nineteenth-century industrial town is intended.

Few publishers would think of issuing a book without the name of the author; but many organisers issue adult learning programmes without the name of the *teacher*. Those who are considering whether or not to accept the learning contract we offer have the right to know who the teachers are and what expertise and experience they possess. On other occasions, a name without further information is provided. It is assumed that the institution will guarantee the individual's expertise as both authority and teacher, or that these persons will be well known to potential participants either as 'a good teacher' or as an expert because of their other activities. In these cases, recruitment of students is largely confined to those who know of the teacher and their immediate circle. At other times, the teachers will be endorsed by the qualifications or position they hold or by the experience they can bring to the task.

More frequently, there is a *description* of the subject matter of the learning programme. This is often short and uninformative. We expect the learners to have some idea about the subject they want to learn before they come to our programmes. A full description of the course may not be possible or desirable, but the prospective participant is entitled to know something of what the programme of work will be about, what sort of learning is expected to take place, what the purpose of the exercise is, at what level and for how long the programme will continue, who the learning programme is intended for and what sort of activity they may expect to be engaged in. For example:

Management for the 21st Century

BF, MBA, IPFA, DMA, MBIM. Six lectures commencing 3 October 2001, 7–9 p.m. Fee: £415 [location given].

The course will explore the range of techniques, skills and behavioural styles available to the modern manager including decision-making techniques; leadership and motivation; communications; personnel and the management of change. It is intended to meet participants' needs as far as possible and will use discussion groups, practical exercises and consciousness-raising techniques.

Course texts: J.A.F. Stoner and R.E. Freeman, *Management* (1991); F. Luthans, *Organizational Behavior* (1992); R.D. Donnelly, *The Role of the Manager* (1993).

Selecting the participants

At times such blurbs spell out the target group or level of commitment, experience or ability that the programme calls for from the participants, particularly any pre-requirements set by the teacher. A school-leaving certificate course provided for adults, such as 'GCSE Biology', makes this clear, as do those programmes which contain specific reference to such levels. From a community college brochure 2000–1:

Title	*Prerequisite*	*Suitable for*	*Start date*	*Day and time*	*Number of sessions*	*Course fee*
Introduction to Excel	None	Anyone	9 May	Wed 4–7 p.m.	1	Free
Excel workshop	Basic Excel skills	Excel users	16 May	Wed 4–7 p.m.	1	Free

At times, the title is the giveaway: 'Italian Beginners', 'Computing for the Terrified', 'Pitman Bookkeeping and Accounts Levels 1 and 2' or 'Drug Therapy Update for GPs'. Or this is done in the descriptive blurb: 'This introductory course . . .' or 'This advanced language course . . .'. However, even then we leave it to the readers to decide for themselves whether the levels *they* have in mind are the same as ours.

At other times more indirect methods are employed – the selective use of language, for example – to indicate the level of the programme and to select the participants. A one-day 'PowerPoint Workshop' will appeal only to those who know what PowerPoint means. Courses entitled 'Assertiveness for Women: Never Say Yes When You Mean No', 'The First Five Years: Mother and Child Relationships', 'Return to Study', 'Bookkeeping for Small Businesses' and 'Law for the Householder' all select their own audience and indicate the level by the choice of words.

Language may be used in the description even more pointedly to select some and to exclude others. The inclusion of specialist names and the presence of long or technical terms will normally put off anyone not already acquainted with the subject. Carefully chosen language is sometimes deliberately employed in this way to exclude some persons (Figure 1.4).

But often the language used in titles and descriptions is careless and inconsistent. For example, courses entitled 'Peace as an Ecumenical Imperative' and 'The Methodology of Consumerism' may well put off precisely those for whom they are intended. On occasion, the blurb can contradict itself. The course on child psychology which states that it is designed to appeal to mothers of young children who have no prior knowledge of child development will nevertheless discourage precisely this same group by sprinkling the blurb with names like Skinner, Laing, Bruner, Maslow and Piaget, as if the teacher wished, even before the classes have started, to

Figure 1.4 A learning contract designed to deter the novice from attending

show how much they know. Such unthinking internal contradictions occur time and again in the programmes offered to adults.

Creating the contract

But the contract to learn is not entirely the responsibility of the person who drafts the programme publicity and information sheet. All three parties to the adult learning experience – the organiser or providing agency, the teacher and the potential student participants – are actively involved in drawing up the contract (Figure 1.5).

Providing agency and the contract

The organiser establishes the parameters to the learning opportunity – the context, including the rest of the programme within which the course is set;

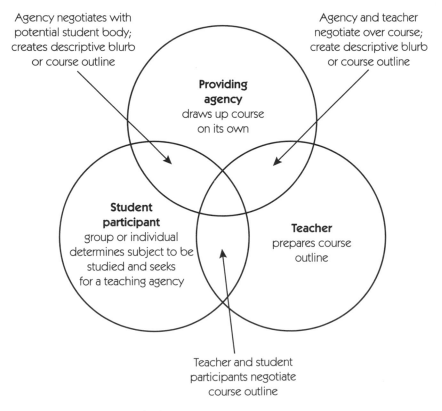

Figure 1.5 Drawing up the learning contract

the subject; the format (location, number of meetings, time and duration of each meeting); the modes of publicity. They may do all of this on their own, or in association with the teacher, and/or after discussion with a prospective student group. Where a professional association, residents' group, local society or similar body exists, it is possible to discuss in advance what they want to learn and in what way, and increasingly adult teaching bodies are discussing future programmes with firms and other potential 'customers'. But on other occasions such opportunities, even where they exist, are not taken. The organisers determine by themselves or in discussion with their teachers what they think the potential student participants should learn and how. Certificated programmes are governed by the regulations of the institution or authority which provides or accredits them, such as the length of terms. Access courses are run in accordance with the requirements of the approved curriculum rather than the requirements of the student-learners; basic skills programmes are bound to some extent by government regulations. The framework within which each adult learning opportunity stands has today an increasing influence on the provision, to the detriment of the other partners, the teacher and/or the participants.

The teacher and the contract

There are occasions when the teacher is excluded from the discussion. The organisers build up a course outline and then find someone to teach 'their' programme. This is especially true of certificated programmes. In these cases, the teachers take over a contract already created and fit their work to that. But it is often also true of more open adult learning programmes. If, for example, we are asked to take a ten-meeting course for beginners on upholstery or an introduction to Excel, the parameters have already been set, irrespective of whether we feel that ten meetings constitute an appropriate length of time for beginners to master anything meaningful about upholstery or Excel, or not.

On other occasions the teacher is a party to the construction of the learning opportunity. This is often our first task – to determine what is to be taught, how much can be covered and at what level, how it should be taught, to whom and to what purpose. Again, like the organiser, we may do it on our own, or in association with the providing agency, or in consultation with prospective learners.

The programme devised by the teacher is constructed for the student participants. The contract to learn is made with them; it is not between the teacher and the providing agency (a different contract may be in force there). The organisers will of course be keen to see what we have in mind to teach; in most cases they will be able to offer advice based on practical experience on matters of both publicity and course content. It is thus worth our while to discuss the outline with the providing agency. But the contract of learning is not directly made with that body. Nor is it made for other teachers, examining boards, professional associations, local education committees, educational institutions or academic colleagues. The contract is made directly with the potential student participants; it is the first point of contact between teacher and learner.

In most cases, we are required to draw up the agreement before we meet the potential student participants, even before we know who the learners will be. This problem is often a severe one. One answer that has sometimes been proposed, and which is probably the worst of all possible worlds, is to do no planning at all – to wait until we meet the student learners for the first time. But normally this is impractical. We need to establish the subject areas of the programme just to call together the prospective participants. Where a group already exists, it is possible for us to meet them and to determine the outlines of the programme of learning jointly; but even here our expertise as teacher or group leader and our experience in this type of programme are called upon to indicate the realistic limits of what can be achieved in any given length of time, and to set out practical proposals for a programme of work. The task of planning the learning programme normally falls to the teacher, however much we may negotiate with the potential student participants in the process.

But we are not completely free in drawing up our proposals. First, we are limited by the context within which we are teaching. The format of the programme has usually been set already – by custom, by the organising institution or by negotiation with the learners – and this may impose restrictions on what can be done. Many aspects may already have been fixed for us when planning our programme:

- the *length of the programme* (frequently determined by traditional school or university terms, although courses other than the 'one-term/semester' or '20-meeting' variety are growing, determined by the time the learners have available, the time needed to master some skill or branch of study, or costs);
- its *frequency of meeting* (often weekly, although more flexible formats are becoming more common);
- the *duration of the class meeting* (usually one and a half or two hours, but again more flexible arrangements are appearing, especially weekend and day-release courses).

The participants may have more say in the timing of the programme and its location, although this seems to be becoming rarer as continuing and life-long education become more institutionalised.

Activity

You might care to indicate, in connection with your own learning programme (described on page 8) whether these areas of planning were undertaken by yourself, were 'given' to you or were agreed jointly with the planner; and whether the students determined any of them:

Teacher Planner Jointly Students

The length of the programme

The frequency of meeting

The duration of the
class session

The timing of the meetings

The location of the
course/programme

Second, we are limited by our view of the prospective students. Consciously or unconsciously, we make a range of decisions about who they will be, how much they already know about the subject, what they want to learn, how much work they will expect to do and what sort of activities they will be prepared or be able to engage in. We may be wrong in all of this. They may not be willing to play games, hand in written work, bring specimens for classwork, even read set texts. They may not be able because of their life circumstances to undertake some of the work we plan for them. But in our planning we make assumptions on all these matters. The programme we draw up is not a question of what we as teachers alone want. Using our experience, we produce a balance between what we have to offer and what we assume the student participants may or may not be looking for, or what they may or may not be willing and able to do.

The learner and the contract

The potential student-learner is fully participant in the contract-making process. Although the terms of the offer are initially drawn up by the provider and/or the teacher, the readers are nevertheless active in interpreting what they read. They are the third party to the contract. They do not passively accept or reject what is on offer, but interpret the material presented to them in the light of their existing knowledge and experience, and their intentions. They assess, often unconsciously, the language in which the programme is set out. They weigh up the context in which the learning programme is being provided – this, as they see it, will control the course or at least give it its orientation. They will bear in mind the building in which it is located, the title of the body that has organised it, what they know about the teacher, and so on. And they will decide on the basis of what they see and what they assume whether the programme will meet their intentions or not.

Potential students have to work with what they are given. In some cases they can deduce from the material provided something about the nature of the programme. But more often, in interpreting the contract, they have to fall back on other experience and knowledge, such as what they know about the institution providing the programme.

The population at large seems to have fairly fixed expectations of what each of the main providing bodies offers in the way of adult programmes. For example, learning programmes organised by statutory agencies and their constituent centres are often (rightly or wrongly) judged to be more directive and practical in nature, while those provided by voluntary bodies are seen to be more participatory and with a measure of social concern lacking in local authority programmes. Programmes offered by voluntary agencies will, it is thought, be informal rather than formal in teaching-learning styles. Those organised by industrial, commercial and other training bodies are considered more intensive and exclusively vocational (even narrow) in content. University continuing education programmes are thought of as being aimed mainly at professional and other qualified individuals who require these programmes for their career advancement. In the UK, programmes offered by further education colleges are in general felt to be more technical and those offered by universities more academic. WEA-type classes are frequently assumed to be introductory in level and university programmes to be more advanced, appealing to those who already have some educational attainments.

None of this is strictly true, but these views influence behaviour. Thus, some people attend learning programmes offered by an advanced training institution because of their expectations of what will happen to them and of how useful the programme will be, while these same people will not go near exactly similar classes offered by a voluntary body such as the WEA – and vice versa. However much one may wish to change the image of the body concerned, it is difficult to do so.

Adult participants thus choose the institution which they deem will best serve their purposes, their agendas. For adults come to learning opportunities and programmes with a goal in mind, to fulfil a desire or intention. They will often search for the programme which best fits their plans and their conditions (the Internet is making this easier for many persons). When presented with a programme brochure, they do not simplistically accept what is printed but make their own meanings out of it – and decide on the basis of what they create whether to join the programme or not.

Understandings and misunderstandings

The prospective learners are, then, active participants in the process of creating the contract by interpreting what they read. Frequently those who prepare learning programmes for adults do little to help them. What may be in the mind of a minister when it is announced that there will be a study group for the next eight Thursday evenings in the church hall (or parsonage lounge) on 'The Letters of St Paul' may not be the same as the expectations that such an announcement will create in the minds of the hearers. Some of them will not come, feeling that they could not cope with the work required; others will attend out of loyalty to person or institution. A number will come in anticipation of getting something out of the programme, but will not be sure what it is they are expected to get. The organisers may well not have clarified for themselves whether the intended outcome will be a greater understanding of that part of the New Testament, or a greater liking of reading the Bible in general, or changed moral attitudes leading to changed patterns of behaviour. A contract exists but it is vague because much of it has been left unformulated.

Much then is presumed by all three active partners to the process of creating the contract to learn (Figure 1.6). There is a range of assumptions in the mind of the organiser – about the subject, about the purpose of the programme, about the student participants, about the teacher. There is a series of expectations and objectives in the mind of the teacher – about what the providing agency wishes, what the student participants want or are able to do, and what are the most important aspects of the subject being studied. Equally, the processes of publicising the programme and recruiting voluntary adult participants arouse a set of expectations in the minds of the potential students. With so much unstated, to expect any real match between these three sets of assumptions is asking too much. The potential for uncertainty, for misunderstanding, for hindrances to learning and even for conflict, when the basic premises of all parties have been so ill-stated, is great. Effective learning calls for the contract to be set out more clearly and if possible agreed by all sides.

Once the group has met, the teacher and student-learners can together explore the nature of the bargain they have made. It is useful for the teacher

Figure 1.6 The contract to learn – hidden assumptions

of any group of adults to try to discover at the start what sort of expectations each of the group members has drawn up in their own mind from the publicity material. We as teachers also need to spell out more fully our own expectations. This can be done through a course outline, presented to the student participants for discussion. Such a procedure enables us to test the assumptions we have made and to amend the proposed schedule of work (if possible) in the light of this reassessment. And it enables the participants to adjust their expectations if necessary and to decide whether to renew or cancel their commitment to the programme on offer in the light of their own intentions.

What this book is all about

We can illustrate this by looking at this book as an example of a contract. It has arisen out of courses I have conducted with various groups of teachers of adults in the UK and abroad. Some were full-time professional teachers of adults; others were part-timers. Several were people who do not see their primary role as educational (e.g. clergy and health visitors) but who have come to realise that they spend much of their time teaching adults. The illustrative material used in the book reflects its origins, and is drawn from a wide variety of settings.

The book follows the sequence of the courses I have taught over many years. The programme starts by trying to define what we mean by the terms 'adult' and 'education' (Chapter 2) and 'adult student' (Chapter 3). It then examines the concepts of learning (Chapter 4) and teaching (Chapter 5).

The second section of the book concentrates on planning the learning programme, setting the goals and objectives of the learning programme (Chapter 6), forming and running the learning group (Chapter 7), exploring the roles of the teacher and the participants in the group (Chapter 8), and choosing the methods used in teaching adults (Chapter 9). The final section deals with making the programme effective – discussing blocks to learning (Chapter 10) and the necessity for constant evaluation (Chapter 11). The book is rounded off with a plea for greater student participation in all parts of what is really their own process of learning – a plea which is even more relevant today than when it was first written (Chapter 12).

The fact that this book has arisen directly out of my teaching has caused some problems in ordering the material. In teaching it is often necessary to repeat what has gone before; in a book, such repetition needs to be avoided as far as possible. I have tried to cut repetition down to a minimum.

Learning to teach
The book is based on the premise that as teachers of adults we have much to learn about our craft. I was pressed to call the book some variation on *Adults Learning* rather than *Teaching Adults* in order to stress that adult learning programmes are student-centred, that teachers of adults should be more concerned with what their students are doing than with what teachers are doing. While I agree with the basic concern being expressed, I have resisted this pressure. Teaching is an activity that calls for a range of attitudes, skills, knowledge and understanding on the part of the teacher, and all of these need to be learned. This book is about learning to teach. It provides a learning opportunity for the teacher of adults – not just to discuss how adult learners learn but how the teacher can so plan and act as to help them to learn more effectively.

I am conscious that to adopt this approach may seem to be too directive. Some will feel that the book allows inadequate scope for choice on the part of its readers, that it seems to be too concerned with 'right' attitudes, 'right' practice, and not enough concerned with personal growth. I hope this is not true, that its concentration on basic principles rather than specific methods will allow for the maximum individual interpretation. But a book is by nature a partial tool of adult education. It cannot establish that two-way learning process lying at the heart of all good adult education. It can build on the experience of the reader only to a limited extent.

Nevertheless, used as a tool it can do something. You can read its various sections in any order you like, starting with the material which is most relevant to your particular circumstances, your immediate concerns. For it is important that you, the reader, control your own learning. You will need to relate the material discussed to your own experience and use it to reflect critically on your experience. A number of activities have been suggested to help you to do this, but you can ignore these and devise your own means of active involvement with the subject matter in these pages. However, without some activity relating the material to your own situation, the discussions will remain remote from real life. Most of the book will be concerned with matter with which you are familiar. It is not trying to tell you anything new. Rather, it attempts to encourage you to make conscious what you are doing or planning to do, to explore it more fully for yourself and to systematise it.

Writing a contract of learning

Many teachers of adults assume that student participants choose to come to our programmes because they understand what it is we are offering them. We are on occasion surprised to find that they have something different in mind when they come. Frequently we put the blame onto them; we allege that they have not read the programme description carefully enough. But we as teachers rarely make enough effort to make the contract explicit. It would be a valuable exercise both for our own sakes and for the sake of the student participants to set it all out clearly: if you (who?) do this (what?) under my supervision (why?), you will learn . . . (what?).

The main medium for setting this out is the publicity notice. It may thus be a useful exercise for you to look at the description, if one exists, for the learning programme that you proposed for yourself on page 8; if one does not exist, you could try to write one now. It then needs to be examined in the light of what we have been saying in this chapter. What does it say, not merely as a piece of publicity but as a learning contract? Whom will it attract as potential voluntary participants and whom will it deter? What image will they gain from it of the course or programme on offer? How much will they be able to deduce from the notice and how much from the context in which the programme is being offered? Will there be contradictions and confusions, or will blurb and context complement each other?

It is then possible to proceed to a fuller version of our learning contract. In this, we will need to be much clearer about the objectives we wish to achieve and the steps to be taken in order to achieve them. The contract is not with our colleagues or our employing agency; it is with the potential student participants even if we have never seen them. The contract will need to address itself at least to the following items:

- What is the learning programme all about? What is its subject? What will it cover and at what level?
- What is the format of the programme? How long will it last? What are the frequency and duration of the meetings? What work will it call for between group meetings?
- Who is the programme for? What preliminary knowledge or experience is required? How will you make sure that the right kinds of student participant gets to know about the programme and are persuaded to join it?

- What will the programme of work be? What sort of learning do we expect to take place?
- What is the purpose of the exercise? In what ways will the learners be different at the end of the programme of work?
  (If you are currently teaching a group of adult students, you could invite them to do the same exercise and see if there is any mismatch between their understanding of the learning contract and yours; at least you can get them to discuss the outline you have prepared in this way.)

Such a statement is not final. Once we have met the participants, once we and they have embarked on the process of learning together, we may find it necessary to renegotiate the contract, sometimes more than once as the programme progresses. This is part of the creative process of teaching adults. But the fact that the contract to learn has to be renegotiated in this way is not a reason to refuse to think about it from the start, to leave it until later. Because our students have chosen to study with us, to accept our package out of all those on offer, we need to make sure that both we and they are clear what that package is.

Our first task, then, as teachers of adults, will be either to draw up for our prospective student-learners an outline of the programme or to interpret in more detail the outline prepared by others. The importance of this is that it will:

- help to determine who will be admitted into and who will be excluded from our programme;
- help the participants to decide whether our programme will meet what they see as their agendas or not; and
- help to create the expectations about the programme with which the student-learners will first come, and which will to a large extent determine whether the programme is effective or not.

We need to be *very careful* when we draw up our learning programme outline.

Further reading

Chickering, A.W. (ed.) (1981) *The Modern American College: Responding to the New Realities of Diverse Students and a Changing Society*. San Francisco, CA: Jossey Bass.

Edwards, R., Sieminski, S. and Zeldin, D. (eds) (1993) *Adult Learners, Education and Training*. London: Routledge.

Stephens, M.D. (1990) *Adult Education*. London: Cassell.

Thorpe, M., Edwards, R. and Hanson, A. (1993) *Culture and Processes of Adult Learning*. London: Routledge.

Tight, M. (ed.) (1983) *Adult Learning and Education*, vol. 2. Beckenham: Croom Helm.

DEFINITIONS

What do we mean by . . . ?

The meaning of the terms we use affects how we view the subject. This chapter discusses how people construct for themselves the concepts of 'adult', 'education' and 'adult education'. It suggests that inherent in all 'teaching' is a tension which determines much of what the teacher is able to do.

Teaching adults is often equated with adult education but the two may not be the same. Education is the wider context within which teaching takes place, so that adult (and now lifelong) education is the context for teaching adults. We therefore need to try to understand what is meant by adult education before concentrating more closely on teaching adults.

The search for understanding: adult education

Much ink has been spilt on trying to determine what we mean by the words 'adult', 'education' and 'adult education' but there is still confusion. Despite the fact that, mainly in the form of continuing education and more recently lifelong education, adult education is becoming increasingly important in the public eye, a good deal of uncertainty exists as to what these terms mean. As Cross (1981), speaking of 'lifelong learning', said to her United States readers: 'It is quite possible that lifelong learning now outranks motherhood, apple pie and the flag as a universal good. Almost everyone is in favour of lifelong learning, despite mounting confusion over the meaning of the term'. But in spite of the problems, it is worth persevering with trying to understand the concepts that lie at the heart of what we want to do – to teach adults.

A number of different terms have been coined in an attempt to overcome some of the problems seen to be inherent in the expression 'adult education', each of them conveying some additional information or idea. It is important to remember that the different terms used represent different ideologies and that the meanings and value systems they indicate change over time:

- *'Continuing education'* – this term has changed its meaning from its emergence in the 1960s. At first, it stressed the unity of education, for children and for adults – 'from the cradle to the grave'; education continues throughout life. Gradually however it came to have a more limited meaning: education which is planned for adults who are returning to the formal educational system of schools and colleges, people who in America are called 'non-traditional students' and who form a major focus of interest in adult education (Davies 1995). And even more narrowly, the term is often used to mean professional and vocationally oriented training programmes at advanced levels for adults who have already received a good deal of education. 'Continuing education' is thus increasingly being seen in narrower, not wider terms, as institution-controlled learning programmes.
- *'Recurrent education'* is another such phrase. It embraces schooling as well as adult education, and stresses the right of individuals to enter, leave and re-enter the educational world at will. In particular, it calls for the reform of the formal schooling system to accommodate the needs of new groups of learners. Special concern has been shown by many of those who advocate 'recurrent education' for older-aged student participants, for whom a number of special learning programmes have emerged.
- *'Lifelong learning'* and the French term *education permanente* are also used, with slightly different meanings; but both see education as built into the process of living rather than as separated into a range of special classroom and study activities.
- *'Non-formal education'* describes all out-of-school education for any group of any age. It refers not merely to the format of this education but also to the contents, which are seen to be more life-related than the traditional school curriculum, and to the processes which are claimed to be more interactive and participatory than directive (see Rogers, forthcoming).

Comparing adult education

Part of the reason for the lack of agreement is the search for a definition that will embrace the very diverse educational cultures of (for example) Ireland, Indonesia and Indiana, so that the practice of adult education in all countries can be compared. Some people hope that an overriding conceptual framework can be devised to cover what is one of the most culture-bound of all activities. As a result of this concern, international statements defining adult education have become longer and increasingly involved in an attempt to suit all places and all conditions. The Organization for

Economic Cooperation and Development (OECD), for example, indicated its belief that

> adult education refers to any learning activity or programme deliber-
> ately designed by a providing agent to satisfy any training need or
> interest that may be experienced at any stage in his or her life by
> a person that is over the statutory school-leaving age and whose
> principal activity is no longer in education. Its ambit thus spans non-
> vocational, vocational, general, formal and non-formal studies as well
> as education with a collective social purpose.
>
> (OECD 1977)

The United Nations Educational, Scientific and Cultural Organization (UNESCO), concerned for the so-called 'developing countries' as well as the West, has a wider view of the scope of adult education: 'organised pro-grammes of education provided for the benefit of and adapted to the needs of persons not in the regular school and university system and generally older than 15 . . . organised and sustained instruction designed to communic-ate a combination of knowledge, skills and understanding valuable for all the activities of life' (UNESCO 1975a: 4).

It thus includes:

> the entire body of educational processes, whatever the content, level or
> method, whether formal or otherwise, whether they prolong or replace
> initial education in schools, colleges and universities, as well as ap-
> prenticeship, whereby persons regarded as adult by the society to which
> they belong develop their abilities, enrich their knowledge, improve
> their technical or professional qualifications, or turn them in a new
> direction and bring about changes in their attitudes or behaviour in the
> twofold perspective of full personal development and participation in
> balanced and independent social, economic and cultural development.
>
> (UNESCO 1976)

Perhaps the broadest definition of adult education is that of the (then) National Institute of Adult Education (now NIACE), England and Wales:

> any kind of education for people who are old enough to work, vote,
> fight and marry and who have completed the cycle of continuous
> education commenced in childhood. They may want to make up for
> limited schooling, to pass examinations, to learn basic skills of trade
> and profession or to master new working processes. They may turn
> to it because they want to understand themselves and their world
> better and to act in the light of their understanding, or they may go to
> classes for the pleasure they can get from developing talents and skills
> – intellectual, aesthetic, physical or practical. They may not even 'go to

classes'; they may find what they want from books or broadcasts or take guidance by post from a tutor they never meet. They may find education without a label by sharing in common pursuits with like-minded people.

(NIACE 1970: 10)

Post-initial education

The term 'post-initial education' for a time came to command a good deal of support as a description of adult education. It is implicit in the NIACE statement of 1970, and the term is used in the Nairobi Declaration (UNESCO 1976), while a number of reports relied heavily on the idea, if not the term itself. The Advisory Council for Adult and Continuing Education (ACACE) wrote that understanding the term 'adult education' would be assisted:

> if a major distinction was made between 'initial' and 'post-initial' education. This is a more basic distinction than such kinds of administrative divisions as 'compulsory' and 'post-compulsory'. The initial education stage would obviously include going to school, including nursery school, but it could go on full- or part-time into the mid-20s. After compulsory schooling, initial education takes a wide variety of forms: full-time study in sixth form, university, college, polytechnic, medical school, military academy and so on; part-time day-release; evening classes and correspondence courses; on-the-job training in the factory.

(ACACE 1979: 9–10)

All education after this is post-initial – that is, adult education. The Alexander Report for Scotland used the term 'initial education' to mean all educational experiences undertaken by a person prior to the time of taking up a first full-time career post (which may of course be long delayed). On this basis, initial education includes:

> all school-based or compulsory education and also the education of those who go straight from school to university or college in pursuit of higher qualifications. In addition we regard those whose immediate post-school employment involves vocational day-release or sandwich courses or apprenticeship training schemes as still undergoing initial education. All educational experience which an individual undergoes subsequent to or additional to this initial education we term continuing education [the phrase Alexander preferred to 'adult education'].

(Alexander 1975)

In Northern Ireland, (adult or) continuing education is seen in similar terms: 'Continuing education is regarded as any education which adults voluntarily undertake, excepting that which they pursue full-time or part-time directly following the period of their compulsory education' (NICCE 1980: 10).

The report of the Adult Education Commission for the Republic of Ireland (Department of Education, Ireland 1984: 9) used a definition that is only slightly different: 'Adult education includes all systematic learning by adults which contributes to their development as individuals and as members of the community and of society apart from full-time instruction received by persons as part of their uninterrupted initial education and training'.

The idea thus implies that an individual engages in a preliminary period of initial education starting at the age of 3, 4, 5 or 6 in most countries, and ending at some age usually between 12 and 24 according to whether they leave school at the earliest possible moment or stay on at college or university, or at institutions offering professional studies. At the end of this period, all people of whatever age who 'return' to education after a gap are engaged in 'adult education' (Figure 2.1).

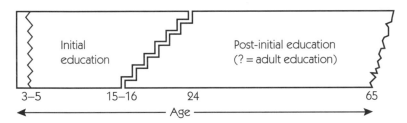

Figure 2.1 Initial and post-initial education in the lifespan of the population

There are however several difficulties with such a definition. First, applying this concept to those countries where a considerable number of people receive no initial education at all, or where there is a high drop-out rate at various ages between 6 and 16, is not easy. Even in the West the distinction between the end of initial education and the beginning of adult education is not always straightforward, especially as new forms of initial education are emerging. Does adult education cover those many young people who nowadays leave initial education for a short period and then return to it in the form of day-release or block-release programmes, part-time courses, youth training schemes and other activities where they may join older persons in search of some means of qualifying themselves for a job? What about those compulsory training programmes that some people are required to take during their first years in post under their contract of employment (in the banks, for instance)? Are graduates who take further full-time training courses to make themselves more attractive to a prospective employer still in initial education or in post-initial education? What about the person who after leaving school does one or two years' accountancy or architecture (for example) and then goes to university or college for professional training? What about those people who continue their initial education through distance or open learning modes while working?

More important, from the teacher's point of view, is the decision as to what courses and programmes constitute 'post-initial' education. Is a training course or school-leaving certificate course (for example, in a college of further education) attended by both school-leavers *and* returning adults (a 'mixed economy' course) initial or post-initial education? This is a matter of considerable import to both provider and teacher.

Activity

Would you define the course in your case study as:

• initial education; or

• post-initial education?

A definition of adult education which sees it in terms of post-initial education – that is, as part of the *structures* of a hierarchical educational system ranging from primary (or pre-primary) through secondary and third-level education, all of which comprise initial education and are followed sequentially by post-initial or adult education – would seem to be unsatisfactory. Perhaps this is the reason why lifelong learning has emerged as a non-sectoral and over-arching concept for all education, and why searches for definitions of adult, continuing and even lifelong education no longer feature so prominently in the publications on adult learning today.

A different way forward may be to try to examine the distinctiveness of education for adults as lying in its *process*. To understand this process, we need to look in more detail at the meaning of the terms 'adult', 'education' and 'adult education'.

Adult

A wide range of concepts is invoked when we use the term 'adult'. The word can refer to a *stage* in the life cycle: each individual is first a child, then a youth, then an adult. It can refer to *status*, an acceptance by society that the person concerned has completed their novitiate and are (or should be) incorporated more fully into the community. It can refer to a social *subset*: adults as distinct from children. Or it can include a set of *ideals and values*: adulthood.

Most people tend to think of 'adult' in terms of age. But no single age can define an adult even within one society, let alone on a comparative basis, because legal and social liabilities come into play at different ages. We have only to think of voting, getting married, fighting for one's country, holding property, buying a drink or cigarettes, being sued, incurring sentences, obtaining credit, driving a vehicle, engaging in paid labour or attending various forms of entertainment – all of which have age-related restrictions applied to them – to see that we cannot say an individual becomes fully adult at any specific age. There are many who feel hesitant about using the legal school-leaving age, which varies from country to country, even in the West; and the legal age of majority is lower than the end of initial education for many people.

Some definitions are clearly inadequate. For example, in one study, an adult 'is defined as anyone either age twenty-one or over, married, or the head of a household' (Johnstone and Rivera 1965: 26). Another asserts that 'The taking on of social roles characteristic of adulthood – roles such as worker, spouse or partner, voter, and parent – differentiates adults from children better than chronological age does' (Merriam and Cafarella 1999: 393).

The problem of defining an adult – and a non-adult – is so great that at times those bodies with greatest experience of making such definitions give up. UNESCO in 1976 determined that adults are those people whom their own society deems to be adult. An adult is both self-recognising and recognised by others. And this is important, for adulthood, like childhood, is a social construct. While in part both of these concepts have a biological basis (physical growth and psychological development), the implications of these changes, how they are understood, and the social reactions to them are cultural. Both adults and children consist of an *experience* (being a child, being an adult). Both too are active in determining their own lives – even children, with their own folklore, language, laws and games etc.

Adulthood seems in every culture to be contrasted with childhood. There are a number of issues relating to the way different cultures construct childhood. In some contexts, childhood is a very short period, in which case adulthood starts early. Among other groups, however, childhood is long, and adulthood therefore appears to be 'delayed'. For some, childhood is a period of innocence, for others it is an age in which self-centredness needs to be disciplined (socialisation), while yet others follow the adage of Shakespeare that there is nothing good nor bad but nature makes it so. In some contexts, it is believed that children need to be isolated from the real world, cherished, kept in dependence, while in other constructs the opposite is felt: children need to be integrated into the society of which they form a part, to be encouraged into independence. All are agreed that adults are different from (indeed, in most cultures the opposite of) children. They are the fulfilment of what is partial in children. Whereas children are 'growing up', adults are 'grown ups'; they have (in that sense) 'arrived'.

Characteristics of adulthood

We need therefore to identify those characteristics inherent within the specific cultural construct of adulthood. In every culture, there is a series of expectations about those who claim and who are recognised to be adults, though these will vary from individual to individual and from culture to culture. Characteristics such as far-sightedness, self-control, established and acceptable values, security, experience and autonomy are among the most common ones advanced, although not all of us would claim that to be an adult a person needs to possess all these traits.

Maturity

Western humanist educators such as Houle and Carl Rogers have developed this theme most fully. Three main clusters of ideas seem to lie within their construct of adulthood (Figure 2.2). First, the term is used in the sense of being *fully grown*. An overriding concept behind the word 'adult' is that of maturity. In the natural world, we speak of a mature tree or mature cheese as being fully developed. When applied to human beings, the word bears stronger overtones than it does in respect of the natural world. Human maturity is not just a state (though we can recognise the characteristics of a mature person) but also an ideal to be aimed at rather than achieved in full. Nevertheless it still includes the idea of the *full development* and utilisation of all the individual's talents; and the process of moving towards ever greater maturity is one acknowledged as being associated with adulthood.

Perspective

The other two clusters of ideas linked with adulthood may be seen most clearly by looking at the opposite construct, childishness. There are occasions

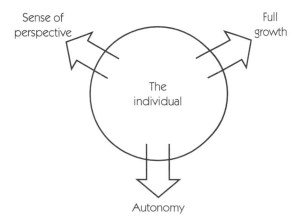

Figure 2.2 The (Western) concepts of the adult and aspiring adulthood

when an older person in many cultures is regarded as behaving 'childishly', in a non-adult fashion. Such childishness may consist of the individual seeing themselves as either being more important than they are seen by others to be, or conversely as less important than they really are. The former throws a tantrum, acts petulantly, makes a fuss and is frequently further infuriated by the accusation of childish behaviour; the latter withdraws, sulks or submits passively, normally accepting the charge of childishness with less hostility. In both cases 'adults' are expected to behave with a greater sense of perspective than is being shown, a perspective that will lead to sounder judgements about themselves and about others. We expect adults to have accumulated experience that, if drawn upon, will help them achieve a *more balanced* approach to life and to society, to be more developed in their thinking in relation to others.

Autonomy
Associated with this is the third element of adulthood, *responsibility*. One of the key concepts of being adult and not being childish is that of being responsible for oneself, for one's deeds and development. One study defines people as 'adults because they have assumed responsibility for managing their own lives' (cited in Merriam and Cafarella 1999: 393):

> To say that someone is an adult is to say that he [*sic*] is entitled, for example, to a wide-ranging freedom of life-style and to a full participation in the making of social decisions; and it is also to say that he is obliged, among other things, to be mindful of his own deepest interests and to carry a full share of the burdens involved in conducting society and transmitting its benefits. His adulthood consists in his full employment of such rights and his full subjection to such responsibilities.
>
> (Paterson 1979: 10)

Frequently the adult is responsible for others as well, but at the very least they are responsible for their own actions and reactions. The adult can decide not to be responsible in some respect or other, but this surrender of self-reference may be seen by others as a denial of adulthood. Adulthood implies some measure of autonomy, responsible decision-making, voluntariness rather than involuntariness. It is important that we do not assume that children do not have any autonomy. They do; and development can be seen as the widening of autonomy from a base which already exists. But in most cultures, adulthood is associated with a major level of autonomy and decision-making.

Adulthood, then, in each of these three aspects is seen by such writers as an ideal towards which each person is struggling – never fully attained but always more or less clearly set out before us. There is in each person, these humanists assert, a drive towards becoming more mature, more 'balanced' and more responsible.

However, such definitions may apply in Western cultures but they clearly are not appropriate to other cultures. Hungry people have not developed anything like their full maturity or potential. Slum dwellers, slaves and refugees are certainly not independent but oppressed. And it is not easy to take a balanced view of life while under conflict or threat from natural disasters. And yet in these contexts there are still adults.

Other cultures therefore see adulthood in different terms, often the opposite to Western cultural values. In many groups in China, for example, adulthood is seen in terms of 'family continuity, socially prescribed roles, the acceptance of hierarchical relationships as supreme, compliance with authority [rather than autonomy and individual responsibility], a value on stability versus change . . . an identity that is externally ascribed, subordinated to the collective, seeks fulfilment through the performance of duty . . . highly malleable', characterised by 'a group-oriented way of thinking [rather than] an individual focus' (Pratt 1991: 302; Merriam and Cafarella 1999: 129–30, 334).

Adulthood and teaching

These three characteristics – maturity, perspective and autonomy – are traits that mark off the socially accepted adult from the non-adult in some societies. If we accept them, they will carry profound implications for us as teachers. They can help to establish both the aims and the curriculum of the teaching we provide for adults (Figure 2.3). Our programmes and courses, if they are to confirm and not deny the adulthood of our student participants, will seek:

- to promote *personal growth*, the identification and full exploitation of the talents of the individual;

Adulthood	'Childishness'	Implications for goals of teaching
Personal growth/ fully developed	Nascent talents, changing interests	Full development and exploitation of talents and interests
Perspective/mature judgements about others and self	Lack of perspective: • over-important • too humble	Development of sense of perspective
Autonomy/self-reference	Flight from responsibility	Development of confidence/ practice of responsibility and decision-making

Figure 2.3 Adulthood and teaching

- to encourage the development of a sense of *perspective*;
- to foster confidence, the power of choice and action, to increase *autonomy* rather than to deny it.

If the content and the material of the learning programmes we conduct and the methods we employ in them do not tend to help our student participants to become more mature, more balanced and more self-determining, then we are denying the adult nature of those we are teaching.

Activity

In what ways does the learning programme you specified earlier (see p. 8):

- encourage the full development of each of the student participants?

- help to develop their sense of perspective?

- help to develop confidence, autonomy, self-direction?

Diversity within unity

But such an approach, useful as it is for teachers of adults, lays stress on the similarities between adults by drawing a clear-cut distinction between adults and younger persons. It treats adults and children more as entities than as collections of different individuals and groups. And it hides the wide range of differences which exist among both children and adults.

In any society, there will be many different concepts of adulthood, not just one. And persons can use more than one concept of adulthood if it suits their particular ambitions and agendas. Studies of indigenous cultures suggest that not only do many of these reveal a concept of adulthood (the ideal self) 'founded upon traditional tribal values, orientations and principles . . . environmental relationships, myths, visionary tradition, traditional arts, tribal community, and nature-centered spirituality' which are missing from Western constructs of adulthood, but that those who live in such cultures will '*simultaneously* use the most appropriate concepts, technologies, and content of modern education' to seek to develop their own idealised self (Merriam and Cafarella 1999: 130–1). Concepts of adulthood are changing all the time and are often mixed.

Thus, being an adult will change from group to group and over time. Studies of groups of women in India show how their concepts of adulthood altered as they met different situations in their lives: 'The pace of the transformation has been relatively "fast" or "slow" for different categories of women, depending on their socio-economic status, education and place of habitation' (Verma 1995: 161). Identifying such diversities may in the long run be more important than deciding who is and who is not an adult in any particular culture.

The importance of all this for us as teachers of adults would seem to be the necessity for us to ask – within our own cultural boundaries – how the concept of adulthood is constructed: how are adults in our society differentiated from children and adolescents? What do we and our students mean by the term 'adult'?

Education

The term 'education', like 'adult', is used in several different (often very negative) senses. For some, it means a *system* of institutions which aim to provide learning opportunities, usually state-run and promulgating state-dominated ideologies. This is too narrow a sense, for 'education' is much wider than a system. For others (especially in the lifelong learning discourses) its meaning has been extended to cover *all forms of learning*, whether inside or outside of any institution. Indeed, on occasion that is how the word is used in daily life. It is not uncommon to hear people say that an activity such as travel or going to a nightclub was an 'education'. What they mean is that they learned a lot from the experience. But this meaning is much too wide to make real sense of what is happening, for education is not simply the same as learning, though it includes learning. A more reasonable position envisions education as a *process* of assisted or guided learning. This too may have a negative connotation in that it often (but not always) implies some form of manipulation which imposes particular views on others. But it is not necessary for us to accept such a negative view; and we may adopt this definition for our purposes.

If, then, we can take education to mean 'assisted learning', it means that what we are doing (teaching adults) is education, even if it occurs outside of any specifically 'educational' context. An adult helping a child to learn cooking in a kitchen is educating that child. A person showing a friend or neighbour how to fill in a form is teaching that friend or neighbour. Teaching is not the same as instructing: it can be argued that someone preparing distance learning materials is 'teaching' as much as someone working in a classroom with a learning group. Both are 'helping others to learn'.

Learning throughout life

Such an approach depends on a distinction between assisted ('taught') learning and unassisted learning. As we shall see in more detail later (see Chapter 5), learning is an activity in which we take part all the time in the course of everyday living. It is the process by which we face, cope with and use our experience. Throughout our lives we face situations in our work, in our domestic settings and in our wider relationships that were not conceived of when we were at school or college, and they all call for new learning. Such continued learning is an informal natural process, performed as we interact with our sociocultural context.

We learn as we enter new *social roles* – as wage earner, as householder, as spouse, parent and grandparent, as voter and member of a local community. What is more, society is constantly revising its interpretation of those roles; today's parents adopt postures towards their children and towards the rest of society often very different from the postures adopted by *their* parents. How we relate to other people is one area that calls for constant new learning.

We need to learn to meet the changing demands of our various *occupations*, whether heart surgeon, historian or handicraft expert. All the tasks we engage in, whether they comprise paid employment or work in the home, call for new knowledge, new skills and new attitudes at various stages. There are some senior posts (e.g. in government and the churches, education and commerce) for which there is no form of initial education and which therefore have to be learned 'on the job'. Some occupations make constant calls for major readjustments and new learning, while others require fewer changes. Even those who are unemployed find themselves engaged in a series of tasks that demand new learning.

As we change and grow older, there are corresponding changes in our personal interests, ambitions and desires. The need to learn as part of our individual development, for our *self-fulfilment*, is a major element in these lifelong learning activities. As some skills decline, new ones are learned; new interests replace earlier ones. Marbles give way to antiques, outdoor pursuits to less energetic ones.

And many of us feel the need to learn before we embark on wider and more structured schemes of self-improvement and education. We read up before we travel; we look at magazines or manuals in preparation for a task we have set ourselves; we develop our study skills before starting a formal learning programme. We learn *in preparation* for further purposeful learning.

These four main areas are not of course entirely discrete. Learning in relation to our job may also be part of self-fulfilment and personal growth; so too may social role learning. But they do provide a general guide to the main groups of challenges which call for learning activities.

Learning and education

Most of this learning is done incidentally, from many new kinds of experience and perceptions: for example, from advertisements, news items, chance meetings and accidents. All of these provide us with learning opportunities (often unintended) which we may seize upon or pass over as we feel inclined. All leave marks on us, some more and some less permanent. This natural learning is part of the process of living.

But such incidental learning that occurs at random throughout life is not 'education'. Education includes learning, which is its essential ingredient, as flour is of bread. Nevertheless, flour on its own is not bread; learning on its own is not education. The OECD definition of adult education as 'learning opportunities for adults' is not adequate, for such learning opportunities exist in a haphazard fashion all around us, whereas education occurs at specific times. There are times when we are not engaged in education, even though we are learning; something more is needed to make learning into education.

Education is planned learning

Education then can be seen as an artificial creation, unlike the natural learning processes. Harold Wiltshire draws a distinction between the two when he describes education as being:

> planned processes of learning undertaken by intent, the sort of thing that commonly (though not by any means always) goes on in classrooms and that involves some who are teachers and some who are taught . . . In much discussion of adult 'education', the word is used much more loosely. Thus in much French writing about '*education populaire*' it seems to be used so as to include the whole range and apparatus of leisure-time activities – cinemas, libraries, television and sports clubs – on the grounds that these exert an educative influence on people who use them and are therefore aspects of education. Certainly there is a sense in which anything that happens to us, from getting drunk to listening to Beethoven, may be said to be 'quite an education'; and certainly we learn (living tissue can hardly help doing so) from our experiences, including those of our leisure. But such learning is unplanned and largely unintended: we do not go into either the pub or the concert-hall with a primary intention of learning. If we intend to learn we behave differently: we join a class or buy an instruction manual; we adopt the role of student and submit ourselves to a planned process of tuition.
>
> (Wiltshire, cited in Rogers 1977: 136–7)

Education, then, consists of planned learning opportunities, constructed and purposeful activities, wherever it takes place. Words like 'structured', 'development', 'cumulative', 'sequential' and 'progress' are associated with the concept of education. To take just one example, the UNESCO report on *Educational Radio and Television* (1975b) stated that 'educational' broadcasts are marked off from other programmes by the fact that:

- their purpose is to contribute to *systematic* growth;
- they form a *continuum* of provision;
- they are so planned that their effect is *cumulative*.

Some broadcasters in their desire to widen the scope of 'educational' programmes have doubted this definition, but it still seems to be a satisfactory one.

The aim of all this planning, preparation and review is to promote and to direct learning. Education may therefore be seen as the provision of organised conditions for learning to take place, a means of providing learner support and assistance. It is aimed at maximising effective learning.

Education involves at least two parties. On the one hand there is the agent (e.g. a formal educational institution such as a college or university, a firm or business, a voluntary organisation or church, a publisher, editor or correspondence course writer) or the teacher, or both. They plan the learning opportunity and assist the learning. They intend certain outcomes to spring from their planning, even though in the process they will themselves come to learn much. On the other hand, there are the student participants. They too usually intend certain outcomes from the activities in which they are engaged; they are motivated by a willingness to engage in a range of activities in order to achieve a particular learning goal. There is in education purpose and planning on both sides.

Much has been written in recent years about 'self-directed learning' (Brookfield 1985). In this process, the learner takes the initiative and plans their own structured learning process. But in most of these cases, there is some outside planner as well – someone who wrote the textbook or manual, who planned the sequence of articles in the magazines or journals used by the learner. There is still someone engaged in 'teaching' (helping the learner to learn). Self-directed learning may on many occasions take place outside the educational sector, but it has many of the characteristics of the intentional, planned, purposeful, and assisted learning that is education.

Characteristics of education

Three characteristics may be identified as inherent within these planned and purposeful learning activities (for more details, see pp. 120–4):

- The process is *sequential and cumulative*. It is not just a number of unrelated 'magazine' items, individual parts without any interconnection. Rather it builds up piece by piece, making relationships between the diverse elements of the learning process.
- The process addresses itself in some form or other to *general principles*. It does not consist of the anecdotal, the one-off episode or miscellaneous facts, but draws from these some conclusions that may be applicable elsewhere. Consumer education, for example, is not a matter of identifying

an individual product or supplier of which particular consumers should be wary; rather, it uses those incidents in such a way that the consumers can make judgements for themselves in a wider range of instances. The result of taught learning is that the learner can apply the new skills, knowledge and understanding acquired in different situations.

- The process is also in some sense *complete*. However open-ended the teaching process may be, there is some 'rounding off' of the material dealt with, some form of fulfilment, of meeting the goals, so that the student participants do not feel left high and dry, incomplete and unsatisfied. Taught learning is of course never complete; it consists of opening doors, leading on to the next stages of the sequence. Nevertheless, each stage has some completeness in itself, some sense of achievement, even of satisfaction and pleasure – as with music, some sense of closure.

The elements of education

Education, then, can be seen as a planned learning opportunity which one party provides for or with another in relation to an agreed objective. Such opportunities can be created anywhere – in the home, at work or in community contexts – whenever guided learning takes place.

There are five main elements to education, which may be seen to be in close relationship to each other:

- the *teacher-agent* (TA), who may be at programme level the institution or organisation that provides the learning opportunity, and at learning group level the teacher/tutor;
- the *student participant* (SP), the individual or group who put themselves intentionally into the learning situation;
- the intended *goals and objectives* (GO), however loosely or closely defined;
- the sequence of events that will enable the student participants to learn, the steps towards the intended goals; that collection of *methods/content* (M/C) lying at the heart of the planned learning process; and
- the *context* within which the activity takes place.

The relationship between these elements may be illustrated as shown in Figure 2.4, although this representation is too static for what is one of the most dynamic of human situations. All elements of the planned learning opportunity undergo change, and each goal leads on to new developments and to new goals.

The role of the *teacher-agent*, whether organiser or teacher, in this process is crucial. It is the teacher-agent who sets up the learning situation, even though the student participants may come increasingly to take control of the learning process. The teacher-agent assesses the needs of the prospective learners, establishes the goals and constructs the programme of methods and contents, the course of action that will enable the participants to 'learn'

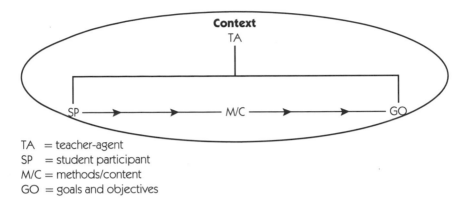

TA = teacher-agent
SP = student participant
M/C = methods/content
GO = goals and objectives

Figure 2.4 The educational process

their way towards the agreed goals. The teacher-agent is the planner – at least in the first instance.

The **student participants** are also active in the planning process. They intend to learn, to achieve their own goals. They, like the agent, have certain outcomes in mind; they come to the learning situation with a set of intentions (sometimes unformulated) and actively set about fulfilling these (see pp. 75–6).

The nature of the **goals** that we set in the planning process (see Chapter 6) will bring in its train a range of implications for the role of the teacher, as well as for the contents and methods used. A narrow objective, aiming at some specific competency or externally moderated achievement, will tend to lead to greater stress being laid on the part played by the teacher than on the learners' activities. On the other hand, a concentration on a wider objective such as the growth of the individual will lead to an emphasis more on learner-centred than teacher-centred processes (Figure 2.5).

Goal	Specific achievement, externally moderated	Personal growth, internally moderated
Teacher's role	Teacher introduces student to subject matter	Encounter between student and teacher
Student's role	Student more passive	Student participant fully engaged
Content	Discipline of subject matter, limited choice	Open-endedness; subject matter less important than activities
Methods	Directive	Interactive

Figure 2.5 The impact of goals on the teaching-learning process: the continuum

The planning agent (teacher-provider) then has in mind certain *expected outcomes* – the results that will flow from the learning undertaken. However, most of the student participants come with their own intentions, which may or may not be the same as those set out by the agent (see Chapter 1). They will use the learning opportunity to achieve their own outcomes. Each of these sets of purposes influences the other. The teacher's planned outcomes help to shape the learners' expectations, and the learners' intentions and hopes should affect the formulation of the teacher's intentions.

Both sets of expected outcomes may well be different from the *effective outcomes* of the teaching process. Since those being taught consist of a mixed group of learners, each of whom responds to the learning programme in a different way, there will always be a series of unexpected outcomes. The teacher-agent needs to keep these differences in mind when planning the learning encounter (see Chapter 11).

We cannot easily separate **methods** from **content**; the two are closely related. But the nature of the goals we set helps to determine whether the emphasis of our programme of work lies more towards content or towards method. Programmes with narrowly prescribed objectives tend to concentrate more on content than on methods; an adult class leading to a certificate in English literature, for instance, or a course on new legislation relating to health and safety at work, define for themselves more or less precisely the content of the teaching-learning encounter. Those teachers who feel it necessary for the student participants to come face to face with a set amount of material will tend to use directive rather than participatory methods, for both teacher and taught expect a specified content to be 'covered'. On the other hand, programmes aimed more at personal growth, confidence building and assertiveness are likely to be less rigidly controlled. Their impulse lies more in the processes involved in the teaching-learning programme. In these cases, we may feel it more important to engage in participatory learning methods than to cover a set amount of material.

Whatever our decisions, which may well change as the course progresses and as we reassess the needs of the learners with their help, methods and content are integrally related in the planning of a teaching experience. They cannot be discussed apart, and neither is more important than the other.

And all of this takes place within a **context** – a context which helps to determine the nature of the teacher-agency and the power relationships involved; which largely determines who the student-learners will be and who they will not be – who will be included and who will be excluded; a context which will certainly shape the goals of the programme; and a context which will determine what content is chosen (for all societies privilege some kinds of knowledge and demean others) and what kinds of methods are used. Learning and teaching do not take place in a vacuum but within a sociocultural context which controls the values inherent in the process.

Education as encounter

Some would argue that what we have proposed is too mechanical a notion of teaching. Instead they see education as an encounter without prior determination of the outcomes. They lay stress on the fact that each student participant reacts uniquely to the material they are meeting or are perceiving anew, and that in any case the outcomes may not reveal themselves until some time after the learning programme has ended. They emphasise the open-ended nature of the meeting of learner, teacher and material, and the unpredictability of learning. In fact, they urge, learning may not take place at all; and in the nature of the encounter, the teacher may learn as much as the student.

All of this is true, but a teaching-learning situation still calls for a *conscious decision* to create such an encounter. Even when that decision is accompanied by a desire for open-endedness, there is still a *purpose* behind the encounter. It still calls for a process of *planning*, of selection of the material to be used as the basis of the encounter. Equally, such a view of teaching as encounter calls for an *intention* on the part of the participants, a willingness to engage in the encounter. The outcomes of our teaching may be different from those we plan for or anticipate, but some element of planning is essential.

The dynamic relationship between all the elements within teaching is not confined to the initial planning of the learning programme. It becomes clearer as the process goes on. The teacher-agent is (or should be) active all the time, reassessing the student participants, evaluating progress made, amending and redefining the goals, reconstructing the methods and content and learning all the time from and with the participants. The learners too are active, clarifying their intentions and changing their objectives. A course once set and never altered, directed towards unchanging goals, can only with difficulty be called 'education'; for education is a process of change in which teacher and learner join together in relation to a third element, a series of agreed but changing goals.

Education, training and indoctrination

Our definition of education as a planned and interactive learning opportunity is not enough unless we also consider whether the term carries with it a value judgement or not. Are *all* planned learning situations 'education'? A terrorist organisation's programme of field training will be seen by most people as very different from a local conservation society's series of visits or a women's group's acting workshop, although all three may be motivated by a desire to change attitudes, and thus behaviour, and ultimately systems in society at large. So we are forced to ask whether, for education to be education, the goals must be 'good'.

The problem is an old one: how to define 'good' in this context. Clearly once again we are in the field of social constructs. 'Socially acceptable' may in some circumstances not be adequate to describe the good that education is intended to do, for many educators of adults wish to use their learning opportunities to encourage some form of change in society, and change is not always 'socially acceptable' (think, for example, of the early Western trade union and the later women's movements). Those of us who have been brought up to think in terms of traditional liberalism will conceive of the good that education can bring as increased freedom. Others may assume that an increased ability to generate wealth (either for oneself or for society at large) is the good that education should achieve, while yet others will talk of the rectification of social inequalities or the increase of cultural richness and harmony, or environmental concern and action.

Rather than pursue this line of thought here (it is discussed further in Chapter 6), perhaps a more useful approach is in terms of 'wide' and 'narrow' goals. In this sense all structured learning opportunities can be seen as lying along a continuum. At one end are those planned teaching-learning programmes with narrow goals, the aim of which is to demonstrate that there is a 'right' way to do something or other. These are largely in the skills area but not entirely so; some people are taught that there are 'right' ways of working things out and of learning. Choice is strictly limited and not encouraged. This is what we usually mean when we speak of *training*. At the other end are all those activities that set out to convince us that there is a 'right' way of thinking and feeling and behaving. Once again there is a limitation, even a denial, of choice; there is only one set of values and attitudes to hold. This is essentially *indoctrination*. Between these two extremes is that large area of education where the goals are wider: to demonstrate that there are different ways of thinking and doing, to encourage the development of choice and self-determination (Figure 2.6).

Our question, then – whether the term 'education' refers to *all* planned learning opportunities or only to those for which the goals are 'good' – may be a matter of personal choice. We can call all learning activities specifically created by one agency for another group of people 'education', in which case we can talk of using education for good or bad ends. Or we can define 'education' as consisting only of those programmes and courses with wide

Narrow goals: the 'right' way to do; no choice

Wide goals: many ways of thinking and doing; development of choice

Narrow goals: only one way of thinking

(Training)   (Indoctrination)

Figure 2.6 Training, education and indoctrination

rather than narrow goals, thus cutting off training and indoctrination from the world of education. It is a question of personal definition.

On the whole this is more a matter of concern to the organiser of programmes than to the teacher. Nevertheless we as teachers have to decide for ourselves whether our goals are wide or narrow, whether we are engaged in education, training and/or indoctrination. Probably elements of all these will come into our teaching at different times, arising from our commitment to our students and to our subject.

Activity

Are the goals of your case study learning programme (see p. 8):

- wide?
- narrow?

Does your course consist more of:

- training: the right way to do something?
- indoctrination: the right way to think?
- education: the increase of choice?

Adult education

Is adult education simply the addition of our definition of 'adult' to our definition of 'education' – that is, the provision of planned learning opportunities for those persons whom society deems to be adults – or does the phrase imply something more? Is there a distinction to be drawn between 'the education of adults' and 'adult education'?

Adult education as content

Some people have argued that the difference between these two concepts lies in terms of the *contents* of the programmes. Thus they see the 'education of adults' as referring to all forms of education for those over the age of 16 (or 18 or 20), whatever is being studied. It thus includes some subjects (both skills and knowledge) better learned at a younger age (e.g. playing a musical instrument). On the other hand they would restrict the term 'adult education' to those topics which can be learned or best learned only as adults, because they rely on experience (politics, say, or interpersonal relationships, or spirituality) or because they relate to adult roles (parenthood or management). Some have suggested that the key ingredient of *adult* education is that it is life-related, that it helps adults to solve their own problems from 'real' situations.

Activity

Is the subject of your learning programme (see p. 8):

- especially appropriate to adults?
- more appropriate to younger persons?
- equally relevant to both groups?

Such a definition would however exclude from 'adult education' a great deal that belongs to it. Literacy and basic skills, for example, typewriting, sports, languages, woodworking and computing are all better learned while young, but they feature in most programmes of recognisable adult education. And there are some subjects – art, for instance – which experience shows do not have age-related criteria for learning.

Adult education as process

Because of this, others have suggested that the difference between what may properly be termed 'adult education' and the 'education of adults' lies less in *what* is being learned (although some subjects are especially appropriate to adults) than in the *approach* to adult learning. They draw a distinction between those programmes that teach adults as adults and those that teach them in ways more appropriate to younger learners. The 'education of adults' can then be seen to cover all forms of education (planned learning opportunities) for those over the age of 16 (or whatever), whether the student participants are treated as adults or whether they are treated as if they were younger learners – taught, that is, as if they were largely or completely ignorant of the subject being studied, without relevant experience, unable to be relied upon to control their own learning, having little or nothing to contribute to the learning process. 'Adult education', by contrast, consists of all those forms of education that treat the student participants as adults – capable, experienced, responsible, mature and balanced people. In this view, the essential difference of adult education from all other kinds of education lies in its power relationships, the equality of teacher and student participants – 'teaching on equal terms'.

We have suggested above that Western societies promote the view that all forms of teaching adults should respect and enhance the adulthood of those who have voluntarily become our students. This makes any approach to the education of adults that does not possess the characteristics of 'adult education' inappropriate. To deny the adult students' adulthood is not just to create unnecessary barriers to effective learning, to deprive ourselves of the most useful resource we have for the learning task; it is to insult them with our own arrogance.

This approach creates tensions for ourselves as teachers of adults. For one thing some of our students may express a wish to be taught in ways that deny their adulthood. They want to go back to school, to surrender their autonomy in order to learn some new thing (this is discussed in Chapter 12). At the same time, our concern for the subject matter to which we have submitted ourselves and to which we hope our students will submit themselves may pull against this concern for the adulthood of the student participants. The primacy of the goal of greater adulthood over all other goals is one of the main problems faced by those of us who teach adults.

Two patterns of education

This distinction between treating participants as adults ('adult education') and failing to do so (what we may call 'adult schooling') reflects a tension deep within education itself. The tension is felt in all sectors but is at its most acute in the teaching of adults. It reflects two contrasting attitudes towards the task in hand and to all elements of that task. The tension can be expressed in a series of polarities:

- between education as content and education as process;
- between education as 'teaching a subject' and education as 'teaching people';
- between education as preparing for life and education as a part of living;
- between education as discipline, conformity to an external standard, and education as liberation.

A useful (though in places overdrawn) summary of these two approaches can be seen in Figure 2.7. This distinction between two fundamentally different approaches to education has been pointed out by many writers, from Houle (1961) with his statement that 'Education either functions as an instrument that is used to facilitate the younger generation into the logic of the present system, or it becomes the practice of freedom, the means by which women and men deal critically and actively with reality and discover how to participate in the transformation of their world', to Paulo Freire with his strongly asserted statement that education cannot be neutral: it either domesticates or it liberates the student participants.

Activity

Are the course you have listed (see p. 8) and the methods adopted closer to:

- the conformist end; or
- the liberation end of the continuum?

'Conformist'	'Liberation'
Make student participant like teacher	*Make student participant independent of teacher*
1 There is an external reality to which student must adapt (subject discipline). Truth is known.	1 There is no externally 'right' way of knowing and behaving. Truth is not known.
2 Student can't be trusted to pursue own learning; teacher takes initiative.	2 Human beings have a natural potential for learning; student takes self-initiative.
3 Presentation = learning.	3 Most significant learning acquired through doing.
4 Material exists on its own, independent of both teacher and student.	4 Significant learning takes place when subject matter is perceived by student as having relevance for their own purpose.
5 Teacher must help the transfer of knowledge to student: students cannot obtain knowledge by themselves.	5 Knowledge cannot be transferred; all knowledge is created by student for themselves.
6 Process of education is to accumulate brick upon brick of knowledge and skills – progression of subject is externally set.	6 There is no set sequence of learning; students engage with material in their own way and in their own sequence.
7 Constructive and creative citizens develop from passive learners.	7 Creativity in learning depends on active involvement; student participates responsibly in learning process.
8 Evaluation by teacher of student's progress is a necessary part of learning.	8 Learning is best achieved when self-criticism and self-evaluation are primary; evaluation by others is of secondary importance.
9 Cognitive learning can take place without affecting rest of person.	9 Learning that involves the whole person – feelings as well as intellect – is most pervasive and lasting.
10 Learning is a one-off experience and need not be repeated.	10 The most useful learning in the modern world is learning how to learn; a continuing openness to experience and an incorporation of the process of change into oneself are necessary goals of education.

Figure 2.7 Two approaches to teaching

The tension that is teaching

It would however be a mistake to suggest that one of these models is wholly correct and the other is wholly wrong. Rather, they represent a tension that is never resolved. This tension impinges on both the teacher and the student participant. Education with adults is both in part a preparation for life and in part an integral element in the process of living. It seeks both to help the student participants to change towards a predetermined goal and yet at the same time to help them to become more independent. It is both training and education, both discipline and free growth. In education the teacher helps the learner to become free, but within the limits of a field of study or expertise. We seek to bring the student participants into contact with the primary material and leave them free to use it for themselves.

The teacher too is torn – between the desire to help the students develop into something they have already indicated they want to become (a painter, a more confident person, a more efficient professional, a more skilled technician or trade union official, etc.) and the desire to respect and encourage the autonomy of the adult. We are torn between the clear vision we have of our subject and our willingness to encourage our students to see it for themselves in different ways. The teacher is aware that there is such a thing as the 'bad' use of literature, bad dressmaking, bad gardening practice, bad history and so on; that there are standards, in fact. Although we may be conscious of the limitations of our own judgements, nevertheless we believe that there are criteria in our discipline to which we ourselves seek to conform and to which we hope our student participants will wish to conform. Yet we want our students to grow in independence, self-determination and self-appraisal.

And it is here that we need to recognise that we as teachers come from a particular cultural background; that we are created beings, built up through many different experiences. It is a culture which privileges certain kinds of knowledge and which discredits other kinds of knowledge (Barr 1999). The criteria we apply to ourselves and to our subject matter are all partial, contingent and contested, even within our own discipline. We are not neutral, not impartial; we are the product of our culture and at the same time we are the disseminators of the values of that culture. It cannot be otherwise – but if we can become aware of this and reflect critically on our situated value systems, we shall become much more open when we meet other cultural value systems among our student participants.

Nevertheless, we need to go ahead on the basis of our expertise, whatever that may be. And there will be times, in the ordering of the material that the student participant handles in order to move towards the agreed goals, when the discipline side predominates; times when the training aspect – the most effective way to do things – is most prominent, when the teacher's role is to point out the good and the bad (the process of evaluation, as we shall see, depends on *values* – see Chapter 11). Even here, however, the ideal is for the participants not just to accept the judgements of the teacher but to come to make their own judgements, to accept the discipline of the subject for themselves.

But education cannot consist of this alone. There are other times when the freedom, the self-determination of the student participant, the autonomy of the adult, has full play. They will create their own approaches, their own strategies, and our task is to encourage such individual initiatives rather than suppress them.

It is not just a question of getting the right balance between these two aspects of education. The tension is inherent within the whole process of planning for learning. The introduction of a purpose, a goal, as a third element into the relationship between the teacher-planner and the learner creates the tension. For this goal makes its own demands on both the teacher and the learner. It directs both the material and the methods used in the learning process. The teacher who has a goal is not totally free, any more than the learner who desires to achieve a goal can be completely free. Freedom in this respect comes from accepting discipline.

The purpose of the educational encounter is to achieve a series of mutually agreed objectives, and this purpose imposes discipline on both the teacher and the taught. Both, but particularly the teacher, will feel the tension between the discipline that education is and the freedom that it seeks to promote. There is no right solution to the problem. We all have to live with both sides of the equation.

Further reading

Brookfield, S.D. (1983) *Adult Learners, Adult Education and the Community.* Buckingham: Open University Press.

Jarvis, P. (1995) *Adult and Continuing Education: Theory and Practice.* London: Routledge.

Wallis, J. (ed.) (1996) *Liberal Adult Education: The End of an Era?* Nottingham: Continuing Education Press.

Chapter 3

ADULT STUDENTS

Who are they . . . ?

This chapter first discusses some approaches to developing a profile of the students in our programmes, including the lifespan approach, and then lists some of the main characteristics of those who join adult learning programmes. It argues that adults, when they come to our learning programmes, construct themselves as 'students'.

Much attention has been given in recent writings on adult education to the adult learner. Whole books have been devoted to the topic, and most general studies of adult education, based on the premise that all forms of teaching adults ought to be student-centred rather than teacher-centred, contain sections dealing with the way adults learn.

STUDENT PROFILES

One feature of this discussion has been the compilation of lists of character-istics of the adult student. The aim is to help teachers of adults to become more conscious of what they are doing when they draw up a profile of their students, to test out the items specified to see which do not apply to their particular group and to identify other characteristics particular to their teaching context. Most of these lists are limited in their application in that they are directed more towards the student in part-time non-vocational, non-qualification adult education of a more or less academic orientation than towards those in basic education, practical skill-based courses, formally certificated courses or advanced professional development programmes.

In many of these descriptions, large generalisations are made about the adult student participant. It has been suggested, for example, that adult students are people well beyond schooldays, full of a mixture of regret, determination, guilt and ambition, but dogged by lack of confidence and self-belief, harassed by noise and diversions, facing problems of time and space to study, tiredness and opposition and mockery from spouses and friends. (These descriptions have all come from a number of recent writings purporting to describe the general principles on which adult education is predicated.) But clearly these do not describe all (or even perhaps many) adult students. Each such description needs to be drawn up with a proper regard to the group in question.

Drawing a profile

We all draw pictures of who our student participants are going to be. We do this as an integral part of the process of planning the programme and the course. Some of us can rely on past experience to help us, but new teachers of adults cannot do this. They may turn to other more experienced teachers to assist them, but even this is not always possible. And such a process is often unconscious. We rarely make explicit the views we hold about the prospective learners, their abilities and motivations, what we can and cannot expect from them. Even in those programmes where the goals are negotiated with the potential learners, the teacher-planner still makes several assumptions: for example, that the participants want to join in, that they are willing to entertain the notion of change and are capable of engaging in the processes put before them.

We thus fall into unquestioned presuppositions about our prospective student participants. We may on occasion assume that the learners are at the opposite extreme from our goals: that they possess no skills at all, if our goals relate to the acquisition of skills; that they are completely ignorant of the subject in hand, if our goals are knowledge-related; that they hold negative attitudes, if our goals are attitude change; that they have not yet begun to comprehend, if our goals are concerned with understanding; that they lack all forms of confidence, if our goal is confidence-building. None of this may be true. Indeed, it is most unlikely to be true. Those who come on a bird-watching course are likely to know something about the subject; those who attend car maintenance classes will invariably have had some experience of a car; those who wish to learn about women in literature are most likely to have done some reading in this field already and will have views (often strong views) on the subject; those adults who come to university degree programmes for 'mature' students often know more than their teachers allow for. Unless we make conscious what we believe about our potential student participants, we are in danger of making false assumptions.

Testing the profile

Having compiled a list of apparent characteristics of our potential learners, it is necessary to test these at the earliest possible moment. In some forms of teaching adults – distance learning, for example, or the educational programmes offered by the media, and the self-directed learning materials prepared by many agencies – the teacher-planners never meet the learners, so that the assumptions made cannot easily be assessed to see whether they are right or wrong. But in most other cases it will quickly become apparent whether we have judged correctly what the prospective student participants are able to do, what they are willing to do and what they want to do. Sometimes we will get it all wrong, so that there is nothing to be done after the first meeting other than to redesign the whole learning package. As with most skills of teaching, we can improve with practice; but even after long experience, because every group of adult learners is different, we still need to test whether the presuppositions we have made about our student participants are correct or not, so that the programme of work can be revised or amplified as necessary.

Teachers are sometimes reluctant to do this in their first encounter with the student participants. It may be that they are hesitant to expose themselves from the start of their relationship with the learners, to give the impression that they are in any way uncertain. Or, having prepared some material for the first meeting, they may be anxious to give it. Such teachers sometimes justify this on the grounds that the participants who have turned up want to have something 'meaty' at the first session so as to judge better the content, level and pace of learning involved in the course. They argue that some prospective students would find a first meeting devoted to a general discussion an unsatisfying experience. Or the teacher accepts at face value the participants' assessment of their own knowledge or ignorance of the subject, their ability or inability to contribute anything useful towards setting the goals and constructing the programme of work. There are many reasons for not opening up to challenge the assumptions we have made about the participants.

Despite this, it might be better to spend at least part of an early meeting with any group of adult student participants listening rather than talking, assessing whether the assumptions we have made about their interests and abilities are right or not. The task will have to be done at some stage during the course, and it needs to be done as early as possible if we wish to avoid a lengthy gap between bringing together their expectations as learners and our expectations as teachers.

The range is wide

In order to test out these presuppositions, we need to undertake the process consciously rather than subconsciously. For many of us, it will be useful to write down our description of the potential student participants. But here we run into the biggest problem of all. Most of us teach in groups, and the wide range of those who join such groups, even small groups, may hinder us from making realistic judgements about what we can in general expect from our student-learners.

Let us take one example as illustration. That which we call 'intelligence' today is rarely now seen as a fixed inherent ability that cannot be improved after the end of formal schooling, or a range of abilities that grow and decline along mathematical curves (see pp. 88–9). Intelligence is now thought of in many circles as being 'plastic', context- and content-related, rising to peaks or falling into troughs throughout adulthood, largely governed by whether the activities engaged in and the environmental factors are stimulating and encouraging or whether they are damaging and inhibiting. Particularly, the development of intelligence seems to be dependent more on the amount of educational experience one has received and on the subsequent use of learning skills in one's occupations than on any basic learning ability inherited or developed when young. Thus persons who have had a good deal of education and who have been engaged in tasks calling for considerable and regular amounts of new learning will be 'more intelligent' at 50 than they were at 25; conversely, those who have been employed in occupations that have not required them to engage in problem-solving and new learning are likely not to have developed their intelligence to the same extent. In any group of adults engaged in a learning programme, the range of learning ability, even among people of roughly the same age and the same initial education, is likely to be considerably wider than in a comparable group of children.

Lifespan studies

Many adult educators use 'lifespan studies' for drawing their profile of adult student participants; for it is argued that if learning can be defined as a process of personal changes made in adapting to changed situations and experiences (see pp. 45–6), the study of different patterns of life is likely to throw light on such learning.

In the 1970s and 1980s, a number of general views of lifespan development emerged based on ideas about the major points of meaningful change that occur during adulthood. These were thought to give teachers a useful basis for the process of drawing a profile of their student participants.

The terms 'change' and 'development' are used in educational contexts in a variety of senses. A number of adult lifespan studies speak in terms of growth, the gradual and natural increase of maturity. Others speak of development – i.e. goal achievement. For some writers, the ultimate goal of adulthood is one of 'rational autonomy', moral maturity or critical reflection. On the other hand, some writers have rejected the concept of 'development' and replaced it with a view of change throughout adult life as a purposeless but time-related process.

Lifespan developments and contexts

Most writers suggest that, unlike the child and the adolescent whose different stages are recognised (even if not universally agreed), adults change and develop more by experience and by the exercise of abilities than by age alone. There are of course physical changes that occur with increasing age, but these are not inextricably related to any specific age, and the changes that take place differ for each individual. There is in the West a strong emphasis on the physical elements in human make-up; thus ageing is frequently seen as a phenomenon to be resisted, something to be overcome rather than valued for the wisdom and status it brings. In other cultures, the spiritual is more predominant and this leads to different perspectives on ageing.

Today, much of the emphasis in adult development studies is on the changes within the social and cultural context of the individual which call for new responses. There has been a tendency among some adult educators to see adults in too great an isolation from the social and physical environment in which they are located, to see society as static while the individual changes, to underestimate the effect of changes in social structures and values on the adult. But increasingly we see that we are dealing with a changing person in a changing world. Change, not stability, is the norm.

Among those changes are variations in perspectives, including the view of the ageing process itself. Because of their emphasis on the physical, Western societies have tended to see youth in positive terms while ageing is often constructed more negatively. In recent years, views in relation to older persons have, it is true, shown significant alteration, with growing positive attitudes towards older age groups, perhaps a result of the increasing number of these persons in society as a whole. In many developing countries on the other hand, influenced by Western cultural patterns, the reverse would seem to be happening; despite the increasing number of older persons, youth is increasingly being glorified and older age regarded with disfavour. Society is not only imposing identity on individuals but is constantly reinterpreting that identity.

Ages of man and woman

Most of us are acquainted with Shakespeare's 'seven ages of man': the infant, the schoolboy, the lover, the soldier, the justice, the 'lean and slipper'd pantaloon', and finally second childhood. Since Shakespeare's time there have been many attempts to better this description of adult changes. Some are very general: Whitehead's successive phases of romance, precision and rationalisation; or Egan's romantic stage, philosophic stage, and eirenic or fulfilled stage. These all display the 'plateau effect' of Shakespeare: growth, maturity and decline. The use of the term 'Third Age' for example perpetuates the construct of a three-stage life consisting of growth, performance and 'completion'.

Cognitive development

A growing field of study lies within adult cognitive development, especially the application to adults of Piaget's work on children. Several have added extra stages beyond the 'performing' stage. A number of these are very elaborate, some having no less than nine additional sequential and hierarchical stages. A sequence is proposed by which adults pass from the performing stage of Piaget into problem-solving and finally to problem-identification and creation. One study talks about five levels of consciousness which adults pass through, while others suggest a total of seven stages: 'to think reflectively does not emerge fully formed but develops in a sequential fashion, with earlier stages building on prior stages and laying the foundation for subsequent stages' (King and Kitchener 1994: 152). But although sequential, none of these stages is exclusive; a number of these authors suggest that adults can operate simultaneously on several levels. A few speak about 'transpersonal development' as the goal of adulthood: transcendental absorption into the Universal Consciousness.

Dominant concerns

Among the more influential group of lifespan theories are those that see changes during the adult phase of life in terms of dominant concerns. These are frequently age-related. Havighurst (1952), for instance, suggested that the individual passes through eight main phases. After childhood and adolescence comes adulthood, a 'developmental period in about as complete a sense as childhood and adolescence are developmental periods'. From 18 to 30, adults are focusing their life; there is a concern for self-image, experimentation, jobs and love affairs. Education tends to be used for occupational advancement. From 30 to 40 is a period of stability and relatively less introspection, less self-doubt. The job is now most important, with child-rearing a close second. From 40 to 50 is a period of self-exertion and assertion, the peak of the life cycle. Public and civic activities are more important than participation in educational programmes. There is a turning out towards society from oneself, the family and the job; action is the means of dealing with the world, and this brings the first consciousness of physical deterioration.

From 50 to 60, adults begin to change roles. Educational involvement is for expressive rather than instrumental purposes. There is increasing physical deterioration (sight and hearing), and larger amounts of energy have to be exerted to avoid losing ground. 'Thought' rather than 'action' is the means of dealing with the world, and short-term rather than long-term achievements are sought. The adult spends the years between 60 and 70 deciding whether and how to disengage, and from 70 onwards is the period of making the most of disengagement. Healthy adults are not too preoccupied with the past, are self-accepting and relatively content with the outcomes of their life, but this period is often characterised by poor health, reduced means and dependence on others.

Havighurst's views, as set out above, are frequently cited by adult educators, for they relate such changes directly to educational activities. But these are too simplistic, too rigidly tied to ages, and they are based on Western male-dominated concepts of a successful work career. Major changes in social structure have rendered such a neat analysis suspect.

These considerations led to other sequential approaches without tying each stage too closely to ages. Neugarten (1977) spoke of adulthood as representing a 'movement from an active, combative, outer-world orientation to . . . an adaptive, conforming inner-world orientation'. Three stages were identified: a period of expressiveness, expansiveness and extroversion, of autonomy and competence (up to about the age of 30); an intermediate period of reorientation; and a third stage of change from active to passive modes of relating to the environment with greater introversion. More recently, others see adulthood as repeated and successive stages of performance which are relatively stable, followed by periods of transition away from these more or less stable states through 'structure building' processes which may include disorientation and reorientation. They relate these stages to different ages, but the view holds even if such ages are removed.

Tensions

Erikson (1965) on the other hand saw the stages of human development in terms of tensions. There is, he argued, the general and continuing tension between 'the inner wishes . . . and the demands to conform to other people's standards and requirements', which all people experience and which leads to compromises if the adult is 'to maintain the integrity of his [sic] personality'. In addition there are a series of developmental tensions: in puberty and adolescence, there is the tension between identity and role confusion; in young adulthood, intimacy versus isolation; in adulthood, generativity versus stagnation; and in 'maturity', the integrity of the self versus despair. The educational implications of each stage are delineated: initial education for the child and adolescent, vocational education for the young adult, social and community education for the adult, and philosophical and creative education for the mature. Others speak of incongruence. The individual has 'two problems; maintaining inner harmony with himself [sic] and with the environment. Incongruence is developed within the person (intra-self) and between the person and other-than-self experiences (self/other) . . . The research of life-cycle psychologists supports the notion that younger [adults] manifest more intra-self and self/other incongruence than older, more mature [people]' (Boshier 1989: 147–50).

Time perspectives

Lifespan changes may also be seen in terms of how time is viewed. Some writers have suggested that the child sees the future as far away; for the adolescent, the future is rosy; for the adult, time is finite; while the mature adult feels that time is running out. Friedman (1972) elaborated this version of the 'plateau' theory of lifespan changes, being particularly conscious that successive stages do not easily correlate with ages. He thus overlapped some stages:

- The *entry stage* (say, 18–25): orientation is to the future – the future will be better than the present; change is good.
- *Career development* (say, 20–50): orientation is increasingly more to the present than to the future; away from interest in promotion towards an interest in the intrinsic value of work, together with participation and achievement in non-work areas.
- *Plateau* (say, 35–55): the main time focus moves to a feeling that time is running out; there is increasing neuroticism, especially among the lower socioeconomic groups, who cope less well than professionals and managers (!).

After 55 comes a period of decline.

Gender and class factors

More recently it has been recognised that these schemata are too closely tied to datable stages, and attempts have been made to break away from this. As these examples show, it is recognised that there is considerable sex and class bias in such analyses, deriving from the origin of most of the studies – among reasonably successful American white professionals, those who on the whole predominate in continuing education programmes in the USA. The gender bias is surprising; all of these theories relate to male careers despite the fact that women predominate in many forms of adult education. The women's movement has been seeking to redress the balance. A major strand has been the exploration of women's development in adulthood which sees one of the key themes emerging as the transition from identity (the self) into intimacy (empathy), moving from the acceptance of other's knowledge to the creation of one's own knowledge. Similarly, it is likely that the lifespan stages and expectations of blacks are different from those listed above.

The class bias has received less attention. Almost all the above descriptions rely upon doubtful assumptions concerning the social and educational background of the participants – the educated, the professionally employed and the ambitious. One attempt to redress this balance towards the working class suggests that:

there is a rough sequence in a working life which the intellectual is too apt to forget. After the first period of school and pure technical training, the worker, for the ten years from 15 to 25, is pitchforked into practical life – finding and holding a job after marriage and founding a home on small resources . . . between 25 and 35, as the worker approaches a more responsible job, education should broaden his [*sic*] ideas of the nature of authority, of the social and human implications of any new job, of the deeper purposes of society. Once this broadening process has been started, it may well lead on into history, literature and art . . . It means at 21 bread and butter and the wage packet. At 30 it may include ideas of status, leisure, civic responsibility; and at 40 and thereafter it may deepen into a concept of the good life.

(Hunter quoted in Stephens and Roderick 1971: 195)

The importance of context

These studies show how the importance of context has come to dominate more contemporary explorations of adult development. The conflicts and contradictions inherent in any lifeworld are part of the creative forces which make for the continuing change in the individual. Dialectic is a more general feature of lifespan studies today. A number of different approaches can be seen. For example, some Western thinkers, perhaps drawing on the thinking of Habermas (see pp. 105–6), have elaborated this into the continuous interaction of a person's work, relationship to others and perceptions of self.

Roles, crisis points and cycles

It is significant how important work is in almost all Western lifespan studies. Attempts to draw up an alternative lifespan sequence to that of the male professional still assume a working life. But the New Work Order, changing patterns of careers in almost all sectors and long-term unemployment on a large scale together with changes in attitudes to work and retirement have thrown doubt on much of the existing research. These changes and the patronising air that surrounds efforts to define working-class life stages, as well as an awareness of other changes (especially in marital relationships) have led to a number of different approaches, some of which concentrate on the pattern of family life and/or lifestyles. Some concentrate on the changing *roles* of the adult which form a unique pageant of life or on the *crisis points* that occur in the life of most adults of a particular generation, whether male or female, working class or middle class, black or white – although reactions to these new roles and crisis points vary considerably according to experience and the culture of the individual. The most common roles and crisis points identified usually relate to the first job, marriage, parenthood, the departure of children from the home, bereavement (especially the loss of parents and spouse), separation and divorce, loss of a job or other role, retirement and (less sequential and more occasional) moving house. Such events have been divided into individual and social, but the distinction cannot always be maintained. These are seen both as events with a specific time frame and also as a process. Among these writers, a common crisis point is seen to occur somewhere about the age of 40 in both males and females.

Others suggest that linear, normative, predictable and at times prescriptive stages are no longer appropriate and replace such stages with a concentration on social forces as the major source of personal change and development. Hudson (1991: 43) sees 'life as a complex, pluralistic, multivariate flow, with ongoing cycles in nature, societies and people. Families, corporations and nations are all part of a larger, often chaotic flow that can be influenced and shaped but not completely controlled . . . adult development [is] adaptation to change – change within themselves and within their environment'. Within these *cycles*, basic themes such as love, achievement and the search for meaning are played and replayed through adult life. Responding to these themes, to changing commitments and to altered circumstances in one's life is what adult development is all about.

Summary

The search for universally applicable stages of adulthood is revealing ever more divergence and less agreement. From our point of view as teachers, it is wise to remember that adults age, and that with ageing:

- physical and some psychological changes occur, to a greater extent for some people than for others and in different ways;
- roles change, all calling for new learning, and there may on occasion be difficulties as well as excitement and challenge in adapting to new roles or to new perceptions of roles;
- various crisis points are passed, sometimes easily, sometimes with difficulty.

But we also need to note two further points. First, individuals are (with very rare exceptions) single entities; body, mind (and spirit) interact with the context to make a single person in a constant process of creation. It is whole persons who change, grow and develop, each unique yet sharing a common humanity.

Second no individual is an island. The adult 'develops in a continuously ongoing reciprocal process of interaction with his or her environment'. It is now much more widely recognised that the culture we inhabit tends to create our thinking and thus our development. We need therefore to explore in each lifeworld 'how the world about us defines who and what we ought to be' (Merriam and Cafarella 1999: 118). The way our culture defines 'work' and 'others' and even our own 'self' will be enormously influential in our development throughout adulthood. A Chinese approach is very different from western approaches, as we have already seen (see p. 43).

But what has not been recognised is that those who write about lifespan development are themselves the creatures of cultural climates, mainly American. It is highly significant that many of these thinkers now claim that the highest goal of adulthood, the aim of personal development, is the construction of one's own knowledge. King and Kitchener assert that in the final two stages of adult cognitive development, knowledge is no longer a given but will be constructed by the person via critical reflection. Belenky and her colleagues aver that the fifth and final perspective which women have on knowing is the construction of knowledge. Others suggest that the most advanced thinking comes not with the certainty from the provision of answers but rather the uncertainty of posing questions, not the elimination but the toleration of contradiction. The move from a deficit approach (the need to receive other person's knowledge) through the disadvantage approach in which the individual explores their relationship with others and into the diversity approach in which each adult creates for themselves a truly unique knowledge of self, of others and of their world may reveal not only the cultural climate of the past half a century (see pp. 1–2) but also how individual interpretations of development during adulthood over the past generation have themselves been constructed.

The implications for the teacher of adults of this multiplicity of views on adult development (and many others have not been listed here) can be summarised briefly. The mixed group that most of us face will not only possess a wide range of ability. It will also contain persons of different ages and at different stages of development, experiencing different roles and facing different crises points. And each of them will react in different ways to the very varied changes they are experiencing in their own life: 'Adults address and solve life events and dilemmas at different rates and times' (Hughes and Graham 1990: 8). The most important characteristic of any group of adult student participants is that they will be very diverse.

GENERAL CHARACTERISTICS OF ADULT STUDENT-LEARNERS

Does this mean that we can say nothing about those we are teaching? I think not. Despite the wide variations that exist between the members of our learning group, it would still seem to be possible to identify some characteristics of the participants in adult learning programmes which appear to apply to most of the group and which will affect the way we teach them. I have selected seven such characteristics, although cultural settings will modify these to some extent. What follows is my list; you may find it helpful to decide for yourself how far each of the categories is appropriate in your own circumstances and to make up your own list:

- the student participants define themselves as adults;
- they are in the middle of a process of growth, not at the start of a process;
- they bring with them a package of experience and values;
- they come to education with intentions;
- they bring expectations about the learning process;
- they have competing interests;
- they already have their own set of patterns of learning.

They all have a self-image as 'adult'

In Chapter 2 we saw that in Western cultures the construct of adulthood represents an ideal, never fully achieved. The concept seems to imply movement, progress towards the fulfilment of the individual's potential, the development of balanced judgements about themselves and others, and increasing independence. Our student participants are people who are becoming more mature, and the way we teach adults can either encourage or discourage this development in self-fulfilment, perspective and autonomy.

The most visible way in which adult learners exercise their adulthood in relation to our programme of work is by voluntarily choosing to come to learning programmes. We need to stress this, for some participants in continuing and lifelong education programmes may be seen as compulsory students, sent there by their employers or other agencies against their will (see p. 14). But even in such cases, these adult student participants have decided for themselves that they will comply with such directives rather than incur whatever consequences would follow from their decision not to do so. They are not like children in this sense of 'compulsion'; for whatever reason, they have chosen to attend.

Malcolm Knowles (1990) suggested that adulthood is attained at the point at which individuals perceive themselves to be essentially self-directing (although this may not be for many persons a single point in time). He believed that there is a natural process of maturation leading organically towards autonomy, but that this is limited by what the social culture permits. In many societies the local culture does not encourage the development of autonomy in some groups of people (women, for instance, especially married women, in many parts of the world). Thus, self-directedness is often partial; it may not extend to all parts of life (including education). Knowles pointed to the gap or tension that exists in these cases between the drive and the ability to be self-directing. Some people will feel more strongly than others this urge to take control of their own lives, to be involved increasingly in the decision-making processes affecting their life choices. But he claimed that it is there in virtually all adults nonetheless. His 'andragogy', to be effective, needs to build upon and foster this process of maturation. A situation that reverses the trend, treating the developing adult as a child to be directed what to do and what not to do, will find itself faced on most occasions with major blocks to learning. Our programme needs to adapt itself to this increasing sense of self-determination if it is to maximise learning.

Knowles' views have been challenged as failing to take sufficient notice of the differences between adults and their contexts, for being prescriptive, a set of normative humanistic values (Hanson 1996). For example, some adults, re-entering education after some time away from school, expect to be treated as children. The expectations of 'being taught' are sometimes strong, and if these expectations are not met in some way or other, once again learning is hindered. However, experience suggests that even the most docile group of adult students, happy for much of the time to be directed as if they were in school, will at the right time rebel against their teachers when the affront to their adulthood becomes too great. It can be a great help to provoke such a situation when we feel the time is right to break up the more formal atmosphere and secure greater participation by the students in their own learning process.

They are all engaged in a continuing process of growth

Our adult student participants have not stopped growing or developing. They are not at a static period in their lives, a plateau between the growth stages of youth and the declining stage of old age; they are still people on the move. Whatever our view about the way adults develop, the key issue is that growth and change are occurring in all aspects of our student participant's life – in the physical arena, in the intellectual sphere, in the emotions, in the world of relationships, in the patterns of cultural interests. This is true of all participants in all types of adult learning – they are all on the move. The pace and direction of these changes vary from person to person, but that it is happening cannot be doubted.

The teacher needs to take these patterns of change seriously. The people we are trying to help to learn are not passive individuals – they are actively engaged in a dynamic process. And they are in the middle of this process, not at the start. They may be at the start of a new stage of the process, but this stage will draw upon past changes and will in turn contribute to the whole programme of development and growth. It is a process that, although continual, is not continuous. It seems to proceed in spurts, triggered off by new experiences (such as the adult learning programme itself) or new perceptions.

We are partially aware of this process of change within ourselves. Indeed, learning about teaching adults itself forms part of the changing pattern of our lives. But we are sometimes reluctant to accept that such a process occurs within the student participants – that they are in the midst of a series of changes when they come to us. It is not practicable for us to know all our student participants intimately enough to assess accurately the position each of them has reached, the way by which they have got there and the different directions they are going. But we can be aware that the process is in every case continuing. Sensitivity to this fact, and to the fact that the educational experience we offer forms part of a number of ongoing change processes, helps a great deal in creating our responses to the varying demands the students make upon us.

They all bring a package of experience and values

Each of the learners brings a range of experience and knowledge more or less relevant to the task in hand. New students are not new people; they possess a set of values, established prejudices and attitudes in which they have invested a great deal of emotional investment. These are based on their past experience. Knowles suggests that, for children, experience is something that happens to them; for adults, experience serves to determine who they are, to create their sense of self-identity. When this experience is devalued or ignored (e.g. by the teacher), this implies a rejection of the person, not just the experience.

This is true in all fields of teaching adults, even in the formal technical and higher educational programmes, but it becomes particularly important for the adult teacher in those contexts where personal growth forms the major objective of the educational programme. The tensions and concerns of both the learner and the teacher in these contexts have been particularly well described by John Wood in his 'Poem for Everyman' (1974):

> *Poem for Everyman*
>
> I will present you
> parts
> of
> my
> self
> slowly
> if you are patient and tender.
> I will open drawers
> that mostly stay closed
> and bring out places and people and things
> sounds and smells, loves and frustrations, hopes and sadnesses,
> bits and pieces of three decades of life
> that have been grabbed off

in chunks
and found lying in my hands
they have eaten
their way into my memory
carved their way into my
heart
altogether – you or I will never see them –
they are me.
If you regard them lightly
deny that they are important
or worse, judge them
I will quietly, slowly
begin to wrap them up,
in small pieces of velvet,
like worn silver and gold jewelry,
tuck them away
in a small wooden chest of drawers
and close.

Such sentiments are not characteristic of all adult student participants. Far from being reticent, some are confident, and a few positively push their views and experiences at the group and at the teacher. But it is perhaps true of more adults in learning situations than we are aware of. The teacher of adults needs to be sensitive to the situation whenever it arises, and it often occurs in the most unlikely of settings and in every class, whether it is a closed group brought together for a specific training purpose, an open-recruitment general interest course, a highly structured formal class or a community education or development group.

What are the implications of students' prior experience, knowledge and values for our approach to teaching?

First, this 'package' determines what meanings are created by the learner. The student participants see all new material they encounter through the lens of their existing experience and knowledge (just as the teacher does), and this may distort the messages. Each participant will test all that they learn against their own experience to see if it 'rings true' or not. Constant feedback from the participants is essential if the teacher is to remain alive to exactly what the student is learning.

Second, in those cases where the student participants do not believe that they possess any relevant experience or knowledge, where they insist that they 'know nothing at all about the subject', it is possible to help them to become aware that they do in fact possess relevant material (see p. 239). For unless the new learning is related to this existing reservoir of experience and knowledge, it cannot be fully absorbed into the person; it will sit uneasily with the rest of the individual's make-up, it will be compartmentalised from the rest of their being and will thus not fully affect their attitudes and behaviour. It is not a difficult skill for the teacher to acquire to explore with the participants something of what they already know about the matter in hand. Words and phrases relating to the subject of the course, collected from the participants and listed on a flipchart or otherwise, can demonstrate to them that they are able to contribute towards the programme of learning. It is usually only necessary for the teacher to make a beginning; once the process has commenced, the participants will normally be able to continue the exploration for themselves and find new ways of relating the content of the course to different parts of their own experience and knowledge. The start of the process is the most difficult step for some of the student participants to take, but it is an essential one before deep and permanent learning can take place.

Third, not all of this set of values, experience and knowledge is correct or helpful to the required learning. Experience of teaching adults reveals that there is often as much unlearning to be done as new learning, and because of the emotional investment in the existing patterns of experience and knowledge, the unlearning process is one of the more difficult tasks facing the teachers of adults (see Chapter 10).

Fourth, this experience and knowledge (some of it unique to the individual participant and therefore new to the teacher and other participants) is a major resource for learning and can be harnessed into the work of the group. Much new material can be drawn out from the student participants rather than be presented by the teacher. Theoretically, we should all start from where the learners themselves are; but since we usually teach in groups this is not often possible except where the contract to learn has ensured that a more or less homogeneous group has been created. But the utilisation of the varied experience and knowledge of all the members of the group is essential, not only to ensure effective learning at a personal level; it will help to bind together the group and make all of its members richer.

They usually come to education with their own intentions

It is often argued that adults come to education because of a sense of need. Being adults, it is said, they come with an intention to do something about changing their world. Unlike children, adults have the opportunity and the means to implement their learning immediately rather than wait until 'they are grown up'. They can use education to change their personal lifeworlds. Adults (so it is argued) come to achieve specific tasks in order to make their lives better.

We shall discuss the question of needs in adult learning in Chapter 4 (see pp. 95–6), but here we must note one or two points. First, it is not always strictly true that the members of our classes are motivated by needs. Some job-related programmes, for instance, contain participants who have little or no sense of need. Perhaps it is more useful to talk of all adult student participants as having a set of 'intentions', an agenda which for many of them can imply the meeting of a felt need (see Chapter 1).

Second, for those who do come out of a want or need, it is on occasion a confused area. Sometimes the participant is imbued with a vague sense of unease and dissatisfaction. The reason for attending that they give to others and even on occasion to themselves is not always the true reason. Sometimes the reason is not related to learning at all but more towards social contact, or getting out of the house, or to please some third person (some research suggests that there is a high correlation between attending some forms of adult education and problems within the marriage relationship, to take but one example). But even when this sense of need is related to learning, there is at times an uncertainty as to what it is that they should be learning. R.D. Laing has expressed something of this in his poem 'Knots' (from the 1972 book of the same title):

Knots

There is something I don't know
    that I am supposed to know.
I don't know *what* it is I don't know
    and yet am supposed to know,
and I feel I look stupid
    if I seem both not to know it
        and not know *what* it is I don't know.
Therefore I pretend I know it.
    This is nerve-racking
    since I don't know what I must pretend to know.
Therefore I pretend to know everything.
I feel you know what I am supposed to know
but you can't tell me what it is
because you don't know that I don't know what it is.
You may know what I don't know, but not
    that I don't know it,
and I can't tell you. So you will have to tell me everything.

Thus, at one end of the continuum of student intentions is the satisfying of some vague and ill-articulated sense of need. At the other end are those who are present out of an intention to undertake a particular learning task – for example, to learn a language for their next holiday; to acquire mastery over a computer programme for job or leisure fulfilment; to understand the development processes of very young children to help them cope at home; or to come to a knowledge of one of the systems of government to enable them to play a more effective role in their local community.

In the course of their own continuing development, some will find that they need a specific skill or knowledge set or understanding to enable them to fit more easily into some existing or new situation. Even those who come to adult education classes in search of a qualification rather than new learning may be there for different motives. For some, it is the necessary preliminary to securing promotion or access to more education; for others, it is part of their pursuit of self-affirmation, a need to achieve a publicly recognised validation. A number come to seek reassurance, personal confirmation of their ability to achieve the goal. There is a wide range of such wants and intentions.

Such purposes are often concrete and meaningful to the participants' immediate concerns, though on occasion the learning is intended for longer-term future application. But others may not be so concrete. It has been suggested that some adults seek learning for *symbolic reasons* (i.e. they want to be seen as educated); some for *opportunity reasons* (i.e. the results of the learning programme will open doors to them not necessarily directly related to the learning programme, including access to further learning opportunities); and some for *practical reasons* (i.e. they want to use the new learning itself). But in each case the participant has a relatively clearly identified outcome from the learning programme.

Houle has represented this as a continuum of adult intentions (Houle 1961). At one end are those who come to achieve a particular piece of learning related to their present pattern of life (the *instrumental-* or *goal-oriented*), who wish to use education to achieve some external objective such as a certificate or job promotion or to solve an immediate problem facing them. For them the learning activity tends to come to an end once the objective (often separate from the learning process) has been achieved. At the other end are those who come for social and/or personal reasons or out of some general or indeterminate desire (the *process-* or *activity-oriented*). They like the atmosphere of the learning group, they find in the circumstances of the learning a meaning for themselves independent of the content or of the announced purpose of the activity. They attend because they get something out of the process apart from the subject matter involved. These people frequently seek the continuance of the activity even though the content of the learning may well change. They may pass from one learning programme to another, searching for satisfaction in the processes involved. In the middle are those who come to learn a 'subject' (the *subject-* or *learning-oriented*). They desire the knowledge or skill for its own sake. They pursue the subject out of interest. These people will frequently pass on to another educational programme in the same or related subject area, or continue to pursue the subject even without the assistance of a formal programme of learning (Figure 3.1). Here are those who wish to learn literature or cooking, painting or bird-watching, material that is specific enough but not directly related to the solution of an immediate

Orientation	Intentions	Learning process	Continuation at end of programme?
Goal-oriented; some end product	Achievement; problem-solving/ attainment	Learning most in certain specific areas	Process ceases on 'successful' completion of course
Learning-oriented	Interest in subject	Learning in all parts of subject matter area	Continued learning in same or related subject
Activity-oriented	Social or personal growth needs; may be indeterminate	Find in activities satisfactions	A new situation or activity is sought

Figure 3.1 Orientations of learning

problem. For them it is a matter of interest, adding to the richness of their way of life (the subject-oriented).

Often no clear-cut distinction may be drawn between these different groups.

The implications for the teacher of the different intentions of each of these three orientations are considerable. For the responses of each kind to the demands of the learning programme will vary. Those participants who are motivated to attend courses out of some sense of internal need may on occasion exhibit anxiety, sometimes mixed with hesitation and uncertainty; for the concept of need is threatening, demeaning both to oneself and to others. Such anxiety can be useful – it can promote learning provided it is not too great (see pp. 243–7). A gentle encouragement to focus it upon particular learning objectives often brings about greater readiness to learn. The development of a sharper consciousness of the nature of the learning task and of the relevance of the material to the immediate concerns of the participant is an essential preliminary to the use of the learning programme to satisfy such objectives. On the other hand, those whose motivation is to achieve some external goal (to pass an examination, for instance) will often reveal a great keenness. Here too, the clearer the awareness of purpose and of the relevance of the task to meet this purpose, the greater the motivation to learn.

They bring certain expectations about education itself

As we have already seen (Chapter 1), adult student participants come with a range of expectations about the learning process, a series of attitudes towards education in general. Using their experience over many years, they now construct themselves as 'students', putting themselves into a position in relation to 'their teacher'. Their focus in coming to our programmes is 'learning'.

This construct is usually based on their experience of schooling and of any education since leaving school. The conception of what education is and what it is for varies widely. Some people enjoyed their years in school; others did not. A number of our student participants assume that adult education will be like school. They expect to be taught everything by a teacher who 'knows everything'; they expect to be put back *in statu pupillari*, which is what education and learning imply for them. On the other hand, some are more willing to engage directly with the material being handled. For some of them the joy of the adult class is that it is unlike school. Even for many of those who enjoyed their schooldays, the value of adult education is often that the contents and the methods employed are different from those experienced in the formal education system (Figure 3.2).

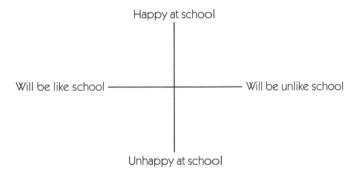

Figure 3.2 Student expectations of adult education

These expectations have different results on the attitudes of the participants. Some tend towards conformism, while others seek for a measure of independent learning. Some look for a more formal structure as a support for themselves, feeling more at home with 'being taught'. They may feel that their ability to learn has declined since they were last in education (and this may be true; on occasion we may have to spend some time with our student participants boosting their confidence and strengthening their skills of formal learning). Some of those who have had experience of education over a longer time may look for a less formal structure or become impatient, wishing to push on faster; they feel able to deal with the material easily.

In particular, both kinds of student participant bring with them a set of *self-horizons* relating to the sort of material they can or cannot master. Most of us believe that there is some subject or other that we can never learn, that is just not compatible with our range of inherent abilities and interests. It is odd that so many voluntary adult students still find themselves in classes containing a good deal of material that from the start they are adamant they will never be able to learn. Students attend courses in religion and yet say they cannot cope with 'theology'; students join art classes with a firm belief that they can never learn to draw. Learning in some parts of these fields is not for them; they confine themselves to the role of 'looker-on', as presumably they were at times in school. They may plead age, using this as an excuse to avoid identifying other causes of failing. By contrast there will be those who see the entering of new areas as a challenge, difficult but not beyond the learning resources they can call upon.

We need to explore these constructs, about schooling, learning, about being a 'student' and what is expected in education, from an early stage in the learning programme. The worst thing we can do is treat all the participants alike, teaching one course to them all. The problem of the teacher of adults, faced with a mixed group of student participants, encouraging those with low self-horizons and keeping the more self-reliant satisfied with their own progress, is one of constantly making choices between alternatives, of balancing the needs of one sub-group with those of another while maintaining loyalty to the subject matter of the course and the group as a whole.

They all have competing interests

Apart from those adults who for a relatively short period engage in full-time courses, adult students are part-time. Education for them is a matter of secondary interest; it is not their prime concern. Even for full-time adult students, their education is constantly overshadowed by the 'realities' of life: their job or lack of job, their family situation, their social life, other competing concerns. Some may come to our programmes with relief, to get away from other pressures. Others may come with reluctance, squeezing in learning time against the pressure of what they may feel to be 'more important' activities.

The adults who come to join us in the learning enterprise come from a complete social environment. They all have relationships such as parents, partners, workmates and friends, as well as being students. Adult learners should not be divorced from their background if their learning is to be relevant and thus effective. We need to take seriously the whole of the context within which our student participants live and where they use the new learning they have acquired. Students in other parts of the educational world may be taken out of their life situation to concentrate on their learning, but adult learners continue to live within their lifeworld and to apply what they learn in that world.

Within that background there are factors supporting as well as some militating against the learning endeavours. Not all of the competing concerns that the participants bring with them to our programmes are hindrances.

Indeed, periods of intensive study can hardly be carried through without the identification of support networks around the adult learner, and it is to the advantage of both teacher and student participant to encourage the full exploitation of these supporting factors. This is particularly true where the class is a one-off episode, not backed up by other studies as it is at school or college. A short course, taken part-time and on its own, will often assume in the life of many student participants rather less significance than it has for the teacher. We must not be surprised if our students' attention is at times distracted towards more urgent problems (see p. 237).

They all possess set patterns of learning

Adults are engaged in a continuing process of lifelong learning, and they have already acquired ways of coping with this. They often fail to see this as 'learning' in the educational sense, but it exists all the same. Over the years, each of our adult student participants has developed their own strategies and patterns of learning, which they have found help them to learn most easily, most quickly and most effectively (see pp. 110–13). Learning changes are not brought about without effort, and the process can be painful. It takes an investment of time and emotions and, once done, no one wants to do it again. We all thus seek ways to ease the pain, shorten the time taken to master the necessary new material, and make the gains acquired more permanent. Experience has taught us what strategies we can adopt to achieve these ends.

Each of us learns in our own way, according to our particular aptitudes and experience. Some handle figures more easily than others. Some have fostered different methods for memorising facts (addresses, telephone numbers etc.). Languages particularly throw up differences of approach in this respect. Some learners need a text, finding it hard to react to spoken words, while others respond easily to oral tuition. Both are valid methods of learning languages, and we should not try to force any learner into adopting a particular style because we prefer it to any other. We must remember that our student participants all have their own ways of learning which may differ from our ways of learning, and opportunities to exercise these have to be created if new learning is to take place.

The pace of learning of each student participant also varies. In general, in those areas where the participants can call upon a good deal of experience – social relationships and roles, for instance – they tend to learn a good deal faster than young people, provided that the new material does not conflict with existing knowledge. But where they have less experience on which to fasten the new material – languages, for example, or computer studies – especially if it calls for extensive memorising, they tend to learn more slowly and have greater difficulty in mastering the material than their younger counterparts.

Such matters are central to our concerns as teachers. There is a wide range of learning styles within any group of adult learners, and we need to devise methods that give each of the participants full scope for exercising their own particular learning method, and as far as possible not impose our own upon them.

Implications for the teacher of adults

We can see, then, that teachers of adults, especially those who teach in groups, are faced with a difficult task from the start. Unless the group is narrowly conceived (as in some forms of industrial training or adults in university courses), our student participants will consist of a wide variety of people all bringing their own advantages and disadvantages to the learning situation:

- Some see themselves as more adult than others; some are still searching in education for autonomy, others are more willing to accept dependency for the purpose of learning.
- All are growing and developing, but in different directions and at a different pace.
- Some bring a good deal of experience and knowledge in different parts of the subject matter, others bring less; and there are varying degrees of willingness to use this material to help the learning process.
- They have a wide range of intentions, some specific, some more general and related to the subject matter under discussion, and others unknown even to themselves.
- They are all at different points in the continuum between those who require to be taught everything and those who wish to find out everything for themselves; and they each have some belief in what they can and cannot do in the way of learning.
- They all have competing interests, often of greater importance to them than their learning.
- They have all by now acquired their own ways of learning, which vary considerably the one from the other.

It is easy to view all of this in negative terms, to see most of what we have discussed as hindrances to learning. The pressure from competing interests, the worry and anxiety students have, especially about their learning abilities, based as these often are on misconceptions as to what education involves, the problem of coping with unlearning and the attack on the personality that this can at times imply – all of these may seem to make the task of the teacher of adults particularly difficult. We must not be surprised if some of the student participants do not move as fast as we would wish them to; if they have difficulty in grasping some of the material that *we* find so easy and have so carefully constructed for them; if they show a lack of responsiveness to all our promptings to engage more wholeheartedly with the subject matter of the programme. We must not be put off if some of the learners require us to demonstrate or lecture when we would rather that they practise for themselves or discuss.

But there are many aspects of this discussion that give cause for hope. Within the group is a well of resources that we can use. Some of these can be quickly identified: the wealth of knowledge, skills and experience gathered together in one room; the fact that all the student participants, whether they know it or not, are already engaged in some form of learning; the awareness, however dim, of purpose and need; the greater use of reasoning powers, and the fact that adult students, when provoked, 'accept' the teacher's word less readily (those of us who prefer to demonstrate and to lecture, to perform rather than to watch, to listen to our own voice rather than to the voice of the learners, will not see this as a resource); the desire of many of the learners to apply what they learn one day to their lives the very next day and the fact that (unlike younger students) they are in a position to do so. All these factors can be seen as combining to form a powerful aid to learning.

We need to try to identify both those factors that prevent us from being fully effective in the teaching-learning process and those resources that we can bring into play in order to overcome the obstacles. In adult education, our students are not there just to be taught; they are our greatest resource in the learning process.

Application

It is important, as you look through this material, that you relate it to your own experience. You may find it helpful to write down what assumptions you made about the potential student participants for the course you have chosen as your own, what characteristics they will bring with them to the programme. It may be possible for you, if you actually run a course, to test this against the group that materialises so that you can assess how accurate your first thoughts were.

A second useful exercise at this stage is to set out for yourself the range of helps and hindrances that you think your students will bring with them to the programme of study. Most of us do this without being fully conscious of it. To make it a deliberate process will help to bring into focus those whom we hope to help to learn.

Further reading

Belenky, M., Clinchy, B.M., Goldberger, N.R. and Tarule, J.M. (1986) *Women's Ways of Knowing: the Development of Self, Voice and Mind*. New York: Basic Books.

Cross, K.P. (1981) *Adults as Learners: Increasing Participation and Facilitating Learning*. San Francisco, CA: Jossey Bass.

Giles, K. (1981) *Personal Change in Adults*. Milton Keynes: Open University Press.

Knowles, M.S. (1990) *The Adult Learner: a Neglected Species*. Houston, TX: Gulf.

Rogers, J. (2001) *Adults Learning*, 4th edn. Buckingham: Open University Press.

Sheehy, C.T. (1976) *Passages: Predictable Crises of Adult Life*. New York: Dutton.

Sugarman, L. (1986) *Lifespan Development: Concepts, Theories and Interventions*. New York: Methuen.

Tuijnman, A. and van der Kamp, M. (eds) (1992) *Learning Across the Lifespan: Theories, Research, Policies*. Oxford: Pergamon.

Chapter 4

THE NATURE OF LEARNING

What is it . . . ?

It is now agreed that 'learning' is the interaction of the learner, the context, the kind of learning task and the processes involved. This chapter looks at the various theories of learning which have been constructed around these four themes.

Some readers may be tempted to give this chapter a miss. They would argue that learning theories are both disputed and irrelevant to their task of teaching. But that would be a pity. For theory and practice do need to go together. Academics need to be challenged by teachers to explain what are the practical implications of their theories. And we ourselves will be more effective in our work if we understand more clearly what is happening when we teach.

Nevertheless, this is a complex and contested area, and to summarise it in such a short space runs the danger of oversimplification. There are I think two main reasons why the area is so complex. First, some theories concentrate on asking *why* we learn, what is it that drives us to learn, while others try to explain *how* we learn, what are the processes involved. For example, some humanists tell us that learning springs from our inner drives (the why), but this does not tell us how we learn. Those who urge critical reflection on experience tell us how we learn but not why. These are two quite different questions.

Second, as we shall see, it is now generally agreed that learning involves the interaction of several factors – including the learner, the context of learning, the learning task itself and the processes involved. Most learning theorists concentrate on one or at best the interaction of two such factors – and that leaves room for others to come along and tell them that their theory is deficient! So we get another theory.

In this chapter, I will outline briefly the main sets of learning theories before turning in the next chapter to a different approach which is emerging.

<table>
<tr><td>

Activity

You will find it helpful to take a case study of some recent learning task you engaged in – preferably something outside of a formal classroom (e.g. learning to swim). Make a note of it; I shall ask you to refer to it throughout this chapter.

</td></tr>
</table>

LEARNING AND CHANGE

In common parlance the word 'learning' carries at least two meanings. There is a general one of some kind of change, often in knowledge but also in behaviour. 'I met Mrs X today and learned that she has just left her job.' 'Today, a new bus timetable was introduced. A spokesman for the council said that he believed the public would soon learn to use the new routes.' But there is also a more intense sense of the verb 'to learn' meaning to memorise, to learn by heart: 'Take this poem home and learn it.'

We may leave on one side the meaning of the word as 'memorising' and concentrate instead on 'learning as change'. To say that 'learning is change' is too simple. First, not all change is learning. Changes brought about by ageing or other physical processes can hardly be described as 'learning changes', though they may in their turn bring about learning changes. Secondly, some forms of learning are confirmation of existing patterns of knowledge and behaviour. But since the knowledge is more strongly held, the skills consolidated, or the behaviour more intensely engaged in after the learning, it can perhaps be said that learning is still change but that it is more reinforcement than alteration of patterns of knowledge and behaviour.

What we usually mean by 'learning' are those more or less permanent changes and reinforcements brought about voluntarily in one's patterns of acting, thinking and/or feeling.

Areas of change (learning domains)

There have been several attempts to describe the different areas of learning change.

The traditional distinction has of course been between learning knowledge and learning skills; but others have elaborated on this. Several point to the need to include attitudes as a third area. In the field of learning objectives, knowledge, skills and attitudes (KSA) is a well-worn path. Kurt Lewin (1935) suggested that learning changes occur in skills, in cognitive patterns (knowledge and understanding), in motivation and interest, and in ideology (fundamental beliefs). Gagné (1972) identified five 'domains': *motor skills* which require practice; *verbal information* – facts, principles and generalisations which when organised into larger entities become knowledge; *intellectual skills* – the 'discriminations, concepts and rules' that help in using knowledge; *cognitive strategies* – the way the individual learns, remembers and thinks, the self-managed skills needed to define and solve problems; and *attitudes*.

Learning then takes place in a number of different spheres. We may categorise these using the mnemonic KUSAB:

- We learn new information that is largely memorised and converted into usable *knowledge* ('I know').
- Knowledge may however be held uncomprehendingly. So that learning new *understanding* (organising and reorganising knowledge to create new patterns of relationships) is a different area of learning ('I see').
- We may learn new *skills* or develop existing skills further – not just physical skills, our ability to do certain things, but also skills of thinking and of learning, skills of coping and solving problems ('I can').
- The changing of *attitudes* (including beliefs and values) is a distinct sphere of learning ('I feel/believe').
- Finally, learning to apply our newly-learned material to what we do and how we live, changed ways of *behaving*, is a separate area of learning ('I do').

The way these five domains of learning relate to each other is complex. Changes in attitude rely to a large extent on changes in knowledge and understanding, and behavioural changes can hardly take place without accompanying changes in other areas. But these relationships are idiosyncratic and uncertain. When new knowledge (e.g. 'smoking can damage your health') meets contrary behaviour (the habit of smoking), one of a number of different reactions may occur. The information may be decried, ignored or rejected ('It's all very exaggerated', or 'I know but I don't care'); the new knowledge may be accepted but rationalised away by other knowledge ('I agree, but less than 30 per cent of smokers die of cancer caused by smoking and I'll be one of the lucky ones', or 'It's more dangerous to cross the roads than to smoke'); or the new knowledge can lead to changes in behaviour. How any individual reacts to learning changes in any one domain seems to depend on personality and situational factors.

Four elements in learning

It is now increasingly agreed (Merriam and Cafarella 1999: 399–403) that learning springs from the interaction between the individual, the learning processes and the sociocultural context within which the learning is set. All of these elements form part of the learning equation. There is a fourth element, the *task* or the content/subject matter of the learning. It will I think be helpful if we can organise our discussion of adult learning theories round these four elements:

- learning theories focusing on who is doing the learning;
- learning theories focusing on the context;
- learning theories focusing on the kind of learning task being undertaken;
- learning theories focusing on the processes involved.

Activity

Look at your chosen learning task and try to see what you did, what part was played by the context, what kind of learning task was involved and what kinds of processes you used.

LEARNER-BASED THEORIES

This is the largest area of discussion among educators, especially those concerned with student-centred learning. All writers agree that learners change over time, some adopting a *growth* model (linear and natural change) and others a *developmental* model (diverse and more purposeful change) (see p. 63). Many suggest that all persons change in the same way – in the same direction and at much the same pace – but others think that this hides individual differences.

Intelligence and the brain

Before discussing these theories, we need to look first at one key area of research, on intelligence. Most writers now accept that, although there are some genetic areas of the brain with learning predispositions (especially those relating to language), the brain is not a high powered engine already designed and unchangeable, simply functioning. The concept of a basic intelligence which after initial growth remains the same and can be measured (an IQ) has been challenged on many grounds (see p. 63), especially by the ideas of crystalline and fluid intelligence (Cattell 1987) and of multiple intelligences (Gardner 1993). A few have gone further, denying the existence of the mind as a finite entity in favour of a dynamic, ever-changing flux with unknown potential, and claiming that those who speak of fixed measures like intelligence, aptitude and personality traits for what may be temporary stabilised states are perpetuating myths and creating blocks to a 'truer' perception of the personality as fluid and active in its own quest.

More recently, the view that each of us is 'growing our own brains' has gained acceptability. The brain is thought to be changing each time we use it. We are able to develop some parts of it by stimulation and use, while other parts may remain underdeveloped or become atrophied (Field and Leicester 2000: 65–74).

How such changed understanding will affect traditional learning theories is not clear, so that what follows is a description of the conflicting views as they stand at the moment.

Behaviourist theories

One group of learning theories which concentrate on the learner suggests that the main aim of learning is to change behaviour. Stimuli from outside the individual provoke responses, and these responses can be directed towards achieving desired behavioural changes. Society (or the teacher) can control this process by selecting the stimuli and reinforcing the approved responses. Learning is thus brought about by an association between the desired responses and the reinforcement (rewards and punishments) through a system of success and failure indicators. Such responses become more complex as the learner grows, in a linear process.

These theories tend to suggest that the learner is relatively passive. Although a variety of responses is offered, only the 'right' (i.e. personally or socially satisfying) response is rewarded while other responses are discouraged. Feedback, the return from the learner to the source of the stimulus or to society around, is separate from and follows after the learning process.

Despite the many attacks on it, this remains a strongly held view, for it seems self-evident that much learning is initiated by external stimuli which call forth responses, and that society confirms or denies the validity of those responses. Behaviourist theories distinguish sharply between right and wrong; they assume that knowledge is truth, independent of both teacher and learner, that it is the same for all learners and can be known.

Stimulus-response is not seen as applicable only to low-level learning; it also applies at more advanced levels. Nor is it confined to skill learning; it forms the basis for cognitive and affective learning as well. Indeed, the general validity of the theory may be seen in the fact that it underlies most of the other approaches to learning. Cognitive theories which stress the inherent demands of the subject matter still rely on an assumption that responses are called out by different stimuli. And some humanist theories urge that stimuli arise from our life context, although our responses will vary, dependent on our individual experiences and personalities; we learn at an early stage of life by a system of approvals and disapprovals whether our patterns of behaviour are socially acceptable or not. Stimulus and response form part of several other theories of learning in some form.

Cognitive theories

During the 1960s, a number of theories emerged that directed attention to the activity of the learner in creating the response and to the nature of knowledge itself. These form a distinct group. They point to the active engagement of the mind in processing data, the instruments of perception, the emergence of insights, the development of memory etc. The concept of intelligence as learning capability underpins these theories, not as a fixed capacity but one which continues to develop throughout life provided it is used and stimulated, so that one could be significantly more intelligent (or indeed less, if intelligence is not used) at age 50 than at age of 30 (see p. 63).

In order to learn, understanding is necessary. The material needs to be marshalled into meaningful units and then mastered. Thus the focus is on how the content of learning is structured, building up from easy to more difficult knowledge and skills, and on the practice of intellectual exercises. Although the learner is seen to be active rather than passive, the activity is controlled by the inherent structure of knowledge itself which the teacher-agent sequences. Words like 'must', 'necessary' and 'discipline' which occur in connection with this view of learning reveal that learners are faced with something bigger than they are, something to which they must adapt themselves. The world of knowledge lies outside of themselves. Growth is linear, the development of the ability to cope with increasingly complex knowledge. Such views are not confined to the acquisition of knowledge or the development of new understandings; they apply to learning skills and attitudes as well.

Activity

Did you, at the time, see any structure in the material of your learning activity?

Hierarchies of learning

Both behaviourist and cognitive learning theories posit that learning advances as more and more learning takes place; there are higher levels of learning which not all learners attain to. These levels are now being extended from childhood into the adult field.

Bloom (1965) suggested that learning takes place not only in the cognitive field but also in the affective, and that a series of steps common to all learners in the cognitive domain parallel those in the affective. Thus cognitive learning consists of the recall and recognition of *knowledge*; *comprehension*, understanding the material, exploring it actively; the *application* of the comprehended knowledge in concrete situations; exploring each new situation by *analysis* of its constituted parts and *synthesis* into new concepts; and finally *evaluation* in which the learners assess the value of the new knowledge in relation to the realisation of their goals. On the affective side, there is a similar progression: *receiving* stimuli, developing awareness, being willing to receive, eventually using selective attention; *responding* willingly, the emergence of a sense of satisfaction with the response; *valuing* the concepts and the process they are engaged in, expressing preferences and eventually commitment; then *conceptualising*, attaching concepts to each of the values identified; and finally *organising* these values into a system that comes to characterise each individual. Gagné (1972) also drew up a progression of learning from simple 'signal' learning through stimulus-response, chaining, verbal association, multiple discrimination, concept learning and principle learning, to complex 'problem-solving'.

Personality theories

In a reaction against such hierarchies, 'personality' theories of learning emerged. Most of these depend on the distribution of personality types along a continuum of one kind or another – between the extrovert and the introvert, for instance, or between those who see the 'locus of control' as within themselves and those who see it as outside of themselves ('I was ill because I ate stale meat' as against 'the food in that restaurant made me ill'), or between the fatalist and the self-confident.

Those who locate people on such external-internal scales sometimes suggest that people at one end have a general expectancy that positive reinforcements are not under their control. They may lack self-confidence, possess feelings of inferiority, even expect failure and rely more on luck, fate, chance or God. Such people may feel that what they don't know is so vast and what they do know is so small that they may be discouraged from attempting to master new fields. At the opposite extreme, it is suggested, are those who believe that reinforcement is contingent on their own behaviour. These are usually thought to be more independent individuals, resisting manipulation; they will act, pay attention and (if they feel it necessary to the achievement of some goal) remember. They draw upon the information and other resources provided by their environment, select activities in which they have already been successful, and feel confident that what they already know will help them to master further skills and knowledge. Most people are thought to occupy mid-points between these two extremes or to display characteristics of both of these types at different times and in different circumstances.

Learning then, according to these theories, depends not only on one's perception of the subject but also on one's perception of self. One example of this is the metaphor of 'learning maps' (Rogers 1993). This view argues that people draw a map in their head with themselves at the centre, and place every experience, concept and activity on the map at a chosen distance from their self-centre. Those who like cooking and feel themselves to be good at it, for example, will locate 'cooking' close to the self-centre, whereas they may well put 'computers' or 'astronomy' closer to the periphery because they feel less at ease with these subjects or because they seem to be distant from their main preoccupations. These are not of course fixed maps – they are constantly changing as events (experience) thrust new material onto them or bring some items closer to the self-centre than before. Learning, it is suggested, is easiest among those subjects which are close to the self-centre; and this implies that teaching includes a process of helping each participant to redraw their personalised map so as to bring the subject closer to the self-centre. So long as learners feel that any subject is far away, 'not for me', they will experience great difficulties in learning.

A different continuum is that between those who are 'high-achievement oriented' (not just ambitious: this group embraces those who seek to play chess or breed pigeons better than their neighbours) and those who are anxious about failure. The former experience an 'approach motivation', a drive towards engaging in some activity or other, while the latter experience an 'avoidance motivation' (McClelland *et al.* 1953). Success encourages the former and failure does not put them off easily, it can become a challenge; whereas both success (generally regarded as a 'flash in a pan' that will not necessarily be repeated) and failure alike encourage the latter to withdraw.

Various learning theories have been built on these analyses of personality types. Houle (1961) drew up a series of different orientations of some learners (see pp. 77–8). But the danger with such schemes is that of assigning individuals to particular categories. Designations of this kind can become a hindrance to learning, if they are thought to prescribe the way in which people will behave; they will certainly determine the way we view other people. There is some value in knowing that such factors are at work, but they are not determinants, only explanations of what is happening.

On the other hand, the importance of attitudes in the learning process and the relationship of attitudes to knowledge form the major contribution of personality theories. Learning is not just a matter for the head. McClintock (1972) described four kinds of learning – behavioural modification, functional learning (the satisfaction of basic needs), the development of consistency (the reduction of inner tensions) and information processing – and suggested that the way in which knowledge (K), attitudes (A) and practice (P) relate to each other in each of these is different.

Activity

Ask yourself how you *felt* about your learning.

Humanist theories

It was as a reaction against the personality theories which seemed to reduce the control of the learner over their own learning and against the hierarchies of the behaviourists and cognitivists that the humanist theories of learning emerged. These are not so coherent as the other groups.

Humanist theories are associated with changes away from the certainties of empirical science, the universally valid conclusions of objective research, the stability and general applicability of scientific laws, the normally accepted values, into a world of living complexity, uncertainty, instability, the uniqueness of individual response and the conflicts of values. These theories reassert the agency of the learner in the learning process; they stress that it is the learner's actions which largely create the learning situation. They emphasise the urges and drives of the learner towards (for example) increased autonomy and competence, the active search for meaning, the fulfilment of goals which individuals set for themselves – in short, the impulse towards being more fully human. Learning and goal setting are seen to be natural, calling into play the abilities that the learners have already developed and which they seek to enhance. Learning then is the satisfying of inner drives and needs. Motivation for learning comes from within, the desire to fulfil one's potential, self-actualisation, individuation (intra-personal); and the material on which the learning drive fastens is extra-personal, the whole of life, the cultural and interpersonal relationships that form the social context.

These views stress the agency of the learner and emphasise that all the other theories talk about the learners being controlled by the stimuli, by the teacher, by the subject matter or by their inherent personality. The humanist views learning as the active engagement of the learners with the world around them and with themselves. For many, it is part of a process of conflict in which the learners seek to take control of their own life processes. The material on which they exercise their learning skills is less important than the goals they have set themselves. The role of the teacher is to increase the range of experiences so that the student participants can use these new experiences to achieve their own desired learning changes.

Experiential learning

There is general acceptance that experience forms the basis of learning. Since Dewey wrote *Experience and Education* (1938) outlining the conditions which govern learning from experience, it has been increasingly agreed that the experiences we have lead us into learning. Experiential learning can be applied to the other kinds of learning theories. Thus the kinds of responses provoked by stimuli are in large part determined by experience. Cognitive judgement about the subject matter of learning is based on prior experience. Humanists suggest that at the heart of all learning is the search to make sense of and control experience.

The problem with experiential learning is that it means many things to different people. It can mean *learning from current experience* – that is, one's experiences create the need for learning. The gap between one's current experience and one's past experience will (it is argued) create the impetus for learning. It can mean engaging actively with one's context in order to learn effectively (*learning by doing*). It can mean *using one's past experience* to challenge the present. It can mean *creating experiences for learners* so that they can 'experience' what they are learning about. It frequently means *learning by reflecting critically on one's experience*. But the main use of the term refers to the way in which current experience creates the learning need and prior experience governs the learning changes made in response to current experience (Boud and Miller 1996).

Experiential learning is a key element in contemporary discussions of lifelong learning. For if learning is embedded in life, much of adult learning will be informal, not publicly recognised. The Accreditation of Prior Learning, the recognition of this informal learning from experience by educational agencies, is one way in which such experiential learning can not only be utilised but can be harnessed to enable the adult to proceed into further forms of lifelong education.

One of the major implications of experiential learning is that the concepts of 'simple' and 'difficult' in learning cannot be absolute, inherent in the subject, as the cognitivists suggest. Instead such concepts are seen to be relative, determined by the experience of the learner. What is 'difficult' in learning terms to one person within one cultural context will be easier to another person in a context where greater meaning or value is attached to the knowledge item involved. This undermines much of the 'easy-to-harder' progression of many educationalists.

Experiential learning has been critiqued by a number of writers. They point out that this set of concepts is confused, depending on whether one is looking at the way the individual learner relates to and uses their own experiences, whether one is creating new experiences to enhance and direct learning, whether one is examining the power relations within experience, or whether one is viewing the totality of experience in terms of the interaction of nature, organisations, cultures and the individual: all of 'these orientations have their blind spots' (Fenwick 2001: 2).

Motivation for learning, then, from a humanist point of view, can spring from inner drives and needs, or from interaction with experience.

Motivation and learning

These views thus assert that people are already motivated to learn. To talk about persons not being motivated is to misunderstand the situation. They may not be motivated to *learn what we want them to learn*, but all adults are motivated to learn their own learning in their own way.

Motivation is usually defined as a drive directed towards meeting a need or achieving an intention, those factors that energise and direct behavioural patterns organised around a goal. It is frequently seen as a force within the individual that moves them to act in a certain way. Motivation in learning is that compulsion which keeps a person within the learning situation and encourages them to learn.

Motivation is seen as being dependent on either *intrinsic* or *extrinsic* factors. Extrinsic factors consist of those incentives or pressures such as attendance requirements, punishments and rewards, or examinations to which many learners in formal settings are subjected, or the influence of other persons or organisations. These, if internalised, create an intention to engage in the learning programme. Intrinsic factors consist of those inner pressures and/or rational decisions which create a desire for learning changes.

Much adult learning is dependent on intrinsic motivational factors, but not all of it is. It has been argued that intrinsic factors are stronger and more enduring than extrinsic. But even within intrinsic motivation, there is a hierarchy. For example, a desire to please some other person or loyalty to a group, which may keep a person within a learning programme even when bored, are seen as motives of a lower order than a desire to complete a particular task.

There are three main groups of ideas behind the development of a theory of motivation. The first says that motivation is an inner impulse based on needs or drives. The second says that motivation can be learned. And the third claims that motivation relates to goals set or accepted by oneself.

Activity

Ask yourself what your motive was for learning.

Motivations as impulse

Needs

There is a large literature which suggests that all learning (certainly all purposeful learning) comes from a sense of need: 'Learning takes place when an individual feels a need, puts forth an effort to meet that need, and experiences satisfaction with the result of his [*sic*] effort' (Leagans 1971: 33–4). The awakening of a sense of need has been identified by many writers as a precondition of effective learning.

But we have to tread carefully here. Not all purposeful learning comes from a sense of need; some, for example, comes from an increased interest or a desire to test some theory. Indeed, 'needs' is a dangerous concept. It can lead to an assumption that 'I know what you need to learn even though you don't know what you need'. And it reduces learner agency. Purposeful adult learning comes as much from learner intentions as from needs (see pp. 75–6).

Many humanists however assert the primacy of needs in learning. Individuals vary in the composition and intensity of these needs. At their simplest instinctual level, they may be the avoidance of pain and the search for pleasure, or the Freudian drives related to life, death, sex and aggression, although all such instincts can be modified by learning. One set of views suggests that many of these needs arise from the demands of lifespan development (see pp. 63–9). Others regard them as a search for the reduction of tension – for example, the inner conflicts between different parts of the self and different experiences (intra-resolution), or the conflicts between the self and the external social and physical environment (extra-resolution). The individual is seeking for harmony, for peace.

Some writers have talked about primary needs (viscerogenic, related to bodily functions) and secondary needs (psychogenic); the latter come into play only when primary needs are to a large extent met. On the other hand, there are those who have described this distinction in terms of needs (physical) and drives (psychological).

Maslow (1968) is recognised as the apostle of the 'needs' school of thought. He distinguished basic drives from temporary needs, and established a hierarchy which is often quoted (Figure 4.1). He argued that all people are driven through the first four stages of basic needs. As each lower need is in part met, the next higher level is triggered. Several levels of need can be in operation at the same time. The highest level of need – self-actualisation,

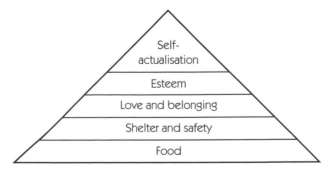

Figure 4.1 Maslow's hierarchy of needs

a need to create, to appreciate, to know and to understand – may not be reached by some individuals on more than an occasional basis. (Maslow indicated in his teaching a further level above self-actualisation: 'self-transcendence', a need to express tangibly concern for others, but this hardly appears in his writings.)

For the teacher, Maslow's work will be a reminder that within any group of adult learners there will be a wide variety of needs, and within each participant there will be a different mixture of needs. This mixture will be constantly changing as the learning proceeds and as the individual's life situation changes. This is why predetermined and uniform learning outcomes can never be achieved in adult learning programmes. Each adult learner will take away from any learning situation what they require; learning is unique to each learner and uncertain.

But Maslow's hierarchy of needs fails us as adult educators precisely at the point we need it most. It offers us an analysis of the *preconditions* to the type of learning we are most interested in: the self-evident truth that the prior personal and social needs (food, security, personal relationships and a sense of esteem) must be satisfied, at least in part, before motivation for the more creative, evaluative and self-fulfilling kinds of learning will be aroused. But it also reminds us that some of our student participants come to our programmes from a desire for social relationships or to gain some sense of esteem, driven by needs that require to be met at least partially before further learning can take place.

Maslow also suggested (in what he called 'pre-potency') that if the lower levels of need are satisfied in part, the motivation to self-actualisation will be automatically triggered because it is inherent within each person. If it is not so triggered, this is because one of the lower levels of need has been inadequately met. This is by no means certain, and in any case, it does not explain the motivation towards the different forms of self-actualisation which occur. To explain this, we need to turn to other work on motivation, particularly that related to drives rather than needs.

Drives

Many writers stress the inherent drives within each individual – drives created partly by the environment and partly by the personality of the individual. They have been variously defined: drives towards autonomy and maturity, to make meaning out of experiences, to satisfy (emotional and intellectual) hunger etc. Whether viewed as goal-seeking (based on specific self-set goals) or ideal-seeking (related to objectives set by the value system the learners have come to accept and hold), inner drives rather than outside imperatives impel the learner to seek out learning changes. As we have seen (p. 41), Carl Rogers viewed this as drives towards adulthood – autonomy, responsibility, self-direction – though the forms such concepts take are culturally bound, varying from society to society.

Such drives are often described in terms of a struggle, a desperate search for freedom. Habermas (see pp. 105–6) viewed human life as a quest for self-emancipation, a striving towards autonomy through self-formative processes. Freire (1972) identified three stages of learning: activities which are task-related; activities concerned with personal relationships; and what he calls 'conscientization', a concept that implies the transformation of the awareness of surrounding reality, the development of a concern for change and a realistic assessment of the resources for and obstacles to such a process, and the conflicts it is bound to provoke, leading to action to transform the lifeworld (*praxis*). Learning is only learning when it leads to action.

A further group of humanist learning theories relate to the drive to make sense of experience, a search for meaning through *paradigm transformation*. This view argues that the environment we live in is the result of our own creative processes; we build, name and manipulate the environment for ourselves. Learning is a process of rebuilding, renaming and remanipulating that environment, the modification and adaptation of those paradigms (i.e. accepted and usually unchallenged world pictures on which we build our lives) that underlie all our actions. Mezirow, the leading exponent of transformative learning, suggested that learning in childhood is laying down socially and individually constructed meanings, a process of finding the keys, making sense of experience, forming perspectives. Learning in adulthood is a continuing process of reconstructing and transforming these meanings through challenging our assumptions, our frames of reference, in the course of active interaction with our environment (Mezirow *et al.* 2000).

Learning then for many humanist writers is dependent on the innate drives of men and women towards autonomy or understanding in an attempt to control rather than be controlled, a search for liberation. Such views are widespread, although they are increasingly being challenged.

Learned motivation

There are however alternative views. One suggestion is that motivation is not inherent, like drives, but learned – the fruit of the reward and punishment systems that people have been exposed to. If this is true, then perhaps motivation may be altered by a new system of approvals and disapprovals, by specific activities accompanied by a change of the learning environment to emphasise achievement rather than failure. Exactly what the factors are that lead to motivation being learned is not clear. Stimulus-response theories may help here; success and pleasure in early educational experiences seem to play a part. It is pointed out, for example, that many of those who liked their schooling and were a success in educational environments return to participate in formal and non-formal educational activities, while those who see themselves as educational failures, although they may often use the lack of education to rationalise their lack of success, are only rarely motivated by this deficit to return to education. Despite the fact that the issues remain unclear, the concept of learned motivation has much to commend it.

Goal-driven motivation

A third group of ideas centres round the view that motivation is related to the goals set and/or accepted by the learners for themselves. Motivation is not responsive but purposeful, an act of human agency. Different levels of motivation can be seen here. The internalisation of goals set by others (e.g. employers) is unlikely to lead to as high levels of motivation as those goals set by the learner themselves. And the immediacy of the goal may also affect the level of motivation. It has been noted that motivation is highest among those who find the learning task itself satisfying, whereas those who have their sights set on goals which are further away (e.g. to pass an examination or to get a better job) tend to have a somewhat lower level of motivation. Motivation may be related to the immediacy of the desired goal.

The context of motivation

Motivation is clearly related to a number of factors: the inner needs and drives of the learner, the interaction between the individual and their experience, the learning which they have already done, and/or the goals they set for themselves. All of these arise from the life situation in which the learner is located. It is important for us to realise that motivation relates as much to the context as to the individual. All learning is located within a particular time and place; and we know that motivation is influenced as much by this setting as by internal drives and avoidances.

Herzberg's work (1972), although related to industrial activities, is of direct relevance to learning. While recognising that all motivational factors will vary from individual to individual, he developed the concept of 'motivators' and 'hygiene' factors (demotivators). 'Motivators' are those factors which make the participants 'feel good' about their work – a sense of achievement, recognition, responsibility, advancement and personal growth. Most of these are internal factors. However, these feelings are not on the whole long lasting, they need to be continually reinforced. But they spring directly from the work in hand. In contrast, the 'hygiene' factors that create a sense of dissatisfaction normally spring from external factors – from inappropriate direction or methods, inadequate working conditions, unsatisfactory relationships within the group and so on. These tend to be longer lasting in their nature.

These two sets of factors are not the plus and minus of the motivational situation. The presence of motivators and the reduction of hygiene factors are *both* necessary to achieve positive motivation. Removing the hygiene factors alone without increasing the influence of motivators will not help the task. Similarly, strengthening the motivators without removing the demotivators will not increase effectiveness.

Kurt Lewin (1947) has a similar approach with his 'force field'. He suggested that in every learning situation, there are forces which promote the learning changes and forces which inhibit the learning changes. He argued that it is necessary for the educator to identify these, to harness the one and to negate the other.

Motivational factors in learning, then, lie as much within the learning situation as within the individuals themselves. In this context, the teacher of adults plays a vital role. We need to be reminded of McGregor's (1960) Theory X and Theory Y (Figure 4.2). The teacher may assume that all student-learners have an inherent dislike of work and will avoid it if they can (Theory X), that they wish to escape from responsibility, that they have a static range of abilities which nothing within the learning situation will improve, and that it is the function of the teacher to direct them to the work of learning. In this case, like all self-fulfilling prophecies, we teachers

Theory X	Theory Y
The average human being has an inherent dislike of work and will avoid it if they can.	The expenditure of physical and mental effort in work is as natural as play and rest.
Because of this, most people need to be coerced, controlled, directed and threatened with punishment to get them to put in enough effort to contribute to organisational goals.	External control and threats of punishment are not the only means to encourage learners to make an effort to contribute to organisational goals. People will engage in self-direction and self-control to achieve objectives to which they are committed through the rewards which the achievement itself brings.
The average person prefers to be directed, wishes to avoid any responsibility, has relatively little ambition, and wants security above all.	The average person, under the right conditions, learns not only to accept but to seek responsibility. The capacity to exercise a fairly high degree of imagination, ingenuity and creativity in the solution of organisational problems is widely, not narrowly, distributed. In most societies, the intellectual potential of the average person is not fully utilised.

Figure 4.2 McGregor's Theory X and Theory Y

become a 'hygiene factor', a demotivator. Or we can assume that learning changes are natural to all human beings and certainly are the expressed desire of our student-learners (Theory Y), that they are willing to accept responsibility for their own learning, that it is external factors such as the educational system itself or patterns of work in society rather than internal factors that are inhibiting the learners from exercising their imagination, creativity and ingenuity, and that all students are capable of breaking out of these inhibiting factors. In this case, the teacher will be a 'motivator' in the learning environment. Motivation depends as much on the attitudes of the teacher as on the attitudes of the students.

Critique of learner-based theories

As we have seen, there are many learning theories based on the individual learner – behavioural, cognitivist and humanist, and whether these are concentrated on the inner drives or the interaction with context in experiential learning.

However, we need to critique such a picture. First, many learning theories are not easy to categorise. One of the most important writers of our time, Mezirow, has been classified as both cognitivist and humanist, whereas he would claim to be within the constructivist school of thought (see pp. 30–31).

Second, they are seen as being normative; they do not allow for the diversity of human responses. They make sweeping generalisations about adult learning which cannot always be justified.

Third, these approaches are decidedly Western. They are beginning to be challenged by other learner-based approaches, especially by some feminist thinkers and writers who claim that women's ways of knowing are different from those of men, based on the fact that women (in general) have experienced greater exclusion and 'voicelessness' than men. These theories suggest that women's learning passes through stages, from silence, to receiving other people's knowledge, to identifying knowledge for themselves, to what they call 'procedural knowledge' (working knowledge), to the highest form of knowing – constructing their own knowledge. Feminist epistemology is a major area of interest today (Belenky *et al.* 1986; Code 1991), but at times it falls into making sweeping and universally applicable statements about matters which others would feel to be contingent and contested. The latter argue that women are not only different from men, but that there are as many differences among women as there are among men. To say that *all* women's learning is related to their higher levels of connectedness is to demean those women who do not conform to these criteria.

The one thing that seems to be clear from these learner-centred theories is that it is the whole person who is involved in learning. Individuals engaged in their own learning episodes use the whole of their being, including their perception of who they are, however that has been constructed. In this way, adult learners bring their individualised concept of being an adult as well as their experience and personality factors to their learning tasks. People differ – in learning as in everything else.

CONTEXT-BASED THEORIES

Most of the learning theories centred on the learner tend to isolate the learner from their social context, 'virtually alone in . . . a world of objects he [sic] must array in time, space and causal relationships'. But increasingly there are others who suggest that the learner draws their understandings and control of knowledge 'under the guidance of or in collaboration with more capable peers' (Bruner 1983: 138–9, 181), who suggest that there may be an element of 'teaching' (helping others to learn) in all learning: we learn with and through others.

The humanists suggest that the self-impelled learning process is called into play by the interaction between the person and the lifeworld, and in turn it calls upon the resources of this environment. But the social learning theorists go further than this. They suggest that learning is created and controlled by active encounter between the person and the outside world more than by inner drives and urges. Behavioural theories thus find themselves being adapted and debated in new conceptual terms of highly individualised instead of generalised responses. Each learning is unique just as each learner is unique. All learning is contextualised, designed to meet a specific situation. The focus of learning lies outside the individual, although the processes by which each learner chooses which role models to adopt is a key element in these theories.

Activity

With reference to your chosen learning case study, ask yourself who helped you with your learning.

Three main sets of context-based learning theories may be identified.

Human communications theory

In brief, *human communications theory* indicates that communication is a transaction, a series of two-way processes which involve a source (initiator), a transmission, a message and a receiver. There is inevitably interference and distortion in the transmission, and feedback is a necessary, though independent, part of the process in order to check whether what has been received is perceived as being equivalent to what has been sent. Interpretation is an essential element of the transaction, and in this the receiver is active, not passive. One example is Berne (1970) who combined communication theory with personality, building a view of learning on the difference within each person of 'parent' (P), 'adult' (A) and 'child' (C). He argued that communication between people may go seriously wrong if these attitudes become confused, if the lines get crossed, if for example one person speaking as 'adult' is responded to as 'child'.

But these theories go further than this. They argue that communication links people together into an organisation to achieve a common purpose. Communication is not just a one-way tool; it is a system or network of events. Learning is a process of change based on reactions to the continuous reception of messages which is the inevitable consequence of each person being part of a human communications network or society.

Social learning theory

Social learning theory stresses learning with others as well as from others. The interaction of the individual and the social environment starts with the members of the family and widens out from there, and much of the learning consists of imitation and the internalisation of value systems acquired from others. The need for direct human contact and the importance of peer group pressure in attitudinal development have become clear. Like human communications theory, this is not just a stimulus-response theory. It emphasises the active engagement of the person with the environment, a dialectic with all the potential for conflict. Role learning and modelling are stressed, but it is recognised that such roles are socially and culturally constructed and are constantly changing and being reinterpreted. Vygotsky (1962, 1978) pointed out how much learning is based on the need to communicate and cooperate with others.

Situated learning

Lave and Wenger's (1991) study of *situated learning*, based on the apprenticeship model, suggests that we all learn by participating in activities with others as social beings. Such learning takes place when learners set themselves in what they call 'legitimate peripheral participation' situations (i.e. on the edge of 'communities of practice') where they learn the language, attitudes, values and practices necessary to allow them to enter into full fellowship with that community: 'Learners inevitably participate in communities of practitioners and . . . the mastery of knowledge and skill requires newcomers to move toward full participation in the sociocultural practices of a community' (p. 29). The term 'scaffolding' has been used for the support and active cooperation of more expert peers, although it is an unsatisfactory term for what is an active rather than a passive support. Such learning can both free us and at the same time limit us to that social context.

These approaches have led to an interest in mentoring in education, the deliberate creation and assumption of role modelling from significant others by which learning of attitudes as well as knowledge and skills is promoted.

Critical theory

The freedom suggested by situated learning theories is challenged by *critical theory*. Each society and each part of each society privilege some kinds of knowledge and some kinds of behaviour, and these power relationships are passed on. When applied to education and training, critical theory concentrates on the power relationships within every learning context (especially situated learning). It explores the ways in which the values and assumptions of the powerful reach out to the less powerful through hegemony. Learning is thus circumscribed by the sociocultural context within which it takes place. Situated learning and mentoring may induct us into the existing power complex; they will rarely enhance our critical reflection on hegemony unless the community of practice itself is one of critically reflective practitioners. Learning in the critical theory sense is the process by which our discontent with the here and now, our search for transcendence, expresses itself in a quest for perfectibility, something beyond ourselves.

Total environment

Some modern learning theories have seen the engagement of the individual with the environment in a more holistic sense – the *total environment*, not just the social environment. The physical world which we inhabit, the built environment which we have made for ourselves, the mental world which we have created as well as the social environment are all elements with which we are bound in a perpetual engagement. Indeed, it goes further than this. Rather than experience being outside of ourselves, something which we can reflect critically on and from which we can learn, these views suggest that we are all made up by our experiences; that experience is us, so to speak: 'Cognition and environment become *simultaneously enacted* through experiential learning' (Fenwick 2001: 47).

Such approaches lie within the humanist tradition. But they are a different school of theories. Learning is not seen by these writers as merely the satisfaction of urges, seeking rest and harmony, the diminishing of anxiety, the relief of tension, the enhancement of satisfaction, creating new and more useful knowledge or more satisfying meanings. Rather, learning through life is an inevitable and active engagement with our environment as a consequence of being a member of a common humanity. This may actually increase tension, a dialectic in which we seek to alter our environment as well as ourselves in the constant search for something better, some ideal, a struggle that will never end.

KNOWLEDGE-BASED THEORIES

In discussions of learning, the influence exerted by different kinds of knowledge, the subject matter of the different learning tasks, is less frequently explored. We have seen in the cognitive learning theories views which are to some extent based on the content or subject matter of the learning. But the interaction of learner, context and processes in learning is incomplete without considering the kind of knowing to be achieved in the learning. For it can be argued that to learn is not a intransitive verb. One is never *just* learning; one is always learning *something*.

The important element here is the conversion of information arising from experience into 'knowledge'. That there is a distinction, and a distinction implying preferences, can be seen from the words attributed to Einstein: 'Knowledge is experience, everything else is just information'. The distinction would seem to be that information becomes knowledge when we process it into a form by which knowing subjects actively use it – in other words, when we experience it: 'Knowledge is information in use, and it is the interaction of information with the human mind that gives it meaning and purpose . . . those insights and understandings that give meaning to information and data' (Sallis and Jones 2002: 8–9).

That there are different kinds of knowledge is well accepted. Knowing about, knowing how to do, knowing to live together, knowing myself (to be) are not all the same kinds of knowledge. Experiential knowing ('I know a building'), for instance, is different from theoretical knowing *about* buildings. To know someone is different from knowing *of* that person (Ryle 1949). Habermas (1978) identified three kinds of knowing[1] which form something of a hierarchy:

- *instrumental/technical knowing* – knowing how to manipulate the environment; the acquisition of skills and understanding needed to manage the world we live in (it is interesting that he places scientific learning on the lowest rung of his scale);
- *communicative knowing* – knowing in the realm of interpersonal relations, increasing social and cultural understanding;

---

1 In his later writings, Habermas changed this pattern, but it remains a valid expression of different kinds of knowing.

- *emancipatory knowing* – self-understanding, awareness and transformation of cultural and personal presuppositions that are always with us and affect the way we act.

These different kinds of knowing (and therefore of learning) have different methods of investigation, of teaching and of evaluation. It is likely that any learning activity will call upon all three kinds of learning in different proportions. Because learning is part of the wider interaction between the individual and their environment, it will involve a transformation of the relationship between the learner, the source or mediator of knowledge and the knowledge itself.

Other content-based learning theories exist, distinguishing between different kinds of learning tasks involving different subject matter. Perhaps the clearest distinction is that between *socialisation learning*, which concentrates upon the internalisation of the knowledge (both instrumental and communicative) which others have, including their value systems, which is an essential part of being human within a human context, and *individuation learning* which concentrates on the creation of one's own knowledge which is an essential part of being an individual. The knowledge involved, the content of learning in each case, will be different and will clearly affect the learning processes. A similar distinction may be made between 'mechanical learning' and 'creative and critical learning'. Anisur Rahman links this distinction with that between education which increases choices and training which limits choices (see pp. 52–3): 'Nor can one be "trained" except to perform tasks which are mechanical, not creative' (1993: 222). Training, memorising, the transfer of knowledge may be suitable for mechanical learning but they are ineffective and dependency-making approaches, and therefore inappropriate to the development of creative adults.

Hierarchies of knowledge

Such views of knowing remind us that 'knowledge is socially created . . . some kinds of knowing have more power and legitimation' (Barr 1999: 117). In western societies, scientific knowledge is normally ranked higher than practical knowledge. To give two examples, a diamond can be known as a carbon crystal, as a tool to cut glass, as a jewel of great investment value, as an ornament and no doubt in other ways. Such ways of knowing can be ranked, with scientific knowledge being deemed by many as above practical knowledge, with investment being superior to fashion. Again, the way that a soil chemist knows 'mud' (as a colloidal solution) will be different from that of the potter or brickmaker, and again different from that of a child using it to dam a stream. To say that a scientist's way of knowing is superior to rather than simply different from that of a child is to apply value systems to knowledge.

Because of the values attached to knowledge, the control of knowledge and the public recognition and accreditation of learning, all become matters which are structured into every society. There are gatekeepers to knowledge, of whom the teacher of adults is not by any means the least important. It is true that today, with information technology, the control of formal educators is being challenged or perhaps reassigned, but such changes are also being resisted. The conflict over knowledge is likely to grow further.

Thus, knowledge-based learning theories not only posit that different processes of learning are brought into play by different kinds of knowledge. They also carry with them sociocultural implications in terms of power. They are not neutral, as the cognitive theories claim them to be.

PROCESS-BASED THEORIES

The final element in our equation of learning is that of the processes of learning.

Much writing tries to suggest that there is one over-arching way of learning which applies to all persons in all situations, with every kind of learning content, at all times.

Critical reflection on experience

The strongest claim in this respect is that made for *critical reflection on experience*. Freire (1972) and others have suggested that learning is accomplished by critically analysing experience and acting on the basis of that analysis. Schön (1983) talks of learning as reflective practice. Freire and others like Knowles have spoken of a learning cycle starting with experience, proceeding through reflection on experience and leading to action which in its turn becomes the concrete experience for further reflection and thus the next stage of the cycle (Figure 4.3a). Action is an essential part of the learning process, not a result of learning, not an add-on at the end. Without action, learning has not effectively taken place.

Adapting the model

Such a cycle needs to be elaborated in three ways.

Search and select

First, the process of reflection is complex. It involves making a judgement on experience, assessing it in the light of some standard drawn from other experience – either one's own or other people's. It means trying to determine how to explain the experience by using other criteria, assessing in

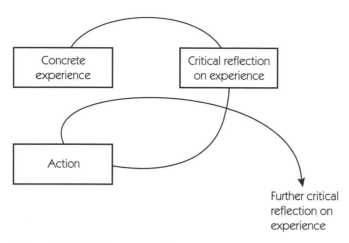

Figure 4.3a The learning cycle

what ways the experience could have been different. To give an example, farmers faced with a new pest or disease will ask their neighbours, 'What is it? We have never seen it before'; they thus reveal that they have first searched their own experience and are now actively seeking to access the experience of others in order to reflect critically on this new experience.

In learning through critical reflection on experience, then, there is an active *search* for new material. Drawing on our own and other persons' past experience, we *select* what we feel to be appropriate to judge the present experience by. This process is of course influenced by the social constructions around us.

The importance of new knowledge from outside the specific learning context cannot be exaggerated. It is against new knowledge, drawn from our earlier experience and the experience of others, however that is mediated to us, whether through teaching, speech, the written word, or observation, etc. that we measure the experience which forms the basis of learning, that we seek to make meaning. Without new knowledge there can be no critical reflection.

Freire's learning cycle thus needs to be adapted as shown in Figure 4.3b.

Conceptualisation
Secondly, as Kolb (1984) pointed out, critical reflection will lead in some cases to the development of generalisations ('abstract conceptualisation'). Critical reflection can be seen as asking questions about experience in the light of other experience; abstract conceptualisation may be seen as going beyond the specific answers to general principles. Only in this way will the new insights generated by critical reflection become usable in other contexts. Hypotheses are formed which can be tested in new situations (Figure 4.3c).

Figure 4.3b The learning cycle and the process of search and select

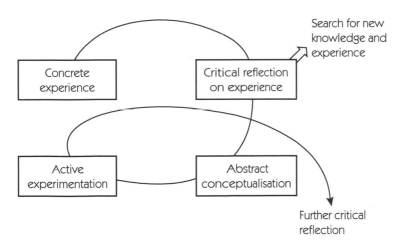

Figure 4.3c The learning cycle and conceptualisation

Decision-making
Thirdly, however, learning includes goals, purposes, intentions, choice and decision-making, and it is not at all clear where these elements fit into the learning cycle. Decisions are needed to determine which other forms of experience are to be used for critical reflection (selection). Decisions are certainly needed before translating some of the possible solutions and not others into active experimentation. And decision-making occurs at other points in the cycle. These have tended to be omitted from discussions of the learning cycle (see Figure 4.3d).

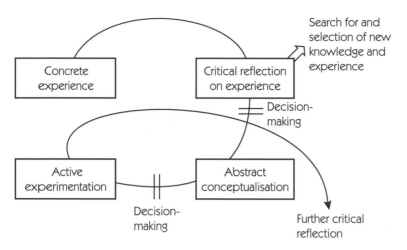

Figure 4.3d The learning cycle and decision-making

Preferred learning styles

Based on the learning cycle as adapted, Kolb identified four main learning styles. Each of the stages of the cycle calls for different learning approaches and appeals to different kinds of persons (Figure 4.4):

- learning through *concrete experience* – an engagement with direct experience (activists);
- learning through *critical reflection* – observing experience from different perspectives and judging experience by a variety of criteria (reflectors);
- learning through *abstract conceptualisation* – analysing experience to create new ideas, concepts and structures (theorists);
- learning through *active experimentation* – using these new ideas, testing theories out in practice (experimenters).

Figure 4.4 Learning styles based on the learning cycle

Activity

You may wish to ask yourself which learning styles you used to best effect during your chosen learning activity.

Some people suggest that there is a progression here: 'in the process of learning, one moves . . . from actor to observer, and from specific involvement to general analytical detachment' (Kolb 1984: 31). Jarvis (1987: 16) argues that 'all learning begins with experience'. Others however suggest that one may enter this cycle at any point, not always start with concrete experience. Thus one may start with a theory and move to trial and error (experimentation), using this as concrete experience which is then reflected on critically to revise or confirm the theory.

Kolb and others argue that every individual develops one or more *preferred learning styles* through experience (Figure 4.5). It is important to stress that we all tend to use all of these styles – we do not confine our learning efforts to one only. But we *prefer* to use one or perhaps two modes of learning above the others; we feel stronger at learning through one approach rather than through any of the others.

Other kinds of learning styles have been proposed, such as the Learning Individual Programme (Rundle and Dunn 1999). But whichever is chosen, these views provide a useful reminder that individual learners feel most comfortable using their own learning strategies. Through a variety of learning activities engaged in over many years, adults have developed a particular blend of learning styles which is stronger in its demand than any such blend in children. The preferred learning styles of children have not yet become established; by adulthood, these have become more crystallised.

Critique of critical reflection on experience

There are real problems with critical reflection as *the* way in which adults learn. First, there is a danger of being normative and prescriptive in this approach. We need to remember that the development of understandings about learning styles was not intended to enable the teacher to put people into a particular category. Rather, they help to explain what is going on.

Second, we need to remember that once again this picture has been drawn on the basis of a limited range of research subjects, mainly white middle-class educated males with successful careers in Western cultures. Whether different styles may be found among black persons, among women, among other cultures (e.g. Muslim, Asiatic, Chinese or indigenous groups etc.) is less clear. And whether such styles change with ageing or with life crises,

We all have certain preferences in the way we learn.

Active learners
Some prefer to learn by doing something immediately. They don't bother to wait to listen to all the instructions, to read the manual first but get on with the job. They try to find out how things work. These people get impatient when someone tells them all about the task first. When they are asked a question, they give an immediate answer without waiting to work it out fully. They tend to be enthusiastic about new things; they like lots of new experiences ('I'll try anything once'). They are individualists in learning; and when they have finished one activity, they want to pass quickly to the next one. They want to see as many new things as possible; they like to meet lots of new people. They will often volunteer to take the lead in any activity. They like short-term goals and are usually bored by the slower work of implementing and consolidating a programme. They tend to believe what they are told.

Reflective learners
Some prefer to 'wait and see'. They sit back and watch others doing the task first, they listen to the talk of others. When they are asked a question, these people don't give the first answer that comes into their heads; they take time to think, they hesitate and are often uncertain. They want more information before they can give a real answer ('I want to sleep on it'). Before making a decision, they try to think through all the implications, both for themselves and for others. These people tend to like sharing their learning with others because this helps them to collect different opinions before they make up their minds.

Theorising learners
Some like to build systems, to get down to first principles. They don't want to deal with 'real cases' – these are thought to be too limited. Rather, they want to understand the whole. They speak in general rather than in concrete terms. They question the basic assumptions. They make rules out of all cases. They usually think problems through step by step. They try to make coherent pictures out of complex material; they often represent ideas in diagrams showing relationships ('What does it really mean? How does this fit with that?'). They try to be objective and detached. They are less sympathetic to human feelings, to other people's subjective judgements. These people want the world to be logical; they do not like too many different opinions.

Experimental learners
Some like to experiment, to apply their new insights. They come back from training courses full of enthusiasm and new ideas which they want to try out. Having been told something, these people do not believe it until they see it for themselves ('It may work for you but I want to see if it will work for me'). They try to find new and more effective ways of doing things. They take short cuts or devise new modes of working. They tend to be confident, energetic, impatient of what they see as too much talk. They like solving problems, and see new situations as a challenge from which they can learn a good deal. They like being shown how to do something but become frustrated if they are not allowed to do it for themselves very quickly.
(adapted from the works of Kolb 1976, 1984; Honey and Mumford 1992)

Figure 4.5 Table of preferred learning styles

or indeed if adults use different styles in different contexts or with different learning tasks, these are questions as yet unanswered. To suggest that all adults have a single set of preferred learning styles based on critical reflection on experience, styles which are used in all situations, is probably going beyond the evidence available.

But more importantly, most of the discussions of critical reflection (e.g. Brookfield 2000: 95) seem to concentrate on great crises in peoples' lives, on 'unexpected events' and 'critical episodes' which cause major disequilibrium 'between biography and [current or new] experience'. But there is more to adult learning than such events (e.g. the learning of languages). Our purposeful learning episodes are not all created by great upheavals. While critical reflection is undoubtedly a process by which we cope with major 'traumas', it also features along with many other strategies of learning in other learning episodes.

It is therefore unacceptable to suggest that critical reflection on experience leading to action is *the* way in which we learn. There are many different processes involved in learning. Critical reflection on experience would seem to be a key strategy in the process of creating meaning out of experience; it is certainly the main way in which critical learning is developed. But there is more to learning than the search for meanings. The learning cycle, which still dominates much of the discussion about adult learning, has come under challenge as being too normative and prescriptive.

Constructivism

A second claimant to universal truth in relation to learning comes from constructivism. Cognitivist views tend to stress the interaction of the learner with a body of knowledge that lies outside of themselves, and therefore the key process is the transfer of information from an expert source to the learner. Constructivism is a response to this view. One of the most influential expressions of this group of theories is George Kelly's (1955) 'personal construct theory'. Learning is not something determined by external influences; each individual creates their own learning. We form personal constructs (units of meaning) from our ideas, feelings, memories and evaluations about events, places and people in our lives or from our cultural background. In this way, we create the world and manipulate it rather than respond to stimuli or to external knowledge. The act of learning is then largely initiated by the learner, exploring and extending their own understanding, holding what has been called a 'learning conversation with themselves', making individualised perceptions of reality, meanings and knowledge.

This school of thought rejects the notion of knowledge existing outside of ourselves, an objective reality to be discovered by research. Rather, all knowledge is contingent, contested and provisional. Learning does not mean uncovering hidden truth but the construction of new perceptions. Those who search after truth are faced with choosing between various 'acts of knowing'. The focus thus switches from trying to establish the validity of the knowledge itself to the criteria by which we can judge the validity of the questions asked and the answers arrived at in each individual case – how can we determine which 'act of knowing' carries with it some experiential validity for ourselves in this particular situation?

Such a view challenges the concept of learning based on the transfer of information. Many modern writers are uncompromising about this:

> Current research has led to . . . a number of widely accepted principles . . . The most general one, characterizing all the current trends, is a well-nigh total commitment to the constructivist notion of the origin of human knowledge.
>
> This means that all knowledge which man [*sic*] has of the surrounding reality is the result of his own mental processes; in this sense, it is of his own construction. The constructivist view is a very different one from the traditional one which is often associated with teaching. Whether consciously or not, learning and teaching have traditionally been seen in terms of a direct transfer of information from the teacher to the learner. In denying the possibility of this kind of direct transfer, the constructivist theory opens up new challenges for teaching. If learning is an individual's active construction process in interaction with the physical and social environment, what kind of role can teaching play in such a process?
>
> (LEIF 1990: 14)

This view has grown widely, not just in adult education circles but outside them as well. For example, in management: 'Learning is not finding out what other people already know but solving our own problems for our own purposes by questioning, thinking and testing until the solution is part of our life' (Charles Handy, quoted in Ball 1991: 29). And in development: 'Development . . . is not possible with somebody else's thinking and knowledge . . . Knowledge cannot be transferred . . . learning is always an act of self-search and discovery. In this search and discovery, one may be stimulated and assisted but cannot be taught' (Rahman 1993: 219, 222).

Indeed, Rahman (1993) asserts that 'transfer of information' is harmful: 'Those . . . who seek to transfer knowledge and skills serve mainly to disorient the capacity that is in every healthy individual to creatively search for and discover knowledge' (p. 222). The distinction is between the 'input' model, in which knowledge, skills and understanding are 'given' or 'imparted' to the learners and the learner responds to these inputs from outside, and the 'action' model in which the learners are searching out the material they need, trying to make sense of their experience. It is not a matter of choosing between two equally effective strategies of promoting learning; the one is seen to be the enemy of the other.

DIVERSITY OF WAYS OF LEARNING

Like critical reflection, constructivism makes claims to universality in learning. But it would seem that there is a plurality of ways in which we learn. Weinrich, for example, lists four main processes: reinforcement through reward and punishment; imitation of role models; identification, 'a process which is more powerful than imitation, through which the [learner] incorporates and internalises the roles and values of the ... significant [other]'; and structuring, in which the learners 'actively seek to structure the world, to make sense and order of the environment' (quoted in Henriques 1984: 19).

Others have suggested the following:

- the acquisition of information through listening, seeing or reading etc.;
- the memorisation of data or processes;
- the changes inspired by watching others and then practising;
- the sudden and apparently unassisted insights which we all experience from time to time;
- the learning that comes from the successful (i.e. the rewarded) completion of some task;
- haphazard experimentation and exploration (trying things out).

There is therefore no consensus about learning. Different theories are espoused with vigour. For learning is a many-faceted activity which incorporates a number of different processes. Some learning may be brought about by the transfer of knowledge from A to B; some by reaction to external stimuli. Other learning may be brought about by drives and intentions (goals), transforming meaning perspectives or transforming social contexts.

This is not to say that all learning theories are 'right', though it may be that they are all valuable. It is to say that in our present state of knowledge and understanding we cannot say with certainty that any one theory is closer to expressing the 'truth' of reality than any other. To look for one over-arching learning theory may be to seek for warriors' dreams after the battle is over.

Therefore, instead of trying to establish one learning theory which covers all situations, perhaps we should be looking for more than one. Indeed, it may be that the learning we do on our own may be different from the learning we do in specially constructed learning programmes. This is the theme of the next chapter.

Further reading

Boud, D. and Miller, N. (1996) *Working with Experience: Animating Learning*. London: Routledge.

Boud, D., Keogh, R. and Walker, D. (eds) (1985) *Reflection: Turning Experience into Learning*. London: Kogan Page.

Code, L. (1991) *What Can She Know? Feminist Theory and the Construction of Knowledge*. Ithaca, NY: Cornell University Press.

Cranton, P. (1994) *Understanding and Promoting Transformative Learning*. San Francisco: Jossey Bass.

Fenwick, T.J. (2001) *Experiential Learning: A Theoretical Critique*. Columbus OH: ERIC.

Held, D. (1980) *Introduction to Critical Theory*. Los Angeles: University of California Press.

Jarvis, P., Holford, J. and Griffin, C. (1998) *Theory and Practice of Learning*. London: Kogan Page.

Lave, J. and Wenger, E. (1991) *Situated Learning: Legitimate Peripheral Participation*. Cambridge: Cambridge University Press.

Merriam, S. and Cafarella, R. (1999) *Learning in Adulthood*. San Francisco: Jossey Bass.

Mezirow, J. *et al.* (2000) *Learning as Transformation*. San Francisco: Jossey Bass.

Ryan, A.B. (2001) *Feminist Ways of Knowing: Towards Theorising the Person for Radical Adult Education*. Leicester: NIACE.

Sutherland, P. (ed.) (1997) *Adult Learning: A Reader*. London: Kogan Page.

Taylor, E.W. (1998) *Theory and Practice of Transformative Learning: A Critical Review*. Columbus, OH: ERIC.

Chapter 5

FROM LEARNING TO TEACHING

What does teaching add to learning . . . ?

This chapter looks at the learning processes we all use in our daily lives. It identifies two different ways of learning: acquisition learning, which is a natural process, and formalised learning, that takes place within any planned learning programme. It argues that teaching adults should build on but at the same time go beyond the natural learning processes by helping the student-learners to become more conscious of their own learning.

LEARNING AND LIFE

Learning is not of course confined to the classroom. The most important thing that 'lifelong learning' has reminded us is that learning takes place throughout our lives *in the course of our daily living*. Learning is going on all the time for all of us and is not confined to planned learning activities.

It is strange how some people use language loosely. They talk about 'motivating people to learn' as if they are not already motivated to learn, or 'getting people to come into learning' as if they are not already learning. By this, they seem to mean persuading people to participate in certain learning activities, but their language implies that these people are not engaging in any learning outside of these activities. They use the word 'learners' to mean those who are in particular programmes, and describe those who are not inside these programmes as 'non-learners'; they speak of 'people who have done no learning since leaving school'. 'Learning' and 'planned learning' thus get mixed up. Even experienced adult educators use the term 'lifelong learning' when they really mean 'lifelong education'. By using this discourse, they suggest that only their approved activities are 'real' learning. They do not appear to realise that 'lifelong learning' is simply that – learning which goes on more or less all the time.

Natural learning

We do therefore need to stress very clearly that learning is quite independent of the classroom or of other kinds of planned learning programmes. People are learning all the time, no one is not learning. And it is vital that all of us who teach adults should understand and build on this natural learning process, not ignore or demean it.

Learning is part of living

Learning is embedded in living. It is closely related to the way in which individuals develop in relation to their lifeworld. We simply cannot avoid learning. And since the experience of living is continuous, so too learning is continuous. It occurs throughout life, from start to finish. Nearly everything we do has been learned and is constantly being relearned.

This means that learning is individual. Although we may learn from and in association with others, it is not a collective activity: 'Each individual is processing the experience uniquely for personal use . . . In learning, the individual is the agent, even though the agent may be subject to the social pressures of the group' (Brookfield 1983: 1–4). Learning is affected and may even to some extent be controlled by society or other collectives, but the learning activity itself – introducing learning changes – is personal.

Learning is also active. It is not simply the passive receiving of knowledge and skills. There are many people who speak about learning as if it were something which a teacher *does to* a learner. They talk of the teacher 'imparting' knowledge or skills to the learners. Learning however is not someone giving information or skills to other persons. It is not filling up an empty pot with knowledge; it is not even watering a plant so that it grows naturally. Learning is a *positive action on the part of the learner*, calling in almost all cases for an act of the will.

Thus, learning is normally voluntary – we do it ourselves. It is rarely compulsory, even among children, although some experiential learning may be less than fully voluntary.

Learning, then, is natural, as natural as breathing. It is the continual process of adapting to the various changes we all face – in our social and cultural contexts, in our social roles, in the daily tasks we perform, as well as in our personal growth and development: 'Learning, like breathing, is among the most basic of human activities. It is the process through which we become the human beings we are, and by which we internalize the external world and construct our experiences' (Jarvis *et al.* 1998: vii).

Another image often used for learning is that of hunger. Within every individual, it is suggested, there is a bundle of unsatisfied learning desires, although some people are more hungry for learning than others. These may spring from inner drives, from half-finished earlier learning activities, or from our own interests and experiences. Some of these learning desires are very pressing, arising from or reinforced by urgent matters, tasks to be done. But most of them lie dormant, overlaid by more pressing concerns, awaiting either a suitable opportunity or an increased sense of need to bring them to life. A spoken or written word or a glimpse of something will arouse this unsatisfied curiosity, cause us to sit up and take notice when certain cues are heard or noticed, make us engage in selective perception (this is the 'I've always wanted to learn something about that' syndrome). For some people, these desires have been damaged or buried deep by other experiences, but they still exist and can in appropriate circumstances be awakened.

Intentional and unintentional learning

Learning, then, springs from two main causes. There are the more or less automatic responses to new information, perceptions or experiences that result in change, and there are more purposeful activities, the result of impulses which lead us to seek out or create new experiences aimed at achieving some kind of mastery. There is a difference in meaning between the use of the words 'to learn' in contexts such as: 'He burned his fingers. He learned not to do that again', and 'I had some trouble with the machine but I learned how to manage it'. The second implies both purpose and effort which the first lacks.

Much of our learning is thus incidental and unintended. A good deal is very casual: it comes from chance happenings (roadside posters, snatches of overheard conversation, newspaper reading or television watching, meeting people: 'adventitious learning [which] springs from accidental encounters with unintentional sources' (Lucas 1983: 2–3). But beyond this, there are occasions when we engage in some more structured process of mastering a situation – learning to deal with a new piece of equipment, for instance, or to adjust to new bus timetables or to cope with a new family situation. At certain times throughout their lives, all adults will bend their energies and attention to achieving some learning task directed towards a goal. Some of these occasions may call for formal methods of learning (learning to drive a car is probably the biggest programme of teaching adults in many countries), but we cope with most of them more informally. It is possible that unintentional and intentional learning shade into each other rather than being completely distinct.

At the same time, there are some 'sources of learning' that equally may be intentional or unintentional. Some simply respond to learning needs, often without appreciating that they are acting as sources of learning. Other sources intend learning to take place – through mass campaigns, advertisements, political persuasion, social propaganda etc. – even though the target

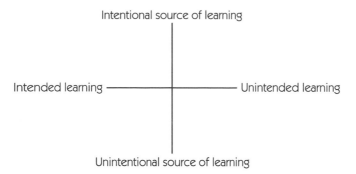

Figure 5.1 Learning matrix

audience has no intention of engaging in learning. Again, these too may shade into each other (Figure 5.1).

Activity

You may wish to place your own learning case study (see p. 8) on this matrix.

Learning episodes

Learning, then, goes on throughout life. But at times there are concentrated periods of learning, dumplings in the soup, so to speak. Some of these 'learning episodes' (as we may call them) come from external requirements: a task set for us by others, for example, or new legislation which calls for changes in our practices, or the need to repair a broken machine in the home or at work. Other such episodes are called for by some of the welcome or unwelcome changes that may come in our personal circumstances. Many an adult has had to learn about new financial matters through divorce or separation. But the majority are undertaken voluntarily and often with some measure of enthusiasm and commitment, although some will be undertaken reluctantly, even perhaps with some anger. Emotions are always tied up in learning episodes. And such episodes are always purposeful – designed to achieve a particular goal which the learners set for themselves.

Learning episodes are therefore distinct from the incidental and unintended learning which characterises the majority of our learning experiences. And they are separate from (though they may at times draw upon) the more formalised learning programmes of education. They form a focus of attention today in the form of self-directed learning (see p. 12).[1]

Learning objectives or 'clearing up messes'?

The fact that these learning episodes are intentional and purposeful, that the adult is active, struggling with reality, rather than responsive to stimuli, suggests that they are directed by more or less clearly perceived learning objectives.

To some extent this is true. When we set out to learn to meet some new situation or to increase our expertise in some field of interest, there will be occasions when we will be able to focus our efforts on defined objectives, when we can see what it is that we are trying to achieve. We clear our mind of all that will block the way and set out to achieve the mastery we require of ourselves. When deciding to trace our family history, for example, or learn a new computer process, we can set for ourselves clear goals, and we can see whether we are making progress towards the achievement of these goals.

But in other cases, the situation is not so clear. Ackoff (1978) (talking about managers) has pointed out that we are often in a more confused situation: we 'are not confronted with problems that are independent of each other but with dynamic situations that consist of complex systems of changing problems that interact with each other. I call such situations "messes". Problems are extracted from "messes" by analysis; they are to messes as atoms are to tables and chairs . . . [We] do not solve problems, [we] manage messes'.

This would seem to be particularly true of many learning episodes which we undertake throughout our lives – for example, moving house. Our task in these cases is not straightforward, simply meeting a need. Rather, it is to unravel a tangle, to sort out a mess.

In these circumstances, how and what we learn depends on how we define the situation we are facing. We analyse the issue, determine what the problem looks like so far as we can see it, and try to solve it. How we do that depends on how much and what kind of experience we bring to the 'mess'. That will determine the way we look at the problem and the language in which we express it. Learning is a haphazard process of trial and error and we often get it wrong. As Schön (1983) puts it in regard to his chosen professionals: 'Problems must be constructed from the materials of

---

1 As Merriam and Cafarella indicate, natural learning episodes form one strand of the current interest in self-directed learning (1999: 288–317). But many discussants of self-directed learning concentrate on whether or not people show 'autonomous behaviour in learning situations' (1999: 310). The argument above reverses Knowles' approach that adults become more self-directed in learning as they progress. I am suggesting that all persons start with self-directed learning but that formalised learning interrupts and can even weaken this natural learning process.

problematic situations which are puzzling, troubling and uncertain . . . [We] are frequently embroiled in conflicts of values, goals, purposes and interests . . . the effective use of specialised knowledge to well-defined tasks depends on a prior structuring of situations that are complex and uncertain'.

Activity

You could ask yourself how clear were the objectives of your learning activity – at the start, and later as the learning progressed.

The importance of learning episodes to the teacher of adults

These structured and purposeful learning episodes will almost always invoke the assistance of some helper. They can thus be of considerable significance for teachers of adults – for our purpose is to create learning episodes for our adult student participants. Since they are intended and purposeful, they reveal more about the sort of learning opportunity that we can construct than does the more ubiquitous, haphazard and largely unintentional learning that springs from the constant interaction of the individual with the environment. The way adults learn purposefully on their own tells us much about the way they will learn in our programmes.

Some adult educators are hesitant about using these natural learning episodes as the basis for building a theory of adult learning. They point out that each of us engages with the environment in ways limited by our experience and existing learning abilities, and that this social environment itself controls our learning. They suggest that what is needed is to break free from the restraints of context. Nevertheless, these episodes show us something of the special features of life-embedded learning as distinct from the processes of formal learning, and thus form a guide as we construct learning activities for those who come to our programmes.

Characteristics of learning episodes

Analysis suggests that there are three main characteristics relating to these self-directed activities that are relevant to our discussion.

Episodic
First, *they are episodic in character, not continuous.* They come in short bursts of relatively intensive activity, absorbing the attention, and they usually come to an end as soon as the immediate purpose has been felt to be achieved. There are some, particularly in the self-fulfilment area, that spring from long-term interests (gardening, for instance, or following trends in

modern or classical music); but even within these patterns of persistent learning, there come more intensive short-term episodes of learning directed towards the achievement of some immediate goal. We cannot keep this sort of pressure up for long. We need to be motivated by an achievable purpose; and when that is over, there may come a rest or a slower pace of learning before the next episode occurs.

Concrete
Secondly, *the goal is usually some concrete task or immediate issue that is felt to be important*. Intentional learning episodes are in general aimed at the solution of a particular problem. The situations they are designed to meet are concrete rather than theoretical, and they take place within a specific context, both immediate and cultural. Particularity is everything in learning episodes. We want to decorate *this* room in a way which will satisfy us and/or *those* whom we wish to please; we need to cope with *this* change in *this* family circle; we are trying to understand *this* new procedure in *this* work context, and so on. Even when the learning is part of a long-term and developing interest (chess, say, or cooking), the individual episode of learning is directed towards a particular goal to be achieved.

There are several implications flowing on from this:

- We do not on the whole *approach any situation academically*. To decorate a room, we rarely study design as such. To cope with a family matter, we do not take a course on interpersonal relations or psychology – although we might well consult books on the subject. We are not concerned so much with a subject as to resolve a one-off concrete situation.
- This means that the learning task is *rarely pursued in a systematic way*. It is not general learning, but limited to the task in hand. Few of us will pull down a textbook to cover the whole field. It is only with those who have had extensive experience of formal education, who have developed and maintained formalised learning skills, that a systematic exploration of a field of knowledge becomes at all common. This is a replication in private of the systems of learning that characterise formal education and is thus confined to relatively few, and to a few occasions in their lives. They too also engage in more limited goal-oriented learning at other times. Most of us most of the time use only those parts of any subject that help us to meet our immediate task.
- This form of learning is *rarely sequential*, starting with an introduction to the field of study and proceeding from A to Z in sequence. Nor do we start with the simple and move on to the more difficult. We tackle the problem with which we have to deal at the level at which it occurs in our lives. We cope with difficult language and terms from the start so long as these are of direct relevance to the learning process (e.g. learning for a planning application or a mortgage).

- The learners do not on the whole draw on *compartmentalised knowledge* such as was learned at school (e.g. history separated from geography or maths from physics). They bring *all* that they know from all sorts of fields to bear upon the particular instance. A more academic approach may occur on occasion, but even here there is often a particular need to be met that leads to the use of knowledge from different fields of study rather than a compartmentalised approach to knowledge.
- Such episodes are aimed at *immediate rather than future application.* There are, it is true, some learning episodes which are intended as a preparation before embarking on a course of action: religious preparation classes, prenatal groups, holiday language courses, pre-retirement programmes, for example. But on the whole, most learning is achieved in the process of doing a particular task or meeting a specific situation, and therefore the material, as it is mastered, is applied at once. We set out to learn how to use a new washing machine by using it; we learn a new bus timetable as we use the service; we learn how to cope with a baby by coping with a baby.

Not generalised
Thirdly, since most of these learning episodes are directed towards specific goals, *there is relatively little interest in overall principles*. Few attempts are made by the learner to draw general conclusions from the particular instance being learned. Once the immediate situation has been resolved, the goal attained or the problem solved, the learner normally brings the process of investigation to a close, storing away the learning gained for another day. What is stored is the way to cope with the particular situation, not general principles. Learning to use a new washing machine will be concentrated on the specific model in hand, not on washing machines in general. The learning needed to cope with a new bus timetable will deal not with the entire transport system but with the one or two routes needed. Learning a new office routine will be confined to what is needed for the moment, not to wider applications. All of these may arouse in our minds wider issues of obsolescence and modern technology, or public and private transport provision, or the demands of innovations as a whole; but these will occur mainly as spasmodic thoughts and grumbles, usually quickly pushed away and forgotten. The efforts are centred on the immediate and the particular, not on the long-term and the general.

Activity

Check this list against your own experience as shown in your learning case study.

TWO DIFFERENT KINDS OF LEARNING

These characteristics enable us to establish a relationship between these purposeful learning episodes and the learning theories we discussed above. For running through most of that discussion is a distinction between two kinds of learning, although the way the difference is described varies. Carl Rogers for example suggested that 'the only learning which significantly influences behavior is self-discovered, self-appropriated learning . . . which has been personally appropriated and assimilated in experience', which he contrasted with 'information assimilation'. He contrasted 'the traditional pattern of schooling' on the one hand with voluntary learning based on the concerns and experiences of the learners, critical reflection on knowledge, beliefs, values and behaviours of society, self-directed learning and the cyclic interaction of learning and action. He set the distinction out as shown in Figure 5.2.

Significant experiential learning	Traditional conventional learning
Personal involvement	Prescribed curriculum
Whole person	Similar for all students
Self-initiated	Lecturing
Pervasive	Standardised testing
Evaluated by learner	Instructor-evaluated
Essence is meaning	Essence is knowing and reproducing

Figure 5.2 Rogers' (1983) distinctions between the two kinds of learning

Knowles, whose view of andragogy (the teaching of adults) has for a long time held the floor in adult education, contrasted this concept with pedagogy, 'the education of youth . . . the [two contrasting] models are probably most useful when seen not as dichotomous but rather as two ends of a spectrum' (Knowles 1980: 43). Constructivist learning (as we have seen) is similarly contrasted with 'the traditional view of learning which is often associated with teaching' (see pp. 113–15). Recent interest in 'informal learning' (Coffield 2000) or 'natural learning' (Eraut 2000) outside of schooling also highlights this distinction. It is the natural or informal learning that is used in the learning episodes, not schooled learning. The distinction between natural learning and taught learning is very widespread.

Acquisition and formalised learning

One of the clearest accounts of this distinction comes from language learning. Krashen (1982) among others distinguishes between the way a person acquires their first language ('acquisition')[2] and the way they learn a second or subsequent language ('learning').[3] These form 'two distinct and independent ways' of learning.

Acquisition learning of initial language, 'the language which every normal human brain acquires with seeming effortlessness' (Cenoz and Genesee 1998), is not really effortless. It is very active learning, initiated by the learner. It employs exploration and experimentation, trial and error, copying and mimicking, and practising. It proceeds by analogical thinking as well as by memorisation. Children play at language; they try out sounds and combinations of sounds, using some form of critical reflection to make their own assessment of what is right and what is wrong, seeking feedback from time to time. It is emotional, based on what *feels right*. The initiative comes mainly from the learner, although encouragement may come from the environment and rewards may be sought by the learner in terms of pleasing significant others. Acquisition learning is contextualised, highly specific, and it uses the ordinary lifeworld as its context. It is not structured or sequential, but works on what comes its way. Each episode ends when the particular task is done, and the recognition of the learning achieved is almost always '*post-hoc*'. But new episodes succeed each other continuously; the individual language learning project is never fully complete. Language in this sense is 'caught' rather than formally learned (Krashen 1982: 9–55).

Formal learning of a language, on the other hand, is based largely on memorisation, practice, external review and evaluation. It relies on the transfer of information more than on experiential learning. The learning content is compartmentalised and irrelevancies are removed, as are the emotional elements, being replaced with reason. Such formalised learning has uniform pre-set goals for all the learners to achieve (which acquisition learning does not have in the same sense), and the evaluation and rewards

---

2 I am not happy with the term 'acquisition' which seems to imply a deficit model by which a person lacks something which they acquire from the outside. But the term does indicate that the learner is active in learning, and I have retained it in the form of 'acquisition learning'; but I hope my hesitations will lead to a search for a better term. 'Active learning' is not right, for formalised learning is also active. 'Informal learning' is a term which carries with it different connotations at the moment. I have on occasions used the term 'natural learning' for this kind of learning as I think that play is innate although its forms are socioculturally constructed.

3 Again I have problems with the term 'learning' on its own, for 'acquisition' is also learning. 'Taught learning', 'guided learning' or 'assisted learning' are all useful terms but they are not right, for some forms of formalised learning are not taught in a formal sense, and acquisition learning is assisted and guided in some way or another. 'Schooling' carries very negative connotations. 'Formalised learning' is nearer the mark. Other terms used for the distinction include 'explicit' and 'implicit' learning (Krashen 1982: 50).

are set by others. It normally takes place in specially constructed contexts and is concerned with general (i.e. decontextualised) content, basic principles and rules (grammar) which enable the learner to find their way through various tasks. It uses specially prepared materials and specially created activities. It is structured and sequenced, planned and externally assisted. It aims at the development of transferable skills.

Such a distinction is not confined to children, as Krashen points out, or to language learning. Both forms of learning continue into adult life. Most social role learning such as parenting, club membership and citizenship (acculturation) is acquisition. When a new member of staff joins an organisation, for example, they learn not only the language of that body but also other things such as how to move through the buildings and how to relate to different persons in that organisation, all through acquisition learning (learning 'on the job'). Recent studies show that refugees in their new context do most of their learning by acquisition rather than by formalised learning. There are many occasions when adults employ acquisition learning rather than formalised learning, just as there are other occasions when they employ formalised learning processes. It is mostly in the form of learning new cultures that acquisition learning is used by adults.

This distinction between acquisition and formalised learning is similar to the distinctions which have been drawn between formal knowledge (i.e. formalised generalised principles) and informal knowledge (i.e. the folklore of what really works), and between explicit (precise and codifiable) knowledge and tacit (personal and intangible) knowledge (see Sallis and Jones 2002). But it is not the same as the dichotomies drawn by Houle (1961 – see p. 92) with his learning which 'functions as an instrument . . . to facilitate the [learner] into the logic of the present system' set against learning as 'the practice of freedom', and by Freire (1972) with his 'domesticating' as against 'liberating' education. For although acquisition learning will normally be domesticating, in the sense that it will induct the learner into the culture in which they are located, nevertheless at times some critically reflective processes are also involved, so that there will be potential elements of liberation in acquisition learning.

Sites and processes of learning

We need to distinguish between these processes of learning and the sites of learning. Resnick (1987) equated the two, suggesting that the learning that goes on inside formal settings (schools and colleges and other situations involving the use of textbooks, distance learning, etc.) is different from what she called 'out-of-school learning'. She suggested that the former tends to be individualised, competitive, mainly mental, decontextualised, generalised and generalisable learning, while 'out-of-school' learning is collaborative, contextualised and situation-specific, and uses tools rather than minds alone. This is characteristic of most of the writings about formal and non-formal education (Rogers, forthcoming).

It may be possible to identify two kinds of sites of learning, formal and informal. But both acquisition learning and formalised learning can take place in both settings. It is probable that when many adults enter formal sites of learning, they tend to adopt formalised processes of learning which they associate from experience with those sites; much formal education encourages this. And those who have been extensively exposed to formal education may also tend to use formalised learning in informal settings (in the home, the workplace, or social settings etc.), because they feel most comfortable with these processes once they have identified that what they are doing is learning. (This may help to account for the fact that most of those who participate in adult education programmes are persons who already have a good deal of experience in formal education.) When adults engage in their own purposeful learning episodes, they choose those sites of learning which they feel are most appropriate to their intentions, and they choose those processes with which they are most comfortable.

There is thus a matrix, which is shown in Figure 5.3.

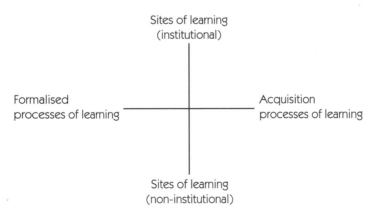

Figure 5.3 Processes of learning and sites of learning

Activity

Look at your case study and see how far you used acquisition learning processes and how far you used formalised processes; and whether it took place in institutional or non-institutional settings.

Subconscious and conscious learning

Acquisition learning reverses some of the sequences we noted above. In acquisition learning, it is argued, people use tools first before they find out what uses these tools may have. We learn both competency and understanding by 'doing' first; only after we have developed competency do we proceed to the making and transformation of meaning. Thus we start with a task which we find before us in our lifeworld and use everything that comes to hand: as Scribner (1988: 1) puts it, in learning, 'people strive to satisfy purposes that have meaning within their community, and in their activities they use tools, symbols and models that are culturally developed and transmitted'. In trying to fulfil this purpose/task, we draw upon our whole selves – our experience and self-concepts, including our concept of adulthood; we draw upon all the knowledge we possess and which we deem relevant in other fields as well. We use the experience and help of others. And we do all of this more or less subconsciously, concentrating on the task rather than on the learning.

The distinction between acquisition learning (task-related) and formalised learning (learning-related) seems to be close to the distinction drawn by Vygotsky (1962) between unconscious and conscious learning. But since consciousness is always present, the distinction may be redefined as to whether the consciousness and the intention are towards the task or towards the learning; in other words, whether it is an activity concentrated on a *lifeworld task* or on a *learning task*. Because acquisition learning is related to an immediate task, it is 'subconscious' or 'unconscious' learning only in the sense that 'the learners are not usually aware of the fact that they are acquiring language but are only aware of the fact that they are using the language for communication' (Krashen 1982: 10). Vygotsky spoke of people 'learning to speak and then finding out what it means, of clumsily taking over the forms and tools of the culture and then learning how to use them appropriately' (cited in Cairns 2001: 20). In what Vygotsky (1962) called the 'zone of proximal development' – i.e. more formalised learning using the help of others – the learner 'gains consciousness and perspective'. It would thus appear that in formalised learning, the learner is conscious of *learning*. In acquisition learning, the learner is conscious of *the task* rather than of learning.

There are of course occasions when the two kinds of learning are mixed. A parent showing a child how to cook, for example, will use a combination. Apprenticeships clearly involve acquisition and formalised learning. Induction into an office may often include both modes. Those who have become most accustomed to formalised learning within formal contexts may tend to use such learning more frequently than those who have had less exposure to guided learning. But they will still use acquisition learning.

Thus we can draw a series of situations in the form of a continuum of increasing consciousness of *learning*. At one end is incidental learning, obtaining knowledge more or less by accident (gossip or the media). Then there is task-fulfilment, without any consciousness of learning. There are the learning episodes which are more self-conscious of learning but are still heavily task-related (e.g. learning to set up home etc.). These are situations where people are known to speak of being 'on a steep learning curve' through some work or other. They may be more structured but the objectives and evaluation lie in the performance of the task rather than in the learning. Then there are self-directed learning episodes where the emphasis is more on learning than on the task (e.g. learning for travel). In these, some of the strategies employed will be formalised (e.g. the use of a textbook) and the growth of the consciousness of learning is more advanced. Distance and open learning contain much more formalised learning. Further towards the formalised end of the continuum lie those guided/assisted/taught learning programmes and activities which rely heavily on the control of others, where assessable learning is the key objective.

Activity

Ask yourself how far you were conscious of the *task* and how far of the *learning* in your case study.

There are then two distinct kinds of learning: acquisition and formalised. They are common to both adults and children. They occur in both formal and informal settings.

The uniqueness of adult learning

We can now try to answer the question as to whether there are forms of learning unique to adults and different from children's learning. This is an area which is becoming more contentious, partly because our understanding of children's learning processes and the processes themselves are changing rapidly under the influence of cultural and technological changes (Vosniadou 2001), and partly because we now understand that more than one learning process is involved. The question therefore is whether the acquisition learning of adults is different from that of children.

Huge assumptions are often made about adults and their learning. For instance, it is suggested that adult learning consists of 'modifying, transferring, and reintegrating meanings, values, strategies and skills' rather than 'forming and accumulating as in childhood' (Brundage and Mackeracher 1980: 33). Mezirow also suggests that the unique element in adult learning is the *transformation of meanings* through experience, whereas children are *creating meanings* from their experiences. But this may be doubted, for children too are constantly transforming meanings as well as creating new ones. Much more research is needed before we can draw firm conclusions.

Adult learning strategies

Some studies have suggested that a range of strategies are used more commonly by adults than by younger learners. For example:

- Adults use *analogical thinking*, calling upon existing knowledge and experience and the accumulated experience of others to see possible similarities that may indicate a solution. Through matching bits and pieces and creating relationships between them to identify where analogies may lie, they explore different ways of dealing with the learning situation. This learning relies upon the adaptation of knowledge and experience gained in spheres of activity *outside of the current issue*. It proceeds by being highly selective of the material felt to be relevant to the task in hand and trying out a number of possible solutions. When learning to mend a lawnmower for example, we may call upon half-forgotten experiences of motorcycles in earlier years. Such analogical thinking leads inevitably to *trial and error*: when learning to cope with new technology, we may engage in all kinds of experiments suggested by our own or other people's previous experiences in other spheres.
- Adults often tend to rely on the creation of *meaningful wholes* in order to master new material. They create patterns focused on key issues. These structured shapes and relationships summoned up by cues enable the adult to incorporate the new material into existing patterns of knowing and behaving.
- Most adults *rely less on memory and rote learning* to retain what has been learned. Along with some of the sensory-motor skills, the process of ageing is often accompanied by a decline in both the ability to remember and the ability to concentrate − a frequent cause of concern.
- Although adults share with younger people the ability and need to learn by *imitation*, and will often quickly grasp something demonstrated to them, in general they will not retain it without constant use as easily as their younger counterparts. Some adults will however seek to move quickly from such imitation (conformism) to experimentation (independence), though others will be content to remain conformist in their learning.

But none of these is exclusive to adults. Children use analogical thinking, trial and error, as well as imitation. They may make less use of creating meaningful wholes (although they clearly search for meaning), and they may use memorisation more easily, but like adults they use whatever processes they feel most comfortable with.

Adult experience and learning

At the centre of almost all the discussions of this issue stands the adult experience. Merriam and Cafarella (1999) claim that there are four ways in which experience is related to adult learning which are different from children's use of experience:

* experience used as a resource for learning;
* learning through the drive to make sense of experience;
* experience used to transform meanings rather than to accumulate new knowledge and skills;
* experience acting as a barrier to learning.

But it can be argued that none of these is unique to adults – that children too use their experience all the time as a resource for learning (indeed much child learning consists of building on existing experience to widen experience); that children too experience a drive to make sense of experience and this promotes much of their learning; that adults accumulate *new* knowledge and skills as well as transform meanings, while children are constantly revising and transforming their earlier created meanings; and that children too on occasion find their existing experience a barrier to learning. Thus it may be that the difference between adult experiential learning and children's experiential learning is a matter of degree. That adults have a greater range of experience (their own and others') to draw upon than children is self-apparent, but this does not necessarily mean that the processes of adult learning are any different from those of children, only that the mixture of processes may be different.

On the other hand, because adults are part of that culturally constructed complex defined as 'adulthood', their experience is qualitatively different from that of being a child. Adult experiences of legal processes, of family relationships and civic roles, of money and its acquisition, for example, are not only more extensive than those of children, they are qualitatively different: 'An adult's sexual or social experiences are of a kind that mark him [*sic*] off from the world of children. The same can be said of his experiences of a job, or politics, or war' (Kidd 1973: 46). A child learns through their experience of being a child; an adult through their construct of adulthood.

Adult development and learning

A more recent examination of this issue (Brookfield 2000: 89–101) is equally suggestive. In summary, it proposes that there are several ways in which adults' learning may be significantly different from that of children. One is *the consciousness of learning*: adults can 'become self-consciously aware of their learning styles'; and 'learning to learn, while evident at earlier ages, is most fully realized in adults and is an important developmental process' (what Brookfield calls, with typical American jargon, 'epistemic cognition' – 2000: 94). The second is *the ability to hold both the contextualised and the decontextualised in harness.* Adults can recognise that specific sites of action may make nonsense of general rules and theories ('dialectical thinking); they can break the rules when a specific situation demands it ('practical logic); they can 'act thinkingly', through critical reflection bringing decontextualised principles into their immediate and contextualised situation. These (it is argued) are the products of developmental processes, a stage beyond Piaget into 'post-formal operations'; younger persons cannot so act until they have gained enough and different experience.

FROM LEARNING TO TEACHING

Both adults and children use acquisition learning and formalised learning. Adult learning may be distinguished from children's learning in terms of their different experience (constructed as either childhood or adulthood), and of the stages of development rather than its essential nature. This then raises the question: how far is the *teaching* of adults different from the teaching of children? What is the role of the teacher in relation to the natural learning process, as revealed in both acquisition learning and in learning episodes?

Building on learning

Most teachers of adults operate in what we have called a more 'formalised' setting in the sense that it is a conscious *learning* activity rather than a task-oriented activity. Both formalised and acquisition learning are accessible in this setting. But the difference between acquisition learning and formalised learning appears to be clear. The formalised (educational) approach is that we learn first, then practice, and then use/perform. Acquisition learning reverses the order: we (try to) do, using our experience and the experience/help of others, and thus learn. Is the one then incompatible with the other?

It would seem that in their own learning episodes, most adults use acquisition learning more frequently and more effectively than formalised learning. It is the more natural process, as natural as breathing. If 'acquisition is central and [formalised] learning more peripheral, then the goal of our pedagogy should be to encourage acquisition' (Krashen 1982: 20). But this does not happen often: much formalised learning (teaching) ignores or demeans acquisition learning rather than builds on it.

I want to suggest that, just as breathing can be improved (e.g. for singing, swimming or boxing), so acquisition learning too can, with the help of formalised learning, be made more effective. This would seem to be the main purpose of the teacher of adults – to *enhance* the student participants' natural learning and to harness it to purposeful ends. And just as enhancing breathing means making the person for a time more conscious of their own breathing (a thing which we do unconsciously for the most part), so one of the tasks of the teacher is to help the learners to be more conscious of their own learning, to help them to bring general principles to bear on specific tasks and/or to draw generalisations from the specific. Consciousness of learning is, as we have seen, one of the features of learning said to be more characteristic of adults than of children.

Building on acquisition learning

There are a number of ways in which the teacher can build on the acquisition learning of their student learners. They can:

- Help the participants to revise their attitudes towards the subject matter and their self-perception (see p. 92). It is important to encourage the participants to build up their confidence in relation to the learning. Adults will tackle almost any new learning if their gaze is focused on a specific task they wish to perform; but as soon as the consciousness changes to focus on *learning*, a new set of confidences is brought into play, a new construct of being a student is created.
- Help the students not only to identify and use their existing learning techniques but also to build these up and enhance them, to make them more efficient, becoming conscious of their own learning.
- Help the participants to move from a concern with the particular to explore the whole field rather than just one part of it. This will mean structuring the field for study in a way which acquisition learning does not.
- Help the participants to explore their own experience more fully and more systematically; and at the same time to increase the range of experience available to the participants, especially knowledge from different contexts. Some of this will be theoretical knowledge. It will mean encouraging the participants to learn in some areas of which they have no real experience except at second hand.
- Help the participants to draw general conclusions from their specific learning, to decontextualise it so as to make it usable in other contexts. This will mean starting with specific issues but then assisting the learner to move from the concrete to the more general, to draw out the principles underlying the particular instances, in order to make the learning more permanent, more available for later use, rather than being simply a one-off incident of learning. Without perceiving the learned material from a decontextualised viewpoint, the learner will only be able to apply the learning to that specific instance.

- Urge that the process should not stop once the immediate task is completed but lead on to further purposeful learning.

Building on the learning episode

The characteristics of the natural 'learning episodes' suggest some of the detailed ways in which these objectives can be met (Figure 5.4):

Characteristic	Implications
1 Episodic, not continuous	• Rely on short bursts of learning activity. • Break material into manageable units; but hook each one on to other items of learning.
2 Problem-centred, not curriculum oriented; immediate goals based on needs and intentions; concrete situation; immediate, not future application; short term	• Make relevant to students' needs for motivation. • Be aware of students' intentions. • Students to set goals. • Start where they are, not necessarily at the beginning. • Do activity now, not prepare for it in the future.
3 Acquisition learning:	• Be aware of different learning styles; build up conscious learning skills.
• analogical thinking; use of existing knowledge and experience • trial and error	• Relate new material to existing experience and knowledge. • Be sensitive to range and use of experience. • Discovery learning; students to be active, not passive recipients. • Need for reinforcement; build in feedback. • Need for practice.
• meaningful wholes	• Move from simplified wholes to more complex wholes. • Help students to build up units to create whole; select out essential units from non-essential.
• less memory; but imitation	• Rely on understanding for retention, not memory. • Use of demonstration.
4 Lack of interest in general principles	• Move from concrete to general, not from general to concrete; encourage questioning of general principles; build up relationships.
• stops when need is met	• Encourage further learning.

Figure 5.4 The learning episode and the implications for the teacher of adults

- *Breaking learning tasks down.* If learning is episodic and not continuous, we should perhaps rely on short bursts of learning activity. Material is more easily mastered if it is broken down into manageable units, provided that each such unit is linked to other items of learning, not left to stand on its own.

- *Who determines relevance?* If the natural learning process is focused on concrete and immediate issues, the material of our programmes needs to be felt to be relevant to the present concerns of the student participants. The best way to determine the relevance of the learning programme is to encourage the participants to determine much of the programme. Their learning intentions will help them to set goals, and their experience and issues should play a large part in shaping the learning activities.

- *Start where they are.* If their natural learning is focused on a specific issue (concrete experience), it will be necessary to start not with the logical introductory material appropriate to the academic study of any subject but with the area of greatest concern to the student participants. To start as it were in the middle of the manual or textbook and to move from there both backwards and forwards, rather than starting at Chapter 1 and moving inexorably to the last page may be more appropriate to many adult learners.

- *To learn by doing.* If learning is more naturally done actively than by passively receiving other people's wisdom, then it will be useful to engage directly with the activity under discussion rather than try to learn about it first and to practise it subsequently. Learning by doing the task at once rather than preparing for doing it theoretically would seem to be more effective. One learns cake-making best by making cakes, not reading recipe books or watching demonstrations; one learns history best by creating one's own historical narrative rather than by listening to or reading other people's history; adults learn literacy, numeracy and basic skills best by engaging in real literacy and numeracy tasks using real materials rather than textbooks.

- *A wide range of methods.* Since all the student participants are well experienced in undertaking learning tasks, and since they have each developed their own learning strategies, it follows that the teacher needs to use a wide range of teaching-learning methodologies. We can help the participants to become conscious of their preferred learning styles and devise activities that encourage them to use and develop these further. It is not of course always practicable to explore with every member of the learning group their own way of working. It is certainly not possible to devise a common learning programme that will incorporate all the different learning styles into one *omnium gatherum*. A range of activities needs to be developed which the student participants can try for themselves, using their own strategies to maximum advantage. The imposition of the teacher's particular learning style on all the student-learners will often slow them down.

- *Learning to learn more effectively.* The reaction of each student-learner will vary. Some will wish to strengthen those learning styles with which they feel less comfortable, which they feel are weaker. Some 'activists' may thus wish to develop their skills of critical reflection or abstract conceptualisation, for example. But others will seek to use their strongest style to maximise their learning. It is never safe to rely upon any one conclusion in adult education. But in building on preferred learning styles, attention needs to be given to the skills of learning as well as to the subject in hand – learning *how to learn* about history and cake-making and management as much as learning the subjects themselves.
- *Participating in planning.* If the participants are accustomed to organising, planning, implementing and evaluating their own learning episodes, then the teacher should not seek to do everything for them. The participants can be involved in every stage of planning, implementing and evaluating the teaching-learning process.
- *Using the participants' experience.* If adults tend to use analogical thinking as a strategy for learning, this suggests that the teacher can encourage the participants to relate the new material to their experience, to assist them to bring that experience into play and to make it available to the group as a whole. Students who discuss their own experience in class are rarely being irrelevant; they are almost always working on the new material, exploring it in relation to their existing knowledge.
- *Encouraging discovery methodologies.* If acquisition learning employs trial and error, the exploration of alternatives needs to be encouraged by participatory and discovery learning methods. The learners should be active, not passive recipients of instructions and information. Practice and reinforcement will form part of the learning programme. Constant feedback can be built into the programme so that both teacher and student learners are able to assess progress regularly. This takes time: adults need time for learning.
- *Using less memorisation and more meaningful wholes.* The decline in memory which many adults face as they grow older suggests that the teacher should rely more on understanding and the creation of meaningful wholes for retention, not memorising. Rote learning on its own is an inappropriate strategy for adults. The learners can be helped to create such wholes for themselves. Together teacher and learners will select out essential from non-essential material.
- *Using demonstration.* Since imitation is as important for adults as for younger learners, demonstration forms an essential part of helping adults to learn. Except in special circumstances (e.g. as a deliberate technique of learning), it is not wise to ask the participants to perform a task without the teacher having first worked through an example with the group.
- *From concrete to abstract rather than from theory to practice.* The lack of interest in general principles which appears in many learning episodes

indicates that the teacher of adults may need to start with concrete issues and move to more general matters instead of the academic process of stating theory first and illustrating this with practical examples. The drawing of general conclusions from particular instances would seem to be a more natural form of adult learning. With many adults, theory tends to *arise from* experience rather than theory *leading to* practice.

- *Promoting continuance of learning.* If adults learn constantly throughout life, the participants need to be encouraged to link the teacher-led learning experience with further learning when the course finishes. Any dependency that the participants may develop, by which they come to feel that the learning process must come to an end when the class or group ceases, ought to be avoided. We should be seeking to encourage them to learn without our help, to make ourselves redundant as teachers. The teacher's main aim is to help the participants to use their natural learning processes to become more effective independent learners.

Is adult teaching different?

If adults and children both use acquisition learning and formalised learning, does this mean that the teaching of adults is no different from the teaching of children?

One answer lies in the accumulations of differences we have seen above as distinguishing adult learning from children's learning. Or we can re-emphasise that adults are able to hold the specific contextualised task in balance with the more generalised knowledge and that this will influence the teaching-learning process. Or we may draw attention to the fact that the preferred learning styles of adults are likely to be much more strongly fixed than those of children. In these cases, the approach of the teacher of adults is likely to meet a much wider range of capacities and motivations among the learning group, and stronger participant determination of *how* they will learn.

Power

This leads to what seems to me to be the key determinant of the difference between teaching children and teaching adults, the different power relationships within the teaching-learning situation.

Constructs of adulthood
These different power relationships spring from the different self-identity of child and adult. In the Western constructions of childhood, as we have seen, children usually see themselves as incomplete, not yet arrived, in transition towards a better (normally more autonomous) life. Much of their conscious

formalised learning is compulsory and tentative (forward-looking). The teaching of children allows for these perceptions. The perceptions of adults, however, are different. Much adult learning is voluntary. Adults therefore are often more able to exercise greater power over their learning than children are. Adults too are often able to put into immediate practice what they are learning rather than wait for some time before it can be implemented. Above all, they are able to challenge the sources of new knowledge more directly and openly than children do, for they bring to the learning encounter their own sense of adulthood. The hierarchical relationships which are implicit and often explicit within the cultural construct of childhood have to a large extent been replaced in adulthood with more horizontal relationships between the learner and the source of learning.

Again we must not overpress this. For, on the one hand, there are areas where children too can exercise some power over their own learning, where they engage in voluntary learning. There are areas where children challenge authority, especially today when different learning methodologies and more self-directed exploratory processes are being encouraged among children using new technologies. There are areas where children are able to put into practice immediately what they have learned. While on the other hand, some adult learning is not voluntary.

Adult constructs of studenthood
There are areas of adult learning where the adult agrees to accept a hierarchical relationship in order to achieve their learning goal. For if the adult puts themselves into the position of being consciously a 'learner', as Wiltshire suggested, many adults today will construct that role as denying adulthood: they 'will adopt the role of student and submit to a planned process of tuition' (see p. 47). Many who come to our programmes set aside their acquisition learning and expect formalised learning, which can make it difficult for us as teachers to make their subconscious learning more conscious. For there will be a clash between their self-image as adult and their self-image as student-learner.

Nevertheless, there is a specific dynamic about teaching adults which is often revealed by a sense of greater equality between teacher and learner, a greater measure of student-learner control which is inherent in Western concepts of being adult. Teaching adults has been described as 'learning on equal terms'; the students have much to teach the teacher as well as the reverse. Unless the adult student participant is valued *as an adult*, formalised learning will deny both the agency of the learners and the acquisition learning they engage in. It is the self-image of the learner, especially the concept of adulthood, which is the unique feature of the adult learning equation, even though this sense of 'adulthood' will vary from person to person. Education which denies to the student learners any power denies their adulthood.

Further reading

Brookfield, S.D. (1986) *Understanding and Facilitating Adult Learning*. Milton Keynes: Open University Press.

Brookfield, S.D. (2000) Adult cognition as a dimension of lifelong learning, in J. Field and M. Leicester (eds) *Lifelong Learning: Education Across the Lifespan*. London: Taylor & Francis.

Daines J., Daines, C. and Graham, B. (1993) *Adult Learning, Adult Teaching*, 3rd edn. Nottingham: Department of Adult Education, University of Nottingham.

Imel, S. (1998) *Teaching Critical Reflection: Trends and Issues Alert*. Columbus, OH: ERIC.

Krashen, S. (1982) *Principles and Practice of Second Language Acquisition*. Oxford: Pergamon.

Rogers, A. (1997) Learning: can we change the discourse?, *Adults Learning*, 8(5): 116–17.

Schön, D.A. (1983) *The Reflective Practitioner: How Professionals Think in Action*. New York: Basic Books.

PAUSE FOR THOUGHT

We have seen that teaching adults in any sphere is a process of providing an opportunity for others to engage for themselves in a more or less intensive bout of individual learning, and of encouraging them to bring about in themselves changes in knowledge, understanding, skills and attitudes – changes that can be reflected in changed behaviour. Such learning depends on the intentions of the learners, and on the range of knowledge and experience they already possess and which they bring with them to the learning task, as much as or even more than on their learning abilities. In coming to us, they bring a range of expectations about the learning task which are in large part created by us as we inform them about the learning programme and its goals.

We have seen that there are many different theories about learning. Most of them suggest that the individual is engaged in learning through a process of active interrelation with either experience, new knowledge or their social or total environment. All these theories have something to teach us about what we are doing, they each contribute to the list of factors that will make for the effective teaching of adults. But none of these commands general acceptance.

Rather than suggest that any one of these groups of learning theories is 'right' and the others are 'wrong', I have directed attention to two things:

- The 'natural learning episode': those incidents in which adults throughout their lives engage in intentional, purposeful and structured learning using their own preferred learning approaches in order to achieve a particular goal or solve a specific problem.
- The distinction between 'acquisition learning' – that natural process which (like breathing) we engage in without thinking about it, where the primary consciousness is centred on a specific task rather than on learning – and 'formalised learning', where we are more conscious of learning. I have referred to these as 'task-conscious learning' and 'learning-conscious learning'. Both forms of learning are used in the learning episode as we

think fit. But when adults come to our learning programmes they construct themselves as 'students', and thus they to a very large extent lay aside acquisition learning processes and instead adopt an approach based on 'formalised learning'. Again such constructs will vary from learner to learner, dependent on their experience and expectations.

I have suggested that these two features remind those of us who teach adults that our student participants are already experienced learners. We need to study these natural learning processes, for they help us to understand more clearly how to structure the learning opportunities we create for adults. I have also suggested that our purpose as teachers of adults is to build upon this acquisition learning, but at the same time to go beyond it – to help the learners to make its results more permanent; to help them to draw out general principles so as to widen application; to strengthen the processes to lead on to further purposeful learning; to encourage them, in short, to become more conscious of, freer and more efficient in, their own learning. We can use the characteristics of these learning episodes as a basis for creating adult learning episodes for our student participants which will fulfil these aims. And this means increasing the use of acquisition learning in our planned learning programmes for adults rather than relying solely on formalised learning. This will be the theme of the rest of the book.

Chapter 6

GOALS AND OBJECTIVES

What is it all for . . . ?

This chapter looks at the difference between goals, aims and objectives. It discusses the process by which goals are set and made more conscious, and suggests that widening the goals may lead to more critical learning.

Teaching adults involves planning a learning programme. I have suggested that within this process, we should build on the intentional and purposeful learning episodes which all our student participants are using regularly in the course of their daily lives. Their purposes are directed towards *self-chosen lifeworld tasks*. The purposes that lie behind our planned learning programmes are directed towards *learning*. Adult student participants have life-related goals; teachers of adults have learning-related goals.

Aims, goals and objectives

A good deal of obscurity is often thought to surround the subject of goals and objectives in education. The matter is however relatively straight-forward. Goals are what we want to achieve in and through the planned learning programme, the reason why we engage in it at all.

Every teacher has goals. If education is the process of building purposeful learning opportunities, then the goals are those purposes that the learning is intended to bring about, the learning changes that will result from the activity. Both teachers and programme planners set out to construct situations in which the student participants undertake certain activities in order to accomplish something: mastering a skill, coming to understand something, behaving in a new way to meet new demands, growing in confidence and maturity. The goals are the *intended outcomes* of the teaching-learning activities, whatever these might be.

Should we have goals in adult education?

Some people, especially some of those engaged in forms of community education, would argue that such a model of education is too directive, that we should not set goals for the learners, that we should seek only to fulfil the varied goals the student participants set for themselves, or that we should provide an open-ended learning situation so that the student participants can each achieve what they want in the programme without undue interference from the teacher. They argue that pre-set prescriptive goals can lead to a simplistic, mechanical and linear concept of progress. There is a good deal of truth in this. It provides a useful reminder of a number of points:

- Because a contract to learn is involved in the process of teaching adults, the student participants have come to the programme bringing with them their own intentions, *their desired outcomes*. These intentions and desires may well change as the learning programme proceeds. The changing objectives of the learners are a real force in the dynamic interaction of adult learning.
- These student objectives will *vary widely* from each other. Each of the student participants will take from the learning situation what they want. It is a salutary lesson for the teacher of adults, especially those of us who have a message to give, that our carefully planned objectives may be set on one side by our students and that they may well go off with some other outcome than the one we have to 'sell'.
- Because the learning situation consists of a dynamic relationship and because four parties are involved in this encounter – teacher, learner, subject matter and context – the *real outcomes* of the process may well be different from both the teacher's planned and the students' desired outcomes. The teacher and the student participants should be aware of the possibility of unexpected outcomes, the unplanned results of the teaching-learning process.
- Sometimes the results of the learning activity are *long delayed* and do not appear during or immediately at the end of the class or course.

Nevertheless, the fact that the goals of the learners may be different from those of the teacher and that the real outcomes (both immediate and long-term) may be different from both of these (Figure 6.1) does not mean that the teacher should not set goals at all. Indeed, in planning any programme of learning, we cannot avoid having goals. Goal setting is an inevitable part of the process of planning learning opportunities for adults. They may be open goals, very general in nature (personal growth, for instance, or 'providing an opportunity for the participants to reassess their own priorities in life'); or they may be more limited goals (to learn to make Carrickmacross lace, say, or to gain an English degree). But they will exist all the same.

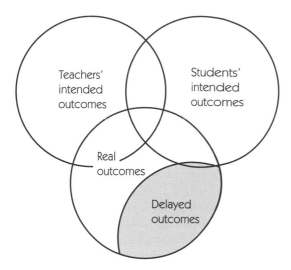

Figure 6.1

The student participants will normally be recruited into the learning pro-gramme on the basis of goals set by the teacher. For example:

Marshes and Moorlands

This class is intended for all those who wish to be able to identify the flora and fauna of these great tracts of the natural environment . . .

The intended outcome of this course is relatively clear. At the end of the course, the participants should be able to identify several species of animals, birds and plants that flourish at different seasons in marshland and moorland habitats. Those who desire to attain such a goal will join this programme of learning (although others, less specifically motivated, may also join).

Despite this selection process on the basis of the goals set by the teacher, there will usually be occasions when the participants – because they are adults, each with their own range of experience and their own agenda – challenge the teacher-set goals. In this lies part of the dynamism of the interaction between teacher and taught, so unlike the work done in most schools and colleges.

Even when accepted, such set goals leave room for a wide range of differ-ent options on the part of teacher and student alike. To take the example above, by the end of that course, the participants may be able to identify some of the most common forms of wildlife in these areas but may be in ignorance of others; or they may have begun to learn the processes of identification so that they can continue to explore and improve their skills when the course is over or during their own field-trips; or they may each have become expert in one particular field (orchids, say, or grasses), the rest being irrelevant to their concerns. These are matters that require a process of negotiation between the teacher and each of the student participants.

Defining the goals

Too often, as we saw in Chapter 1, the goals are left undefined. It is assumed that the potential student participants will understand what is implied when they read the course blurb or programme. But an adult class labelled 'Dress-making' with no further indication of what is intended to be achieved will recruit students with a wide range of expectations. Even when the programme of learning has been negotiated with the student participants, the goals frequently remain vague. But since goals play such a large part in the learning process and since they are one of the keys to learner motivation, it is important that they are not left unstated, assumed or uncertain.

- The more clearly goals are defined, the more effective the recruitment is. Those who join the learning programme on the basis of clearly defined goals are more willing to engage in the learning activities and contribute fully to the work of the group.
- The more clearly goals are defined, the greater the learning that takes place. The student participant needs clear guidance as to the direction in which the learning programme is heading. If the goals are left vague, the learner is uncertain what learning changes are intended.
- The more clearly goals are defined, the better the teacher can choose appropriate teaching-learning strategies, materials and methods. If the goals are left vague, the teacher too tends to flounder about.
- The more clearly goals are defined, the easier it will be for the student participants and the teacher to evaluate progress, to assess how much and what kind of learning is going on. If the goals are left vague, neither party is sure if they are achieving anything or not.

It is precisely here that the issue we raised earlier (see p. 121) on learning objectives being seen as 'clearing up messes' will be most important. In association with the student-learners, the teacher will need to try to determine just how the participants are structuring the situation which has caused them to enter the adult educational programme, what sort of 'mess' they see and what kind of answer they will be seeking. Objectives may thus vary from one student-learner to another – which does not make for an easy life for the teacher. It is easier if we can help them to come to a clear-cut commonly agreed learning objective, although that may not always be possible.

Levels of goals

There are different kinds of goal. Some people have tried to describe these distinctions using different terms – *aims* being general, overall goals, frequently ultimate in nature; *goals* being the main purpose of the activity; and *objectives* being nearer still, those targets which, once achieved, contribute to the goals. This is perhaps an unnecessary sophistication; the words have often been used more interchangeably.

Nevertheless, the distinction has some value; for while we may specify clearly our objectives at one level, we often leave the other levels unstated. Much of our work thus is based on unexplored goals that we have accepted for ourselves and we assume others have also accepted merely because they are present in our classes and groups.

We need to examine each level of goals.

Overall goals (aims or ends)

Overall goals (aims) are those longer-term goals that inform as a whole the programme within which we teach. They consist of those ideals (e.g. a more just society, a richer quality of life, greater professional efficiency) to be aimed at, even if never fully realised, and which may be used to test our work by. In many cases, these are established by the organisation (if any) providing the programme or the setting in which it is placed – the church, local authority adult education agency, voluntary society, development organisation, community association, university or training agency, for instance – and the public image it presents.

Thus behind every learning situation contrived by the teacher-agent is a set of assumptions about the nature of personality and society. We are vaguely conscious of the range of desired changes we would wish to help bring about in order to make our lives in particular and the world in general better. This is our value system which informs much of what we do, the purpose for which most of us engage in teaching adults at all. A teacher of gardening, for instance, can hardly teach the subject without a belief that gardens are a 'good thing' and that gardening practice and appreciation need to be improved and become more widely distributed throughout society. The same is true of most of the subjects we teach; we 'believe' in them in some sense or other.

These aims are rarely made explicit. They are assumptions that we imagine others (especially our students) share. But such assumptions may be challenged by the student participants at any stage in the learning process, because their assumptions may be different from our own. We may believe that training for health and safety at work or a knowledge of certain religious writing is in itself a desirable thing, and assume that our students share these judgements. But we may be wrong. Sometimes the challenge is open: 'Why do we have to do these tasks, learn all this stuff?' Or it may be more polite, a withdrawal with the comment: 'I couldn't see the point of it all.'

Specific goals

These are the shorter-term goals we set, sometimes fully consciously, for our courses. Teachers have, in most forms of teaching adults at least, a fairly clear idea of the kind of changes in skills, knowledge, understanding and attitudes they may wish to encourage the student participants to bring about for themselves. Thus they may plan to offer the student participants the opportunity to become something they are not yet: a better geologist, a 'fitter' or a more assertive person, a more effective teacher, a more efficient and happier worker, a more literate individual, a more critically reflective professional. The more clearly these specific goals are seen and the more closely they match the agenda of the student-learners, the more effective will be the learning process. When the learners' intentions (goals) and those of the teacher are far apart is when a learning group is most ineffective.

This is the area where the tension that we have seen to exist within all education – between learning as discipline and learning as growth into freedom – is felt most keenly. Setting the goals out clearly will on occasion cause us a good deal of concern about being too directive in relation to our student participants. It is also in this area that the assumptions we ourselves make about the nature of knowledge and reality and the role of the teacher express themselves most fully. Making clear and precise our goals at this level will not only help us to construct a more effective learning experience for our students. It will also enable us as teachers to see how we work and what assumptions we make, and thus to test the validity of these assumptions for ourselves; and it will enable us more easily to renegotiate these goals with the student participants. Discussing goals is part of the process of making learning more conscious.

Immediate goals (objectives)

In order to achieve our specific goals, it is necessary to break down the task in hand into manageable units – to learn how to handle wood, to learn how to relax or to read old documents, to use new machinery, to write notes, to read and discuss, to master new concepts or to decide between various viewpoints – in short, to do all the multitude of things that go to make up the learning activity. These objectives lie within each teaching session or each learning exercise. For the learning to be effective, it is necessary for the student participants not only to see the desired learning change clearly but also to see the relevance of the present task to the specific goal.

A hierarchy of goals

Setting goals is a more complicated exercise than this threefold division might suggest. For it is important to remember that there are various levels of goals that come between each of these three main tiers (aims, goals and objectives). Nevertheless, the distinction between overall, specific and immediate goals may be helpful as we plan our programme of adult learning.

There is a relationship between these three levels. The lower levels are usually based on the assumptions and contribute towards the attainment of the higher levels. On occasion, however, one level may contradict the assumptions held at other levels. It is possible for teachers of adults to engage in some forms of teaching because they believe (overall goal) that the participants should be encouraged to become more confident and self-reliant, and yet the immediate goals they set in each teaching session deny the learners the opportunity for self-expression and independence of thought and action.

One of the problems of taking any particular example is that there will always be those teachers who say that such an example is a special case, that the exercise doesn't work for their subject (e.g. music appreciation, degree programmes, industrial training, adult literacy or flower arranging). But it is possible to ask three simple questions about any piece of teaching you may be thinking of undertaking:

- *What* is the purpose of this piece of teaching? (*specific goal*)
- *Why* do I want to do it? (*overall goal*)
- *How* can I best help the students to achieve the purpose? (*immediate goal*)

Activity

Most teachers of adults start setting their goals with the specific goals. An exercise, based upon the course or class you listed earlier, may help you to see this more clearly. Across the middle of Figure 6.2a, put down in one sentence what you see as the specific goal of the course. It may well take the form of completing the sentence:

'The purpose of this course is/was to . . .'

Once you have done this, draw a short arrow upwards and try to answer the question 'Why?' Then ask 'Why?' again, and then again, if possible, until you reach into the area of your overall goals (to make people happy, to build a more just and less unequal society, to help people become better workers etc.) when the question 'Why?' no longer seems relevant, the answer is self-evident.

Then below the central statement, the specific goal, draw an arrow downwards and try to answer the question 'How?' This too can be done time and again until you have reached the smaller elements (immediate goals) of the learning activity.

It may be helpful to give you an example from my own experience (Figure 6.2b).

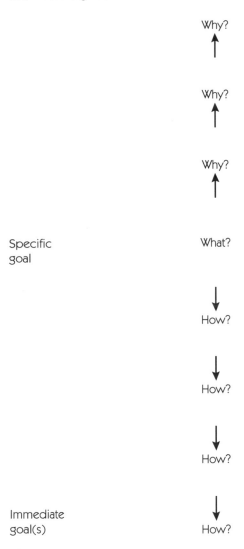

Figure 6.2a

We can note from our case study activity two general points about object-ives. First, there is no single 'right' answer to any of the questions. Each of us might give a different response. For instance, in reply to the question, 'Why do I want the student participants to learn about local history?', some teachers will answer, 'Because the students have expressed a desire to learn about the history of their local community, and I see my role as helping them to do what they want to do, nothing more'. This is for them enough justifica-tion; whereas (as Figure 6.2b shows) I see a social purpose in the task as well.

Because I believe that strong local communities will benefit all their members

Why?

To help build up stronger local communities as support groups for all of their members

Why?

To help build up groups of people who are interested in and concerned for the amenities of their local communities

Why?

The aim of this course is to help people to understand and (if they so wish) to practise the tasks of the local historian

How?

↓   ↓   ↓

By asking intelligent questions about the past of their own community	By coming to know about the range of source material available and searching for it	By developing the skills of analysis and interpretation of the sources and of writing up the results of their studies

How?   How?   How?

↓   ↓   ↓

By reading about the background to their history	By visiting record offices, libraries and museums	By discussing examples of local records in class
By reading other local histories	By visiting surviving monuments	By trying to read old handwriting under supervision (practice, exercises)
By looking around them and questioning what they see	By looking at other local histories to see the sources they have used	By practising writing up small parts of the work under supervision
By asking questions about the local community today	etc.	etc.

Figure 6.2b

Second, most of the 'How?' questions lend themselves to a 'doing' response. This may be expressed as the teacher doing something (lecturing, talking, presenting etc.) or as the student-learners doing something (reading, practising, discussing, writing, visiting, asking etc.). It is worth repeating that adult learning is most effective when the student participants are active, not passive, when they are doing the various activities that will lead to the attainment of the goals.

Setting the goals

Lying behind every adult class and every adult course, in every context, is a set of objectives, an understanding of which can be arrived at by asking ourselves as teacher-planners *what* we are trying to do, *why* we want to do it and *how* we plan to go about it. Two questions arise in relation to these goals:

• how does the teacher set them; and
• how do they relate to the students' goals?

But this implies a prior question: whether the teacher has the 'right' to set the goals. For it can be argued that goals and purposes of this kind can be seen as an act of manipulation, of aggression against the minds and personalities of our students.

By what right?

The main basis for a teacher setting the goals is normally that our student-learners have chosen us to provide them with help in learning. That is the way it operates in acquisition learning and as we have seen, most forms of lifelong learning for adults are voluntary – the participants have chosen to join our programmes. Constructing themselves as 'students', they have put themselves 'under' our instruction.

The basis for this decision is our perceived expertise. We are teachers precisely because we have some form of expertise. It may be a *direct* expertise; we may be a qualified joiner, cook, archaeologist or engineer. Or it may be an *oblique* expertise; we may have experience of groups, tools or methods of study without being an expert in all aspects of the subject under discussion. But whether direct or oblique, a recognition of expertise is essential if we are to acquire that measure of respect needed for the voluntary learner participants to accord us the role of teacher or group leader, to accept our creation of the learning opportunity, our guidance, our conduct of the class, our goals.

There will be those who object to such a statement, to the teacher adopting such a role. They may assert that our task as 'teacher' is to lay our experience and expertise at the disposal of the group of adults who may wish to learn with us, reminding us that we are a resource for the student participants.

This is true, but such a role is common to *all* members of the learning group. In adult learning programmes, each person brings their experience and knowledge and shares these with all the others. The teacher's role, however, goes further than this. We are not just a member of the group like all the others. We have been given the role of creator of the purposeful learning opportunity and director of the programme of work; we set out and generally oversee the activities (the *immediate* goals) through which the participants can move towards the more (*specific*) goal, and to do this we have to determine the nature of this specific goal, the purpose of the programme of learning, first.

How do we set the goals?

As teachers we set not only the 'specific' goals for the course, the purpose of the activity, but also the 'immediate' goals, the programme (schedule of learning) for the participants to follow. There are many different paths to tread, and from our experience and expertise we select those that seem most useful if the participants are to learn what they have indicated they want to learn.

The choice of these paths is revealed by the various answers we have given to the question 'How?' in the exercise above; and they may be set out in some form for the participants to see – in a *syllabus* or programme incorporating the ground to be covered and the methods to be employed. It is not an unchanging syllabus, a permanent programme of immediate goals, to be ticked off automatically in sequence. For as the intentions of the student participants become clearer or change during the learning process, so the programme will change. As the field is explored, as the subject is learned, as the varied experience of the student participants is harnessed to the learning task, so the range of enquiries and the activities to be pursued will develop. As time passes, so the world (even of dressmaking or Christian understanding) will change.

The immediate goals are expressed in the 'methods/content' part of the learning situation. Adult education is as much a process as a system or a set of structures. So the teacher (in negotiation with the student participants wherever possible) has to decide what the learners need to *do* in order to achieve the specific goal. Do they need to watch? To practise? To listen? To read? To write? What *they* need to do will determine both the methods and the content of the programme of learning. If, for example, the goal is the performance of a skill – to learn how to use a set of tools, for instance – then they need to watch a demonstration, to handle, practise and in the end use the tools meaningfully. If the goal is to understand, then they need to grapple with the various concepts that form part of the subject matter, play with them, rearrange and use them in writing and/or discussion. If the goal is the production of a community magazine, then they need to debate (the contents), to explore, to collect or create material, to write and draw, to discover information, to select. If the goal is to pass an examination, then they need to understand, to memorise, to practise writing under restricted conditions. The construction of the sequence of immediate objectives is part of the role of the teacher. It is our job to devise, modify and reconstruct the series of steps (the learning schedule) by which new skills, knowledge and understanding are acquired and developed. This is as true of literature and music, of computers and labour studies, of health and craft training, of bridge, fencing and flower arranging as it is of advanced engineering and accountancy updating courses.

Types of objective

This emphasis on activities, on 'doing', as part of the adult learning process leads us to ask whether all goals and objectives can be expressed in behavioural terms or whether there are other kinds of objective. Bloom's (1956) taxonomy of learning objectives distinguished between cognitive (information and knowledge), affective (attitudes, values, feelings and emotions) and psycho-motor (physical and mental skills) objectives.

Eisner (1985) suggested two types of learning objective: behavioural and expressive.

Behavioural objectives are the changes in behaviour arising from the learning which can be precisely stated and assessed: an ability to swim or to draw or to write a report. They are used particularly in learning skills (e.g. technical training) and are of especial value in helping the teacher and learners to assess the course arrangements and design and in measuring progress – the effectiveness of the curriculum in achieving these objectives. Indeed, some recent writers, influenced by Mager (1991) have claimed that all teaching-learning can be expressed in terms of *competencies*, so that the learning can be precisely evaluated. But this is hotly disputed by other educationalists.

Many behavioural objectives have been pre-set by the teacher, stating what the student-learners are expected to *be able to do* at the end of the course. Brochures continue to proliferate with statements such as 'At the end of this course, you will be able to . . .' and there follows a list of activities which the participants should be able to undertake, the new skills/knowledge/understanding and/or attitudes which will be expressed in action when the programme has ended (Rogers 2001: 88–9). But such a normative process is not really adequate. For the aim of any adult learning programme is to affect actual behaviour, not potential behaviour. It is not important what the student-learners *can* do after the end of the course; what is important is what they *do* do. When, in an adult literacy programme, the participants at the end of the class show that they *can* read but after a short time it becomes clear that they are not actually reading, that programme will be regarded as a failure, not a success. More is therefore needed than just competency objectives – some mobilisation of the student-learners in order to carry out the learning into their daily lives.

Some writers have suggested that the term 'behaviour' can refer to feeling, perceiving and thinking, but most people still draw a distinction between behavioural outcomes and affective outcomes.

Eisner's other kind of goals are *expressive objectives*. Whereas behavioural objectives are usually set by the teacher as 'predictive' goals and can be precisely stated, expressive objectives are more unpredictable in their results. The nature of much adult learning (e.g. increased awareness of self and context) cannot be prescribed. Each of the learners seeks to expand on, elaborate and make unique to themselves the skills, knowledge and understanding they acquire through the learning opportunity. They often do not know in which direction they will 'take off', and each of them will 'take off' in this sense in different directions.

Expressive objectives are therefore complex. They relate to attitudes, values, beliefs, aesthetics, appreciation, perspectives and insight. Behavioural objectives can tend to be simple and linear in nature; once the learners can complete one task, they can move to the next. Such objectives can be assessed by a series of increasingly advanced tests. But for adults particularly, many activities are not only unique to the learner concerned, they are unique to the occasions they are engaged in. Reading a text, for example, or sewing a piece of fabric, are not just simple skills. On each occasion the actions engaged in operate on several different levels at once. They may be done hesitantly or confidently; they may be done at an elementary level or at a more advanced level; they will be done for a particular purpose, unique to that occasion; and they may or may not achieve the desired result (Figure 6.3). These dimensions behind each learning activity form the expressive objectives of the adult student participant and accompany all behavioural objectives.

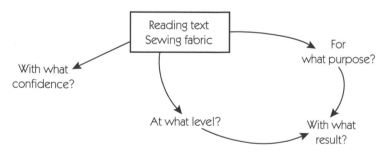

Figure 6.3

The value and limitations of behavioural objectives

This division of objectives into behavioural and expressive corresponds with the distinction that can be drawn between the *public* effects of our teaching (the way the learning will display itself in public) and the *private* effects (those internal changes in understanding, attitudes or skills of learning that contribute towards the overall development of the individual).

Behavioural objectives (the public face of learning) cannot encompass the whole of the learning process. There is much going on behind the behavioural changes, and a good deal of it we can never know. But 'this is not to say that we cannot recognize the existence of such forms of learning through observing alterations in behavior' (Brookfield 1986: 213). Indeed, it can be argued that we cannot see any part of these learning changes unless they result in some changed patterns of behaviour. 'Inner' learning will reveal itself through actions or expressed preferences. Learning in the appreciation of literature, music or art will reveal itself in a number of different ways, not least in a desire to have more contact with the subject. Learning to understand the historical process will express itself in the range of concepts used in discussion and possibly in other activities such as visits to historic places. Learning new attitudes towards other people or coming to understand some scientific process will equally reveal itself in changed practices and behaviour.

Different outcomes

While remembering that such objectives cannot describe all that is going on, it can be argued that all inner learning changes can be outwardly expressed in terms of some behavioural changes. Such observable changes will however be different for each individual adult learner and cannot be prescribed. The activities that will reveal the deeper levels of learning will take a wide variety of forms. One person may express their new understanding of local history and the new attitudes this understanding has brought with it by joining a local history society; another may become an ardent conservationist, while still others may prefer to work on their own, reading more, writing or collecting artefacts. All will display in their lives the learning changes that have sprung from the common achieved objectives, the acquiring of more knowledge of and insight into the history of their local community. In music appreciation, the outcome may be not just going to more concerts or buying more records but listening with discrimination, and this will express itself in decisions about the kinds of music preferred and discussed as well as in other ways. One of the tasks of the teacher is to try to determine with the student participants some of the many different ways in which the inner (private) learning changes may express themselves in (public) actions – in other words, what the participants wish to do with their new learning. And these desired purposes will become part of the objectives for the course, not as pre-set uniform and unchangeable goals but as some of the multiple expressions of the inner learning changes.

To help the student participants to achieve their own behavioural object-ives, they need to be provided with opportunities to engage in these activ-ities under supervision *during* the course. They do not need to wait until the course is over before they begin to practise their new competencies or to express their new learning. The tasks involved need to be seen to be real-istic, useful and purposeful, not meaningless exercises. They should not, except in a few circumstances, be activities that will never be tried again outside the class. To develop the ability to write an essay is perhaps rarely an appropriate objective (except of course in examination courses where this is one of the key objectives), for writing essays is not for most people an activity they will engage in in real life (some people however may like to do it; they may wish to contribute to some publication, even perhaps to earn money writing for local newspapers or magazines). If such a con-structed activity is set before the learners, then they need to be able to see how the task contributes to the whole programme of learning, to the gen-eral goal. We do not want pre-set behavioural objectives; but we do need some behavioural objectives set by the participants.

Conditions

Objectives at all levels can therefore be expressed in terms of accompanying behavioural changes. But not just in simple words of action. We need to set out not only *what* the learners themselves hope to be able to do but also the contextual *conditions* under which the behaviour will need to be practised (how fast or slow, perhaps, or with or without help, and so on) and the *standards*, the level, of the activity – not just that they should be able to do something but as far as they can to do it to a certain level of competence. Such performance indicators help to establish the criteria for evaluation of the learning achieved. Today many such criteria are set out in the form of targets to be achieved. This is of course relatively easier for those programmes designed to achieve a particular skill – courses such as crafts, art or languages; but even in these cases we will need to spell out the conditions under which we anticipate that the task will need to be performed. Academic courses have (often unstated) standards for work done (within a set time frame, with a particular level of accuracy, covering an understood range of subject matter and avoiding irrelevancies, without plagiarism etc.). In adult literacy, the goals have been expressed not just in terms of the learners being able to 'read' in a vacuum but that they should read *something specific*, read it *fluently*, and read it *with understanding* (Charnley and Jones 1979).

The teacher in association with the participants needs to set the objec-tives of the programme of learning in terms of *multiple* observable behavi-oural changes as well as in terms of the unique inner learning. Both sets of objectives will be needed. We cannot afford to concentrate on just the competencies arising from the learning without any concern for changes in understanding and attitudes, or on the internal personal changes in appreciation without any concern whether these express themselves in changed patterns of behaviour or not. Of the two, the inner learning changes are the more important. It is not a question of what we as teachers expect the learners to be able to *do* after the course is over; rather it is what we and they hope they will *be* and how that will express itself in action. Our aim is not simply a trained person but someone whose personal understanding and attitudes have been enhanced. Equally, we want someone who reflects that enhancement in practice in a way which they find most appropriate. Above all, we want to help them to continue to learn purposefully after the end of the course. Developing learning skills further needs to form part of every course for adults.

Activity

Is it possible to express the goals of your course in terms of:

- expressive objectives (private effects)?
- behavioural learning objectives (public effects), stating the conditions under which such achievements should be performed?

How do the goals relate to the learners' intentions?

The teacher needs to give attention to the relationship between their goals and the student participants' goals. Adult students come to achieve particular purposes. They bring goals with them, and they usually express these goals in behavioural rather than expressive terms. They are used to setting their own goals in their own learning episodes, although these may not always be expressed very clearly (see pp. 75–6). For some of them, their objectives will be concrete and immediate, for they will be thinking in terms of some learning change that they can recognise and use at once. They will want to be able to do something new or better at the end of the learning programme. But this is not always true, and the teacher will need to explore just what the students have in mind when they come to the course.

Further, they have usually selected themselves for the learning programme according to the expressed goals of the teacher/agent – the specific goals (Figure 6.2a) rather than either the immediate or the overall goals. They will tend to leave the setting of the immediate goals, the various stages of the learning process, to the expertise of the teacher, while the overall goals are, as we have seen, largely unspoken. The student participants have come in order to join in the stated activity of the group, to produce a particular product (a pot or a report), or to learn how to keep fit, how to market a new product or pass an exam.

Two caveats must be entered here.

First, there will almost always be a *wide range of student intentions*. In many adult learning programmes a number of student participants will say that they have joined a group in order to achieve the same goals as the teacher-planner has set out, but in reality they are there for some other reason. Student participants come to classes from all sorts of motives and for all sorts of purposes, often unstated.

Thus adult student groups contain a wide spectrum of differing intentions related directly to their individual situation (Figure 6.4a). At one end of the spectrum is the person who has come in out of the cold or whose regular night out is to attend some form (it does not much matter what) of adult class. At the other end is the person who wants to do just one part of the whole exercise. In a commercial subjects class, for example, we may

T = teacher
G = teacher's goals
E = expectations and intentions of learners

Figure 6.4a

have at one extreme the attender who seeks companionship and comfort without disturbance, who has no real goals of learning, and at the other extreme the participant who wants to learn how to use a particular word processor programme and nothing more.

If the aim of education is to meet such 'needs' alone, the task of the teacher in these circumstances would be impossible. But we have seen that education is not just meeting needs, it is purposeful learning. So the teacher has a purpose, a goal. Those of the learners whose goals are closest to the teacher's goals will learn most quickly, most efficiently and most permanently; those who are further away will have greater difficulty in learning and may even prevent the other participants from learning. We will see later how a learning group can help to deal with this situation.

The range of student intentions is not evenly distributed throughout the spectrum; they will tend to come in clusters. Nor will the teacher's goal necessarily be at the centre, it may well be to one side. This can be explored only once the teacher has met with the learning group. If the preponderance of student intentions lies away from the teacher's goal, then it would make for more effective learning if the teacher were to move their goal nearer to those of the majority of the student participants. If in a woodworking class we intended to focus on making bookcases, and the majority of the participants want to make garden furniture instead, it would be in the interest of all parties including our own to change our goal rather than expect the learners to change theirs. But this is not always possible.

But we need not change the *specific* goals, for these lie behind the immediate goals. It may be that the purpose of the class is not just to make one type of furniture but for the student participants to learn general approaches to woodworking. In this case, the teacher can accept and go through the widely varying goals of all (or at least most) of the student-learners and still direct them to the goal of the course as a whole (Figure 6.4b). It will however be difficult to do this for those at the very edge of the spectrum, who frequently do not want to learn much or who are willing to learn only over a very narrow territory.

Activity

Write down some of the intentions and hopes of the student participants in your class; try to grade them on a scale of closeness to or distance from your own goal.

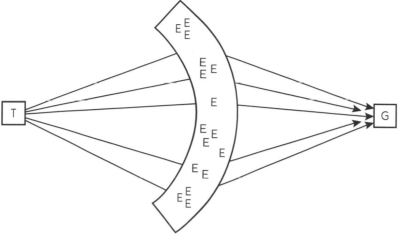

T = teacher
G = teacher's goals
E = expectations and intentions of learners

Figure 6.4b

The second caveat is that some of the participants may see *a different picture* from the teacher. The table, the level of fitness, the type of writing to be arrived at may all be very different in the minds of the learners and of the teacher. How many clergy have failed to realise that the lay view of a practising Christian is very different from that of the parsonage? It is a valuable exercise for us to spend some time exploring the minds of our student participants to discover their perception of the task in hand.

Nor should we assume that, once we have done this, the picture we possess will remain static or that the goals will remain unchanged. One of the main characteristics of goals is that, the nearer one comes to achieving them, not only does the picture of them change but they exert less and less pull on the learners who begin to look beyond that goal to the next one. We should listen and explore with our student participants what goals they have and how these are expressed; and we should continue to discuss this as time goes on to see how the students' goals are changing. We will learn much of misapprehension in our students and in ourselves as a result.

Activity

Try to write down some of the different pictures of the 'end product' of the course that you think your student participants may hold. How can you test if you are right?

To summarise: in order to create purposeful learning, the teacher will set a series of goals for the learners and from them construct a programme for the student participants to arrive at the goal of the course. But the participants may have their own goal or, even when they indicate that their goal is the same as the teacher's, the picture they may hold of that goal may be different. Only as the teacher and the student participants interact can these ambiguities become clearer and be removed.

The relationship of the various parties to the different goals is set out as in Figure 6.5.

Widening the goals

So far we have concentrated on the 'How?' side in our discussion of setting the goals. A consideration of the 'Why?' aspect will also help us to be more effective in the programme we draw up for our student-learners.

There is space for only one example, which is taken from woodworking, though it could just as easily be drawn from geology, health and nutrition, music, computer studies or industrial training programmes. For here we consider the longer-term purposes of teaching adults. The purposeful learning opportunities that we plan for adults will, we hope, lead to permanent learning changes, which in turn will lead to changes in the way of life of the individual and thus contribute towards change in society at large.

Our goals may be narrow, specific and limited, measurable, or they may be wider, designed to extend and maximise the changes in the individual. We can express this in a series of scenarios.

Scenario 1
A class comes together to learn to make a table. The goal is limited: *to make a table* (specific goal). The programme is therefore also limited: to learn how to handle the wood and tools, and to make those joints which are needed to make a table (immediate goals). The achievement too is limited to the skill of making tables (overall goal). This is expressed in Figure 6.6a.

	Teacher-agent	Student participant	How set out
1 Overall ultimate goals (aims)	Usually set by the programme organiser, but the teacher will possess own version of these goals	Students rarely directly interested in this level	Rarely spelled out, usually assumed; implicit in whole programme
2 Specific goals	The main purpose of the teaching-learning situation as the teacher sees it; usually devised by the teacher in association with or independent of the organiser	Usually what the learners will hold as their goals, the reason for attending the course; what they are most interested in	Usually set out more or less briefly in the course publicity or information sheet
3 Immediate goals (objectives)	The narrower goals of each learning task; usually determined by the teacher	Students will have an unformulated version of these goals, but this will usually become clearer as the course progresses	Sometimes set out in the syllabus or schedule of work, but often discussed class by class, task by task

Figure 6.5 Levels of goals: teacher-learner interaction

Figure 6.6a

Figure 6.6b

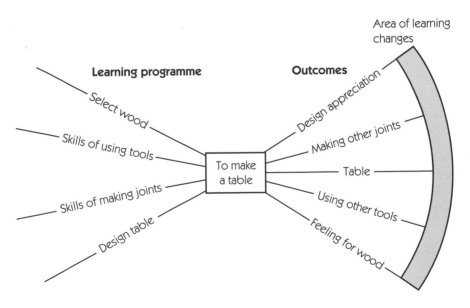

Figure 6.6c

Scenario 2

We may widen the specific goal: *to make a range of furniture* beginning by making a table. The programme then is wider: to learn a wider use of wood, tools and joints, going beyond making a table. The achievement too is wider: the learner is encouraged to innovate with new tools and new joints, to make new furniture (Figure 6.6b).

Scenario 3

We can widen the goals still further, though still using the table. The goals will then be *to understand and appreciate furniture* through making a table. The programme in this case will be much wider: to learn how to design a table and make a comparison with other tables; to study and analyse wood and develop a feeling for it; to acquire a wide range of skills of using wood, tools and joints. And the area of achievement, of learning changes, has also been widened so that the student participant is being encouraged to develop critical attitudes as well as technical skills (Figure 6.6c).

Goals, then, may be set on a narrow or a wider basis, and as a result of these goals, learning will tend to be either narrow in confine or wider. We must allow for the active involvement of the adult student participants. Some will seek to use even the narrow goal-based teaching to learn over a wide front, but their task will not be easy. In any case, it is the intention of the teacher-planner that concerns us most at this point: whether we plan that our student participants should learn over a wide field or over a narrow field. This is our choice.

The value of training

We saw on pages 52–3 the distinction between training, education and indoctrination. I suggested that the main purpose of education is to help the participants to become free to innovate, to develop critical reflection, to increase the range of choices before them. The increase of the ability to achieve in one field will contribute towards a sense of achievement in general. In this respect, training – the acquisition of a particular skill, the growth of knowing how to do something, the development of competence – has greater long-term benefits for the learner than has a process of 'informing' that will lead to a sense of dependency of the learner on the teacher.

In this we can see one of the distinctions between training and indoctrination. Training, that development of knowledge, understanding and skills leading to mastery over some narrowly defined area of activity or study, can become one of the steps towards education as freedom and may be used as a basis for a widening approach to learning. Indoctrination, in contrast, a confinement of ways of thinking and behaving, can never lead to freedom.

Elements of training will inform a good deal of what we do in teaching adults. A balanced view would suggest that some of the goals of the teacher will be narrow (the acquisition of particular skills or data), and some will be wider (building awareness, developing understanding of relationships, furthering a sense of appreciation and the like). It will help the learning task greatly if both the teacher and the student participants are able to distinguish the wider from the narrower goals. Both will be involved in our teaching. Training is an essential element of education. The use of training objectives, the development of specific skills, will contribute to widening the perspectives and increasing the confidence of the learners. But it is not education; more than this is needed. The pursuit of critical learning will not be achieved if teachers of adults confine their goals to specific narrow training goals. Part of our aim in all forms of teaching adults is to widen the horizons before the individual participants, to encourage them to become more conscious and effective learners.

Should the teacher attempt to lead the student-learners from the narrower to the wider goals in this way? Is not such an approach in itself indoctrination? This question has received a good deal of attention. We need to remind ourselves

- that as teachers we inevitably possess goals as we pursue with the student participants their purposeful learning – such goals are inescapable;
- that in treating the student participants as adults, the teacher will seek to make sure that they are aware of what these goals are, so that they may (a) opt in or out of the learning situation and (b) contribute to their formulation and reformulation.

Without this transparency, such teachers will be denying the adulthood of the learners. The continual modification of the teacher's set goals in the light of the changing goals, aspirations and intentions of the student participants is part of the dialectic of teaching adults. Setting and modifying goals is paradoxically a process by which the teacher may contribute towards the students' growth towards greater consciousness of learning; but equally the surrender of autonomy by the teacher in this area is part of the process of building up the autonomy of the learner.

Further reading

Davies, I.K. (1971) *The Management of Learning*. London: McGraw-Hill.
Davies, I.K. (1976) *Objectives in Curriculum Design*. London: McGraw-Hill.
Knowles, M.S. (1980) *The Modern Practice of Adult Education: From Pedagogy to Andragogy*. New York: Association Press.
Mager, R. (1991) *Preparing Instructional Objectives*. London: Kogan Page.

Chapter 7

THE ADULT LEARNING GROUP

How does it work . . . ?

Adults learn naturally from others, individually or in communities. The formation of
a learning group is therefore a valuable tool for helping adults to become more
conscious of and more effective in their learning. In such a group, all its members will
engage in both acquisition and formalised learning, bringing together the specific tasks
and the generalised principles.

The importance of groups in adult learning programmes

Learning is individual. Each person comes to claim for themselves something new and in the process changes their thought patterns, their competencies and their behaviour to a smaller or greater extent. Such learning
changes come from direct interaction between the individual learner on the
one hand and their environment, including the subject matter, on the other.

Much of the teaching of adults, however, is done in groups. There are
a number (probably a growing number) of one-to-one teaching-learning
situations – in adult literacy programmes, for instance, or with community
and social workers, health visitors and the like who engage in systematic and
structured programmes of learning at work, in the home or other settings.
Apprenticeship forms of adult learning are also spreading again. And there
are the increasing distance and open learning activities which many adults
engage in, and individual learning through modern information and communication technologies. But the majority of the planned learning opportunities for adults are still undertaken in some form of group.

There are a number of reasons for this:

• Schooling has habitually structured itself in this way. We ourselves learned
  a great deal in groups (classes), and on the whole we expect and even
  prefer to teach in groups.
• The use of a class seems to be the most efficient way to use the resource
  of a single teacher.

- Most adult students seem to prefer groups as a context for learning. Much of their own acquisition learning is undertaken through associating with others. Although opportunities for individualised learning are increasing (the increasing use of libraries and manuals at home are signs of this trend), a reaction against these forms of 'lone-ranger' education can often be seen in the demands for more face-to-face contact between teacher and taught and between the learners themselves. And in joining a taught learning programme, the participant is deliberately constructing themselves as a 'student' (see p. 47) – and since being a student is (in our society) equated with 'education', part of this construct is an expectation of joining a class, a learning group.
- There are sound educational advantages in group learning. The learning group can often achieve more for its members than a one-to-one situation can.

Whether the existence of learning-teaching groups is more a question of habit or economics or gregariousness or educational effectiveness, the fact remains that learning is individual even when the teaching is a group matter. Here lies tension. The group may be a great help towards achieving learning; but equally it may inhibit the sort of individually determined learning change we hope will be achieved. The teacher of adults needs to balance the usefulness of the group against the growth of individuation, discrimination and self-reliance which constitute the goals of so much of what we set out to do. It is another form of that tension between education as conformity and education as liberation.

Activity

Before we go on to explore the nature of learning groups, you may find it helpful to write down in your own words and from your own experience some of the practical values of a group for your student participants and some of the hindrances that the learner might find in a group.

Values	*Hindrances*
e.g. viewpoints of more than one person (teacher) are available	e.g. learners might be put off from trying by the presence in the group of others 'better' than themselves

Before we analyse groups in the context of teaching adults, we need to note two things about recent studies of groups and the way they work. First, much of the work done on groups during the 1960s concentrated on small informal (learning or therapy) groups, and in particular on group dynamics. More recently, attention has come to focus on larger organisations.

Second, many of these discussions have generalised and decontextualised the groups. It is assumed in much that has been written that most groups function in certain ways in all circumstances. The diversity of groups; the diversity of responses within groups; the diversity of interactions within each group; the importance of the immediate and more general contexts in influencing the ways in which groups form and perform – these have been largely overlooked. It is possible that there is a similar tendency in what follows, but we need to identify the ways in which our learning groups are unique as well as the ways in which they conform to contemporary understandings of how groups work. For each group exists in a social context which to a large extent determines the way they see themselves and the way they behave.

What is a group?

A group is more than a collection of individuals. It is an entity, something whole in itself. There is a continuum of groups: at one end, the tightly knit team, the integrated group where all the members have submerged their individuality; at the other, the loose-knit bundle. There are elements beyond each end of this continuum – the *folie à deux* at the integrated end and the collection of isolates such as a cinema audience at the other – but these lie outside most definitions of 'group'. The classes or other types of group we teach will be at some point along this continuum (Figure 7.1).

For a group to exist, there must be some form of common identity, but of itself this is not enough. The group has to be distinguished from the 'set' (all redheads, for instance) which although possessing a common characteristic cannot be classified as a group because it has no interaction. So two features are essential to a group: a common identity (usually a common purpose), even if it is unspoken, for all of its members; and some interaction between the members allowing for the sharing of attitudes and feelings,

Figure 7.1

some emotional involvement and the emergence of a minimum set of agreed values or standards. However, groups are not static but dynamic. They grow, they develop within their specific context and to meet their specific tasks. Successful groups are those which feel that they are moving forward in one way or another.

The term 'group' covers a wide array of social units, from very small working parties to large organisations. Even in the field of formal education, groups are not all the same. A lecture audience is frequently large and loose-knit. A class is usually rather smaller but at times it is equally loose-knit, closer to the 'collection of individuals' end of the spectrum as each of the members works on their own (the 'no-talking-in-class' syndrome). A discussion group/seminar is often smaller still and closer. A task-oriented group, focused on problem-solving or producing a collaborative piece of work (as in group project work) may be even smaller and may generate a good deal of warmth, if not heat; while a 'buzz-group' is usually smaller still, but it is unlikely to be able to maintain its strength of interaction for any length of time.

Moreover, groups do not stay still. Any group may well pass through a number of stages at different times, changing its nature according to its function. Groups may move up and down the continuum continuously, and it is useful for the teacher to ask at each stage, 'What is this group doing now?'

Activity

You may find it helpful before we go further to jot down one or two groups (not necessarily educational: they can include a committee, for example, or a band) with which you are associated, so that you can test the characteristics to be discussed against your own experience. (Fill in only the first two columns at this stage.)

Name of group	Size (approx.)	(a)	(b)	(c)	Comments

Types of group

Some analyses of groups suggest that there are different types.

Formal groups

In these groups the structure is set before any member joins, and the new recruit does not contribute materially (e.g. the army). Sanctions may be brought to bear on the members, and the group is not altered in any way by its changing membership, only by outside influences. Such groups do not in general concern adult education – though it has been suggested that some schools and classes even in higher education on occasion display some of the characteristics of formal groups. Most forms of adult education groups, being voluntary and participatory, are informal.

Informal groups

These are usually divided into primary and secondary groups. *Primary* groups are normally small face-to-face groups, a close-knit team based on mutual acceptance of roles. A family, a committee, a house church are usually primary groups. Each member is influenced by the others and a sense of loyalty exists, founded on regular contact. In this group, a member may have a strong sense of affiliation, but at the same time the individual will be very exposed to the group.

Secondary groups are usually too large to have regular face-to-face relationships. It is even possible for them never to meet, despite the fact that the ties are clearly felt. The members of an order of monks form a secondary group. More often, however, the secondary group will meet in some way or maintain some other means of contact (newsletter etc.). This group will affect the behaviour, attitudes and outlook of its members, and although the individual will not be so exposed as in the primary group, the influence of the group will still be strong.

Primary and secondary groups are not two clearly distinguished forms; rather, once again there are shades of grey between black and white. As we have suggested, any group may be mobile, moving backwards and forwards along the continuum. A group may display at different times some of the characteristics of a primary group and some of a secondary group. Groups have a life of their own, to a large extent independent of the wills of the individual members. Also, primary and secondary groups overlap; they are not mutually exclusive. A Methodist will belong to their chapel and even to the choir within that chapel – two different primary groups – and also to the Methodist circuit, district and communion (secondary groups). All those who come to learn in adult education, teacher and student participant alike, bring with them many different and overlapping primary and secondary groups.

A general point concerning the members of groups may be helpful. Those who seek to use the group to defend themselves from the outside world can do so only by exposing themselves more and more within the group. Those who reject the openness demanded by the group will find themselves unable to use membership of the group as a defence against the outside. It is not possible to belong fully to a group without being willing to open oneself in some measure to its influence. This is an important point in connection with motivation.

Reference groups

The reference group is hardly a group at all, but it concerns us for the influence it exerts on us and our student participants. The reference group covers the people from whom we draw values, standards, aims and goals by our own sense of affiliation. The group itself doesn't know we belong to it (we may not even be official members of the group) but *we* know. The reference group of our Methodist friend is the Christian Church (or more likely the Protestant branch of the Christian Church). Other such reference groups might be socialists, cricketers, farmers, teachers, clergymen – a sense of identity towards whom will help to determine the range of attitudes we possess.

Adult learning groups

Our adult learning group, to begin with, may not be much of a group at all. Rather, it may consist of a collection of individual hopeful word processors or French-language speakers. In many cases, however, especially in adult education contexts, it will quickly become a primary group with secondary and reference attachments. One secondary group to which the members may belong could consist of all the other adult students in the centre or institution where they are learning (e.g. 'mature students' in a university). Another may include those elsewhere who are engaged in the same sort of activity as that of the class. Participants in a natural history group, for example, will relate to other adult students nearby, if there are any, and/or to other people interested in ecology in the region. Managers taking an advanced course will each bring with them to the primary learning group the secondary groups of their own businesses as well as the institution within which the course is being held. Beyond these there is the reference group: the world of environmental concern as represented by journals and other publications, for instance, or all managers, or all adult education students (the 1980s Save Adult Education campaign in the UK for a short time brought a sense of coherence to this reference group, and Adult Learners' Week is currently doing something of the same).

Activity

It will now be useful for you to determine for each of the groups you have listed (p. 170) what are its primary – column (a) – and secondary – (b) – forms. Do not worry if you have difficulty in determining between them, but have a try.

Most adult learning groups seem to work most effectively as small primary groups (suggestions vary between 10 members as a minimum and 30 as a maximum) that meet regularly (say, once or twice a week) or for short intensive periods of a few days and share common tasks between each meeting. A larger group than this may prevent effective interaction between all its members; a smaller group is often too vulnerable to sickness and other causes of absence to ensure continuity of learning, and this inhibits the growth of group coherence and performance.

Group structures

It has been suggested that a primary group will structure itself in a number of different ways. The first is the *task group* – i.e. the way the group members relate to each other in order to achieve the common aim. A cricket team illustrates this. It has its own structure, and the members play mutually recognised roles to fulfil the task. Task groups are usually primary groups, only rarely secondary groups, and they are distinguished by two features: a defined goal and a recognised leadership structure.

Task groups are made up of individuals who may be willing for a time to submerge their own preferences in order to achieve the task but who remain individuals and relate to each other independently of the task. Some of them may dislike particular members with whom they work closely, while they may interact with others at deeper levels. At some distance from the task, then, the primary group may adopt another structure; its members may fill roles different from those they occupy in the task group. Such a group has been called a *socioemotional group*, and it has its own rewards as well as its own structures. It is, for example, not always the case that the cricket captain is the team's best after-dinner speaker; that leadership role off the field may belong to another member of the group.

An amateur dramatic society, to take another example, has a particular structure during rehearsals. The producer or director is the recognised often tyrannical leader of the task group. But after rehearsal in a more convivial atmosphere, they may as likely as not sink back exhausted and remain silent for long periods; the leadership role comes to be adopted by another member of the group. Many new roles emerge in a different social environment that are not displayed in the rehearsal hall.

The task group and the socioemotional group are the same group acting in different ways. The former stresses the function of the group, the latter its social relationships. Some groups have no task orientation or structure. My drinking partners who meet most evenings in the corner of the bar that I frequent are there only to enjoy themselves and to exchange useful and useless pieces of information. It is clearly a socioemotional group but hardly a task group. On the other hand, few if any task groups will fail to have socioemotional aspects.

A primary group committed to a task at times swings in its activities and in its structures from one aspect to the other. It can rarely remain all the time in the task aspect alone. Such a switch is healthy. It helps to facilitate the task and to increase the strength of the bonds in the group by relaxing the tensions created by the task orientation.

Such changes seem to be most easily made when the task structure and the socioemotional structure are not too far apart. If however the structure of the task group and the socioemotional group become too distant, or if the socioemotional structure becomes too strong – if for instance the leader of the socioemotional group is expected to play a clearly subordinated role in the task group with no recognition of the position the rest of the group accords to them – then the performance of the task group can be damaged. If, in our example above, the producer or director of the play and the leader of the socioemotional group clash over the task and their respective roles in the task (if, say, the leader of the socioemotional group objects to some of the casting), then the whole production suffers. A group appears to work best when the two structures are different but not too different, and when the socioemotional structure is subordinate, with everyone's consent, to the task.

When this happens, the socioemotional group will serve as a *maintenance group*. It will seek to help the task group to attain its goals. A maintenance group and a socioemotional group can at times be distinguished, for the maintenance group has the task before it and ceases to exist once the task has been completed, whereas the socioemotional group seeks to keep itself in existence, perhaps by choosing another task. In this case, the task comes to serve the ends of the socioemotional group, whereas the maintenance group exists to serve the task.

Activity

We can now ask of each of the groups we listed (p. 170) whether they are predominantly task groups or socioemotional groups; which of these two structures predominates – column (c). In some cases, it will be half and half, but in others one type of group structure will stand out clearly.

Groups in adult education

How can we adapt all of this to our adult courses and programmes? Apart from the important but often overlooked point that all of our student participants will bring with them a number of overlapping primary, secondary and reference groups of which they are members, what is the relevance of this discussion to our teaching? Do we need to convert a set of individual learners, which most of us teach, into a primary group with both task and socioemotional orientations; and if so, how do we go about it? What are the advantages of adults coming together into groups to learn? How can the presence of other learners help, and hinder, our student participants?

The discussions above will be helpful here. We have seen that part of the task of the teacher of adults is to build on the natural learning processes which all adults engage in, making these processes more conscious and more effective. In our learning episodes, we rely on the experience of others as much as on our own experience to engage in critical reflection, using search and select techniques. Much acquisition learning is done with and from other people. Imitation, comparison of ourselves against others, and feedback are essential elements in our natural learning processes. The importance of 'communities of learners' in adult learning is increasingly recognised, as social learning theories point out. Situated learning suggests that in many forms of learning we set ourselves, or are set, on the edges of 'communities of practice' from whom we learn and into which we are drawn. And Vygotsky's 'zone of proximal development' is insistent that our major learning is accomplished through working with others. Human beings are social animals and our learning, although individualised, is best achieved in association with others. Simply being a member of a community will bring about some learning.

This applies also to our adult learning groups. Simply belonging to such a group will bring some learning. Much of that learning will be acquisition learning – learning the language, values, practices and structures (roles) of the group informally and subconsciously at the same time as we are learning its subject matter more formally and more consciously. Teaching adults is itself one form of socially embedded activity. Membership of the learning group (a class or discussion group) therefore carries with it the same kinds of informal learning as does membership of a community group, a church or mosque, a pub drinking set or a local dramatic group, *at the same time* as it carries more formalised learning of the subject matter which forms the focus of the learning programme.

Advantages and disadvantages of groups in formalised learning

Views differ about the advantages and disadvantages of groups in formalised learning. What will seem to some to be a help will be a cause of concern for others. Nevertheless, four main values appear to flow from the use of groups in teaching adults:

- they provide a *supportive* environment for learning;
- they provide a constant *challenge* to the learner;
- they provide resources to build richer and *more complex* structures for learning;
- they have a *life* of their own, which can assist the learning.

Each of these needs elaboration.

Advantages of groups for learning

1 *Supportive environment*. There is a sense of solidarity in a group in which the participants can undertake the task (in our case, a learning task) more easily. The social context is one where all the members of the group are engaged in the same activity. The individual will be supported by the group. For example:

- The group calls for conformity to its norms. In this way the group provides a measure of *suggestibility* and reinforces patterns of change. If others in the group can relate to the subject matter and cope with it, strong encouragement is given to individual members.
- The group can establish the *status* of the learner and thus provide encouragement. Endorsement of one's worth, acknowledgement of one's potential, recognition of the role one is capable of playing within the group (especially a task group) and which the group is willing to accept – all of these can enhance the learners' self-image and encourage them to greater effort.
- The group supports experimentation. The shared empathies that spring from the awareness of others in the same situation encourage the student participant to launch out and innovate. In this inner circle, ideas can be tested out first before their assertion in the outside world, skills can be practised prior to their demonstration before all and sundry. With many adult students, it is their vulnerability that is most touched upon in learning; and the group can provide the security needed for personal development.
- The group *rewards* success. The warmth of fellowship and other emotional interchanges help to overcome the anxiety over changes that some learners experience. The group gives confidence. It is even possible for fellow participants to criticise another student at times when it is not possible for the teacher to do so. The group can provide much of the evaluation and reinforcement needed for learning.

All this depends on the members accepting and internalising the group goals and norms.

2 *Challenge*. The group provides an additional challenge to the learner. It creates a new setting calling for novelty in interrelationships. 'Newness' is in the air from the start. Most of us are accustomed to changing groups

and joining new ones – from our family to school to work and leisure groups, new family groups and so on. We accept all of these, usually willingly, and build up new norms. An adult teaching-learning group is another such group. We meet new ranges of views, prejudices and experiences, all of them calling for learning changes and widening horizons. Some adults come to educational programmes more for the experience of newness than for anything else. Much of this acculturation is done informally through acquisition learning. This is particularly true for changed attitudes; the existence of the group often provides the stimulus for change, for increased awareness and critical reflection, for the internalisation of values.

3 *Building complex structures*. The group, drawing upon the increased variety of experience possessed by its members, can build larger and more complex cognitive structures, can create more satisfying products, can present a wider range of possible solutions to problems, can bring into play more evaluative judgements than can any learning environment consisting of teacher and student only. Because all the participants have their own well-trusted learning styles, the methods available in the teaching-learning process are greatly multiplied. It has not been unknown for a student participant to teach another member of the group a particular skill or concept when the teacher's methods have failed. The resources that both student participant and teacher can call upon are greatly increased by the existence of the group.

4 *Dynamic*. The group has a life of its own, a momentum that carries the participant along, helps to create and maintain motivation, and sets a pace of learning that is satisfying to most of its members. Loyalty to the group will often bring about greater effort at particular times than any demand the teacher can make. The teacher's task in these areas is greatly eased.

In this way, a learning group can become something of a community of practice which will draw all its members in.

Disadvantages of groups for learning
However, each of these same characteristics of learning groups may also act as a hindrance to learning in certain cases.

1 *Learning environment*. The pressure to conformity, the *suggestibility* that the group exerts on the individual member, can promote imitation, not the free exercise of experiment. The group may smother the individual. At times (this often happens in an adult learning group) pre-existing prejudices and expectations are confirmed and strengthened by the presence of other participants who share them. Thus conflict between some or all of the student participants on the one hand and the newer ideas and ways of other student participants and of the teacher on the other may be generated and made more bitter. Trying to convince one or two students out of ten that their way of holding a chisel is inefficient and dangerous is relatively easy

– until they are strengthened by the presence of even a few other people who share their idiosyncrasy. The group, in whole or in part, can thus become a new form of authority to which the individual is expected to conform.

The *status* offered by the group may become restrictive. The individual may become typecast by the group into a set role and may thus find it hard to break out and adopt another role (see Chapter 8).

What is more, the success of the group in providing *reinforcement* for its members can lead to some of the participants experiencing anxiety and fear of isolation, of being an outcast from the group if any of them experiments with a new way of doing something or expresses a divergent point of view. Many a participant has refused to express an opinion because of the strength of opposing views held by other members of the group. The participant can so easily become dependent upon the group, and even come to fear the rivalry of other groups. Such dependency can lead to learning ceasing rather than continuing when the group disperses.

2 *Challenge*. The closeness of the group, as each member engages in the similar 'new' activity, can become a threat to some of the more individual-istic learners. At times the challenge of the group may be strong enough to deter experimentation by those who are less confident.

3 *Building complex structures*. Some learners may find it difficult to cope with the wide range of experience and views that others see as the richness of the adult learning group. The more elaborate structures that the group builds may in their case lack the necessary foundations for compre-hension and acceptance.

4 *Dynamic*. The pace set by the group may not be that needed by the individual member. Thus additional pressures can be created by the group. Some learning groups can be very intolerant of those who are felt to move unusually fast or slowly. Again, the relationships within the group may be inimicable to the personality traits of the learner.

Forming the group

Economics, educational considerations, student expectations and existing traditions of schooling all help to create a situation in which most of us find ourselves teaching a number of student participants at the same time. Each of us will have to weigh up how far in our particular circumstances a coherent learning group is necessary or whether we will teach our students without encouraging them to form themselves into a group, a cooperative for learning. A great deal will depend on the context within which our teaching is taking place – the overt and covert aims of the programme. Learning programmes for adults which lead to some form of examination or which focus on enhanced work-related practices will tend to remain closer to the set than the group, as individual and competitive rather than collaborative learning tasks form the staple of the learning activities. Courses which aim more at community development will tend to move quickly to group formation. Courses which concentrate on personal development (from keep fit to music appreciation) will vary considerably according to the underlying beliefs of the teacher and the student participants as to whether adults learn individually or collectively.

If we do decide that both the learning needs of the student participants and the objectives of the programme are best served by helping our disparate students to become a more cohesive group, what steps do we need to take to help turn these separate individuals into a group? Will it happen by itself?

There are several different models of how groups coalesce and develop. The one that has most currency would appear to be as follows. The first stage is when a collection of socialised individuals, seeing a common goal, come together and express their need and willingness to interact. There is a common bond. Then comes an exploration stage, during which the individual members set and explore goals, when their inner inclinations become aligned onto the agreed goal. During this stage, members interact because they see that others are looking towards the same (or similar) goals as their own. They express their mutual dependence and begin to explore other bonds they may share, such as common interests, concerns or acquaintances. Third, the group begins to structure itself. Its members start to adopt roles, and these – after a period of experimentation, jostling and even conflict – stabilise into the formation of agreed role identities and the acceptance of common rules for all members of the group. Finally, the organisation completes itself into a working group – dynamic, not static, with interlocking roles, specialisations and division of functions. In other words, the group has become something of a team, dedicated to the achievement of commonly agreed goals. (Some have added a final stage to this structure – 'mourning' as the group disperses).

Not all groups, nor even all adult classes, pass through all of these stages, though many will. Perhaps the first lesson for us as teacher or leader of a group of adult learners is to watch what is going on in the group, not to be worried when conflicts arise, and to do all in our power to help the group achieve a measure of self-consciousness in identifying and achieving its goals. Nor must we assume that, once the group has begun to perform in relation to the common task, its structure will remain stable. As we shall see (Chapter 8), roles will constantly be changing in the group, and this will make some of the members feel uncomfortable. It does not harm most groups to get them to discuss from time to time the nature of the interrelationships within the group.

Forming

Informing

Storming

Norming

Performing

This becomes particularly true of the group that takes off on its own, that begins to move towards the formal end of the continuum. The mutual identification – in which the group meets the socioemotional needs of the members as well as the task needs – can on occasions lead the members to join with each other against outsiders. Praise, good luck, blame and even persecution of individual members are shared, and the concept of 'we' becomes exclusive. Loyalty and solidarity are expressed in a group symbol (a name, headed notepaper etc.), then a badge, insignia, tie, dress or uniform. It is not long before ranks and titles emerge; taboo behaviour is laid down and jargon encouraged. The group is still a group; standards, values, attitudes and customs are shared, and norms are learned. But it has become more formal.

This is a very powerful tool of conformist learning but it scarcely leads to self-development, to increasing the choices before the members or to critical learning. Formal groups of this kind have their uses and are especially effective in achieving some goals (e.g. political change), but they are hardly education making for autonomy. Nevertheless, some long-running adult education groups seem to have gone a good way down this road.

The teacher and the group

What can we as teachers of adults do within our own contexts positively to encourage effective learning in the group? First, we may be able to help the group to emerge from the collection of individual learners who have joined the class by encouraging the members to coalesce. Frequent face-to-face exchanges, together with some emotional involvement (for instance, collaboration on a common short-term or immediate task) will help in this. People who have nothing to share will never become a group. Students who come to classes and sit saying nothing, waiting for the teacher to begin to teach, with a coldness that suggests a lack of emotional commitment to the exercise, will remain a collection of individual learners, not introducing each other to the combined riches of the group. Equally, dominance of the group by one individual will not help at all. Without a shared ownership of the task and a sense of achievement arising from its completion ('*We* did it'), the learners will remain in loose affiliation.

Seating patterns can help. Figure 7.2 suggests that such arrangements can contribute to the interrelations between group members; but we must be careful not to be too deterministic in this.

Second, it may be possible to watch the balance between the personal self-development of each participant and the supportive/challenging role of the group. Both are desirable, but the needs of the student-learner should perhaps take precedence. Each group member needs to be given opportunities to exercise their skills and express their views without fear of criticism, contradiction or exclusion by the group. As teachers, we will constantly try

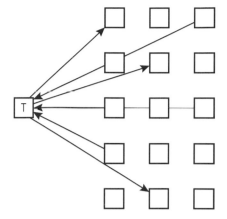

Figure 7.2a Seats in rows prevent members in the front from talking to those behind them, while the only face that all the learners can see is that of the teacher.

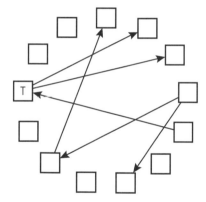

Figure 7.2b Circular seating helps all members to talk freely with each other as well as with the teacher. Even when engaged on individual tasks, such an arrangement allows for interaction (computer terminals can with advantage be set out in this rather than a more formal format, though often only with some difficulty).

to be aware of the pressures the participants in our groups are under. All of them can be enabled to experiment and practise, to play their own games and explore their own concepts. Each will have their particular contribution to add to the common pool. But equally, the capacity of each individual for affiliation varies, and no one ought to be pressed too hard.

Third, we can pay attention to both the task structure of the group and its socioemotional structure. It is not always necessary to discourage the emergence of informal, non-task related interactions (a short break from

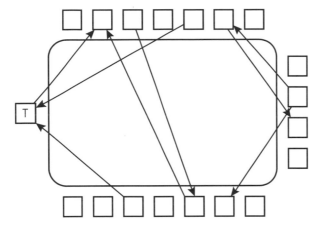

Figure 7.2c Even a large table doesn't always help. The members at the far end have formed their own group; watch out if the same people sit there every time.

the task, such as for refreshments, is a great opportunity for this, as well as the periods at the start and end of each session). Nor is it necessary for the teacher to occupy the leading role in the socioemotional group; indeed it may be helpful if a different leadership could be encouraged. But we do need to ensure that the socioemotional structure is subordinate and contributory to the task group, that it helps with the work of the group as a 'maintenance group'. The task is, after all, learning, in whatever field of activity the class is concerned with. If both structures are contributing towards the task, the teacher will not be unduly worried when the group continually moves in and out of its different aspects, not even when the socioemotional structure seems to predominate for a time ('What about our party this year?'). But it is not always easy to keep a balance, to keep the common goal before the group when so many of its members seem to wish to engage in anything except the learning task.

Sometimes it may be desirable to break up the group, to form sub-groups or create new roles and new structures, in order to encourage the learning task. But this can lead to the formation of cliques. When the participants appear to be reluctant to come back from their sub-groups into the full group, it may well be that the sub-groups are satisfying some need that the full group isn't meeting. If such a sub-group becomes permanent, especially if it gets between the group and the goal, conflicts will arise. In these cases, setting a closer subordinate goal, a short-term task with its own sense of achievement, will sometimes help to recreate the whole group.

On occasion, however, it can be the teacher who wittingly or unwittingly encourages such a division in the group. An in-group centred on the teacher (especially one who adjourns to a nearby bar with some of the members after each meeting) and a consequent out-group frequently occur in adult education. The out-groupers may be willing to accept the role assigned to them, but they will not be as keen on the learning task as they were when the group was whole. The in-groupers for their part will often assert their role, either displaying a proprietary interest in the teacher (asking specialised questions, for instance) or preserving an attitude of aloofness during the class as if to keep their contributions until later when the out-groupers are excluded and they can have the teacher to themselves.

Throughout this minefield, we will need to tread carefully. The most important attribute for any teacher to develop is *sensitivity*: awareness for example of the group members' non-verbal as well as verbal interactions; awareness of group tension and its release symptoms (jokes, laughter etc.); awareness of its signs of satisfaction. The way a group member sits on the edge of (or even outside) the group, the way they lean forward or draw a breath preparatory to taking the plunge into the common activity, anxious to make a point as soon as there is a reasonable break – these and other signals will be absorbed, often half-consciously, by the teacher. Some teachers are born; they seem to take to this naturally. But all of us can increase our awareness by understanding the ways groups operate and by learning to watch.

Conclusion

A learning group is therefore a valuable tool for promoting adult learning. It builds on the experience of the student participants in their own learning episodes; it becomes a site for horizontal learning. It will form a community of learners, providing an immediate context for situated learning. All its members will engage in acquisition learning as they enter more fully into membership, while at the same time they are engaging in formalised learning. It provides an arena in which the specific and the general are brought together (the dialectic of contextualised and decontextualised learning) which, it is claimed, is specifically adult. And it enables the power relationships inherent in taught learning to become more visible and to be challenged in a way appropriate to adults. All of these elements can be made conscious through the group.

Note: killing the group

The sensitivity of group dynamics has been expressed with sardonic humour in Clyde Reid's book, *Groups Alive – Church Alive: The Effective Use of Small Groups in the Local Church* (1969). Although intended for church discussion groups, it can be applied to many other situations. I have used the following extract from the book with several groups of teachers of adults; its sardonic humour pleases many of them.

The Fine Art of Squelching Small Groups

The ability to squelch the life out of a small group may be thought of as an art. Because of the strong interest in this new art, the following ground rules are offered to give direction and purpose to would-be squelchers who wish to develop their talents in this direction.

1 Keep the small group too large for the members to really get to know each other. By all means have at least twenty or twenty-five members in order to do this.

2 Complain at every meeting about how few people have turned out. This will give group members a size-consciousness and sense of guilt. They will either quit coming or they will invite their friends and the small group will soon grow into oblivion; it will become a large group.

3 Arrange the seats in formal rows like a classroom. Don't permit informality to sneak in by sitting in a friendly circle. In that situation group members might feel encouraged to express themselves and not want to give up the group.

4 Include a long business meeting with each group session and bore everyone to tears. The group will rapidly wither.

5 Dominate the group from the beginning. Establish yourself as the authority on all matters that may come before the group. Make all the basic decisions yourself, while giving the impression of a democratic spirit to the group members.

6 If possible, establish yourself as the teacher of the group and deliver a learned lecture at each meeting. (Our rock-bound guarantee: the group won't last more than three months this way or your money back.)

7 Pay no attention to the needs and interests of the group members. Most people don't know what is best for them anyhow.

8 Answer all questions yourself. Don't let group members speak to each other or answer each other's questions. What do they know that you can't say better?

9 Don't permit the fiction to arise that group members should take turns leading the discussion. They're liable to get too deeply involved and interested and keep the group alive in spite of your efforts.

10 Never allow group members to share anything personal. Change the subject to a nice safe intellectual discussion when this happens. That way they won't get too involved with each other at a depth level. Groups in which this happens become devilishly hard to squelch.

11 By all means, don't encourage members of the group to express themselves. Limit the participation to the more vocal, intellectual members to keep the conversation on a high plane of sophistication. They will bore each other to sleep.

12 Keep the discussion on a theoretical plane, preferably in the realm of theology and philosophy. Mention names like Kant, Schleiermacher and Tillich occasionally to make the others feel inferior.

13 Allow one or two persons to dominate the discussion. That way the others will become quietly angry and the group will fold up in no time. By all means, don't point out to the dominators what they are doing. This might lead to some hurt feelings and personal growth – things to be avoided at all costs in squelching a group.

14 Don't urge the silent members of the group to speak up. They might get the idea that you really care about them and that their ideas count after all. They will be more difficult to discourage as a result.

15 By all means don't let the group members express any hostility towards each other. You may find them understanding each other too well as a result and the group will become tenacious of continuing.

Note. It is recommended that every group leader express his [*sic*] own unique personality in using the above rules. There is a squelching method that is uniquely yours. You may have found ways to squelch a group that haven't even been thought of yet. But follow any one of these rules with dogged persistence and you need not fear. You will have expressed yourself. The group will certainly collapse, for you will have violated a principle of human nature.

Further reading

Barron, R.S., Kerr, N.L. and Miller, N. (1992) *Group Process, Group Decision, Group Action.* Buckingham: Open University Press.

Blumberg, A. and Gloembiewski, R.T. (1976) *Learning and Change in Groups.* Harmondsworth: Penguin.

Douglas, T. (1983) *Groups: Understanding People Gathered Together.* London: Tavistock.

Imel Susan (ed.) (1996) *Learning in Groups: Exploring Fundamental Principles, New Uses and Emerging Opportunities.* San Francisco: Jossey Bass.

Jacques, D. (1991) *Learning in Groups,* 2nd edn. London: Kogan Page.

Shaw, M.E. (1981) *Group Dynamics: Psychology of Small Group Behavior.* New York: McGraw-Hill.

Zander, A. (1982) *Making Groups Effective.* San Francisco: Jossey Bass.

Chapter 8

ROLES AND THE TEACHER

What part shall we play . . . ?

In joining an adult learning programme, the participant is constructing themselves as a 'student-learner'. This chapter looks at the roles members of a learning group may play, at the importance of helping them to change roles, at the roles that the teacher of adults will play and at the importance of the teacher changing roles. Again it is a matter of making conscious what we do in natural learning.

We have already seen (p. 47) that when pursuing an intentional piece of learning, the adult deliberately constructs themselves culturally and experientially as a 'student'. The basis for this personalised construction is both general (the cultural climate of their social context) and individual (their personal experience of other forms of education). For some, it will mean adopting a 'pupil' status. For others, it will imply a willingness to 'study', to work under guidance. For all, the role seems to involve some (temporary) abandonment of autonomy, a willingness to accept direction in order to achieve a (normally self-set) goal.

As we have seen (p. 168), being 'a student' carries with it, for those who come to our taught programmes rather than go to distance or open learning, a willingness to join a learning group, a class, and to play whatever roles are implicit in being a member of that group. Just as adults seek different social settings for different activities they wish to pursue (mosque, cinema, community hall etc.), so they put themselves into a new environment in order to achieve learning. They are willing for a time to divorce themselves from their other environments and join a learning environment for the purpose of learning.

Roles and changing roles

Every group has a structure, and this fact implies roles. Groups rely on roles, mutually recognised and accepted, both to achieve a task and also to work effectively in their socioemotional and maintenance aspects. In the learning group, all of the members (including the teacher) will play some part in its functioning. Such roles are fulfilled in meeting different situations, performing various activities and engaging in patterns of behaviour.

The way each of the members of the group views their role may differ from how others in the group see the same role. To ensure group coherence and performance, it is valuable if there can be a measure of agreement about, and acceptance of, roles. This will normally be achieved without being fully explicit – through the pressures of suggestibility, through conformity to and internalisation of the assigned place in the group – although, as we have seen, the capacity for affiliation that each member possesses will vary. The roles of student-learner and of teacher are socially constructed over many years, and their interpretation will vary according to the individuals and to the context of the learning programme.

Equally, engagement with the new material on which the learning changes will be based will call for each group member to adopt new roles – at first in relation to the new material and subsequently (and consequently) in relation to the other group members. Part of the learning process for each of the group members (including the teacher) is to change roles, to try out new situations and perspectives. Much of this is of course undertaken through acquisition learning – it is done subconsciously and derives from the community which is around the individual group member. Acquisition learning is going on in the learning group at the same time as formalised learning. Part of the teaching process is to encourage and help all members of the group (again including the teacher) to enter new roles and to interpret old roles in new ways. This is part of that process of making task-conscious learning more learning-conscious.

Group roles

There is a wide variety of roles that will exist in any one group. In the exercise below is a list collected from a number of teachers of adults of some of the titles they have used to describe individual members of their learning groups. There is no particular significance in the order in which they are given, and in most cases the meaning of the epithet is clear.

A few comments on this list may be useful. First, such a list can never be complete; the roles are too diverse, and in any case we will each see them in different terms. To a large extent, the range of roles and the way they are defined will be set by the context within which the learning group is set. Secondly, titles like these describe a series of activities undertaken by the group members and depend on judgements made by other members of the group. Some of them will be adopted roles, some of them ascribed by other members. Thirdly, since these roles depend on reactions to different situations, all members of the group in their time will play several parts – roles in relation to the teacher (or group leader), to the subject matter and to the other members of the group. A given title must not imply that any person will adopt that role to the exclusion of all others. Fourthly, there are dangers in giving such labels (which some people will in any case see as patronising). They tend to be more negative than positive (although the value to the learning group of the 'jester' and the 'expert' is often substantial). Equally, they may lead to stereotyping and even to self-fulfilling prophecies. But such titles can help to point out the wide range of reactions within any one group of adults engaged in learning under our supervision. Finally, the *teacher* will be called upon to adopt some of these roles during the learning group (you may find it useful to mark these items on your list).

Activity

This list contains 'titles' given to particular roles which some adult student participants have adopted. You can do two things with this list: use each title to describe how you think such a student participant will behave, both in and out of the group; and add to this list other titles from your own experience, if possible.

Title	*Description*
Student leader	Speaks for the group
Questioner	More interested in asking questions than in listening to answers
Queen/King	
Jester	
Professional simpleton	
Leader of the opposition	
Expert	
Prefect/monitor	
Cynic	
Know-all	
Last-worder	
Eavesdropper	
Ignoramus	
Special disciple	
Deviator	
Arguer	

Now add your own list.

Breaking roles

Each member of the adult learning group, be it class, lecture course, training group or voluntary body, will play a role in the group. All these roles
need to be accepted by the group in some way if the person is to feel fully
a member of that group. Rejection of the role is interpreted as rejection of
the individual. However, the role may be tolerated only in so far as it helps
in the achievement of the goal; and this fact can create tensions between
those members who have set themselves roles that do not directly contribute
to the task and those members who are committed to the group objective.
It will be the teacher's task to try to identify and minimise these tensions.
Part of our work is therefore to watch for the signs of these roles, to be
sensitive to the cues that indicate the nature and strength of the role being
played.

Perhaps the greatest problem with these roles, and with giving titles to
them, is that they may quickly become fossilised. The 'talker' at the first
meeting may remain for ever the 'talker' and thus stop the 'listener' from
becoming for a time a talker. The 'show-off' will continue to demonstrate
their skills to all and sundry, in the process not only limiting their own
learning changes but undermining the confidence of other group members
not so proficient. There is often considerable group pressure on members
to keep to their roles, although equally it is sometimes surprising how
much effort a group as a whole will expend in its attempts to limit trouble-
some roles (to quieten down the 'joker', for instance) and to encourage the
'quitter' ('I-know-I-can't-do-it-so-I'm-not-going-to-try') or the 'quiet one'
to join in.

These actions of the group, when they occur, are valuable and show the
contribution of the whole group towards the learning task. They will complement the efforts of the teacher to encourage changing roles in the course
of learning. The teacher's main aim is to help the student participants to
learn, both through the group and also independently of the group. Learning must not become dependent on the group or on the role played within
the group. Role changes will be necessary if learning is to take place. So the
teacher needs to resist any tendency for roles to fossilise, joining with the
group when it seeks to urge some of its members to break roles, and even if
necessary being willing to break up the group structure if it will help members to change their roles.

Although some of the student participants will change their roles willingly, in a spirit of exploration and experimentation, others will be more
hesitant. They may feel that their sense of identity in the group, their security, depends on the role they have acquired, which has been accepted by
the other members. One useful way around this is the use of smaller sub-
groups, dedicated to achieving a significant part of the task yet providing
opportunities (even perhaps the necessity) for members to adopt roles

different from those they possess in the full group. Those who are very quiet in the full group will often speak more easily in smaller syndicates. And some of those who are over-assertive within the full group may become less assertive in sub-groups. It is also possible to use the group itself, its loyalty and sympathy, to encourage such changes in individual members.

It will be desirable – indeed perhaps necessary – at times for the group as a whole to become more aware of what is happening within the group, to become critically reflective on the activities and roles within the group. Only in this way can the group change and grow as its members change and grow.

The roles of the teacher of adults

Just as each of the student participants brings with them a package of experience, expectations and concerns, a self-image of being a 'learner' which does not exist in acquisition learning, so too the teacher brings their own package – and this fact needs to be recognised and acknowledged. Every teacher is at the same time an adult learner, engaging in learning episodes with their own preferred learning style. All that is stated above about the adult learner applies to the teacher as a learner in their own life. However, making learning conscious will alter the nature of the self-image of the teacher; they will see themselves as 'teacher' in their own construct of that term. The way that the role of teacher is constructed in any context is one of the key elements in the teaching-learning situation, and you may well wish to give some thought to how you (and the agency within which you work, if appropriate) see that role.

It has often been suggested that the teacher is the most important single element in setting the whole tone of the learning group – although this can depend on the setting of the learning opportunity. But if there is a tension inside the group between its coherence and the call for individual learning, so too there are a number of tensions within the role of the teacher in relation to the group. Teachers will have at least four main parts to play:

- as *leader of the group*, whose purpose it is to keep the group together, to keep things going;
- as *teacher*, an agent of change;
- as a *member of the group*, equally subject to the pressures which the group itself exerts;
- as *audience*, outside the group, the person before whom the group members will perform their newly acquired learning in search of evaluation and reinforcement.

It is a daunting role and there will often be some clash between these different roles, but the rewards more than compensate for the difficulties.

1 ... as group leader

The teacher is the group leader. Our role in this respect is clearly recognised and accepted by the group. We cease to be a teacher when we abandon this role. There have been many, and increasingly complicated, attempts to describe the role of the group leader. One way to discuss this subject is under the three subheadings of task, interaction and maintenance, as suggested by Ivor Davies (1971).

Task

The group leader identifies and clarifies the learning task ahead, whether it be improving skills, learning a subject or solving a problem. The leader – with the participants – also clarifies the goals that they set for themselves. The leader keeps the worthwhileness of the whole enterprise constantly before the group. The leader evaluates with the group, as the learning process goes on, what progress towards achieving these goals has been made and is being made.

Interaction

Although part of the group, nevertheless the teacher is the one person who can watch what is happening from a position of committed detachment, involved and yet an observer. The teacher, through participant observation:

- monitors the interactions within the group and the structure it builds for itself;
- sees the roles each of the group members adopts, and seeks to assert that all the individual members of the group count;
- acts as arbiter if necessary so as to ensure that monopolies or persecutions do not arise;
- watches out for special relationships that occur and seeks to use them creatively, so that in the end every member will contribute positively and meaningfully towards the achievement of the common task, the learning.

The teacher as group leader can, and often should, help the group to see for itself what is happening. This is part of the process of developing a learning-centred consciousness.

Maintenance

The teacher assists the group to identify the resources available to them and the constraints under which they operate. They encourage and help the group to mobilise the necessary resources and materials (equipment, books, speakers, exercises) needed for learning. This may often include persuading individual group members to utilise the resources that are at their disposal.

Most of these functions can and often should be shared with the participants rather than kept to one person. But the person ultimately responsible for seeing that these tasks, necessary for the performance of the group, are carried out is the teacher acting as group leader.

Problems sometimes spring from the creation of dependency syndromes. The group as a whole may come to rely on us in direct proportion as we act effectively as its leader; and individuals in the group, especially those given special attention in the course of the group's activities, frequently develop an attitude of reliance on 'their' teacher. Some measure of dependency may be desirable, even necessary, in the production of a play, but in an adult learning class or group it will in most cases inhibit real education. This danger exists even where the teacher is attempting to develop the self-sufficiency of the learners, for group members will often try to keep us in the role of group leader against our wishes. We need, as time goes on, to play a less dominant role as leader of the learning group, whatever pressures the group members may bring to bear on us.

At other times or in other situations, groups will strike out on their own. And some teachers of adults find a problem here. It is not always easy to accept – after a lengthy period of nurturing the group – the decision of the group that it does not want us to continue in that role, that they wish to pursue their own agenda, that they can manage without us. Some teachers of adults, subconsciously fearing such a situation, try to prevent such independent action being taken by the group members – 'in the interests of the group', we often argue. But the interests of the group will best be served when they have come to a large extent to control their own learning programme.

2 . . . as teacher

The teacher is the promoter of learning changes, the encourager of the learners. The term 'change-agent' has been used for the teacher in some circles. We aim to use the group to help bring about changes in knowledge, understanding, skills, attitudes and ultimately in behaviour. Teachers thus have to be 'stirrers', to achieve change without breaking up the group.

The teacher operates in two ways: as manager of the learning process and as instructor.

Manager of learning
In this role, four main types of activity may be identified: planner, organiser, leader and controller of the learning process for each of the members of the learning group.

- *Planner* – the teacher analyses the programme of learning, identifies the skills, knowledge and attitudes required, sets out the learning objectives and the individual learning tasks that need to be completed in order to achieve these goals, determines what resources will be necessary and constructs the learning sequences (the curriculum). Most or all of this can be done with the student learners.
- *Organiser* – the teacher organises the learning tasks, subject always to the context within which the learning takes place, the environment of the class or group, the conditions under which the student participants engage in their work. The end purpose is to make it easier for the participants to work and learn together. It is thus important that such organising should be done to meet the requirements of the learners rather than for administrative convenience or for an easy life for the teacher.
- *Leader* – the teacher encourages the student participants, selects and uses appropriate teaching-learning methods and materials. For this part of our work, we need the most effective social tools we can find.
- *Controller* – the teacher to a large extent determines the relevance of the activities and the material to the task in hand and to the ultimate objectives of the learning programme, revises the programme and changes direction when necessary. They rule out irrelevancies and help to create and maintain the momentum of the learning group. It is here that one of the key differences between adult learning programmes and those for younger persons can be seen. For in many programmes (although not all) adult participants exercise much more control over the learning programme than do younger students. They will frequently determine what they want to learn, when and how – and they will reveal these decisions in their own study patterns. In the end, they will simply cease to participate fully when they feel that they have achieved their own learning goals.

Instructor

Several attempts have been made to categorise the different styles teachers adopt in relation to their learners, ranging from what has been called the 'sheepdogging' approach to teaching (herding the flock by constantly snapping at them) to the opposite extreme – allowing the student-learners to 'free-range'. Some writers have divided teachers in their personal approach to the student-learners into different types such as 'lion-tamer', 'entertainer' or 'cultivator'; it is not difficult to see the force of these terms as they apply to teaching patterns. Others have reflected on the contrast in modes of relating to the group: the autocratic, the *laissez-faire* and the democratic, for example. Others again have spoken of those teachers who 'tell', those who 'sell', those who 'consult' and those who 'join' the group of learners. Such descriptions attempt to depict some of the different

Figure 8.1 The continuum of approaches to teaching

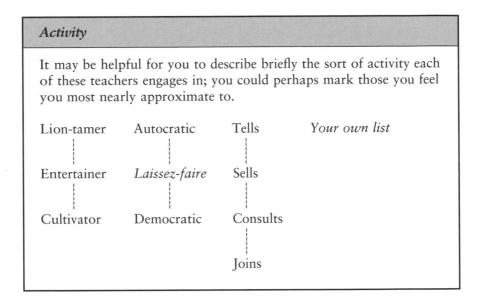

continua of approaches to teaching (Figure 8.1); they are not distinct categories.

Others have spoken of the teacher's manner: of those who on the one hand are aloof and egocentric as opposed to those who are friendly and understanding; of those who are dull and routine as against those who are stimulating and imaginative; of those who are evasive and whose work is unplanned as against those who are responsible and highly organised. Such characteristics are major factors in creating the atmosphere within which we all have to work in a learning group.

Class climate
Teaching styles help to create a 'climate' for the adult class or learning group. The atmosphere of the learning group may be relaxed, warm and friendly, or it may be tense, cold and hostile. The responses of the student participants could be on the one hand apathetic, obstructive, uncertain and dependent, or on the other alert, responsible, confident and initiating.

Attempts to assess the different elements to this climate have been made on the basis of four main characteristics:

- *Warmth* – the strength of emotions and identification between the teacher and the student participants; is the group welcoming, affirming, encouraging to the learner, not dismissive or exclusive?
- *Directness* – whether the interactions between the teacher and the student participants are direct or indirect, whether the teacher does all the work or whether the group stimulates the learners to do their own work.
- *Enthusiasm* – the way the teacher feels about the subject being taught, about the students and their learning; the commitment of both teacher and student participants to the learning task.
- *Organisation* – how far the teacher demonstrates competence in organising; the strength and efficiency of the process of managing the learning situation, devising carefully planned and purposeful exercises so that all involved feel they are not wasting time.

It is the teacher (as well as the learning programme setting) who to a large extent controls these elements and who helps to create the climate of the learning groups by their own styles. Their concern is both to promote the emotional well-being of the student participants and to ensure learning.

The climate of the class or learning group may be stable, with a consistent style used throughout; or it may fluctuate as the teacher swings from one style to another. Sudden and unexpected changes of climate may leave many of the participants uncertain of their roles and less able to cope with the learning tasks; but some modifications of climate are probably desirable for learning changes to take place. A static climate may not encourage the experimentation that is necessary to much learning.

Implications for the teacher

The fact that there are different ways of depicting the relationship between the teacher and the student participants prompts a number of thoughts. The first is that there can be no universal descriptions of the very complex series of relations that go on within a learning group. So much depends on the learning context, on the individual values of the teacher and on the student participants. Each of these may define these interactions in different ways. It is easier for us to describe and classify the relationship of other teachers to their students than it is to do so for ourselves. We are aware how far such categories fall short of the complexity of reality in our own case.

Figure 8.2 sets out a possible matrix of two of the main sets of factors controlled by the teacher and the sort of activity that may result from the varied teaching styles and class/learning group climates. You might consider where you prefer to operate on this matrix.

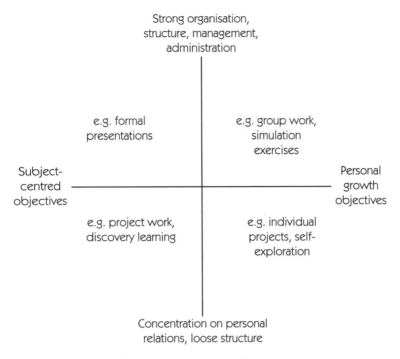

Figure 8.2 Matrix of class/learning group climate

Second, most of us as teachers do not adopt any one approach consistently. We move about throughout these styles as the need presents itself. The effective teacher will probably use many of these different ways of relating to the learners in the group during the course of teaching, just as the students also move about.

Third, we will sometimes find ourselves torn between the style adopted in relation to the whole group and the style needed for certain individual learners. How for instance shall we handle the situation of the slow learner who holds up the group? Or the very able who speed ahead and thus begin to distance themselves from the group? Which comes first, the welfare of the individual student participant or of the whole group?

And finally there may be – and often is – a tension between the role which the teacher wishes to adopt in relation to the adult learning group and the role which the student participants wish the teacher to adopt. Many students want their teacher to teach formally, to present information; they sometimes regard discussions as a waste of time. But some teachers find this a role which they cannot easily adopt. A conflict can arise from the dissatisfaction felt by those teachers of adults who are unable to reconcile themselves to the teaching-learning approaches which their student participants desire.

It is impossible to answer such questions with universal rules. Each teacher must think about them and answer them for themselves in the context of their own style of teaching and institutional framework. If each of the participants in our learning groups has their own learning style, which they have come to use effectively, it is also true that each of us as teachers has our own particular teaching style that we are happiest with, and this will to a large extent determine how we react in our learning groups. We need to recognise our own particular style for what it is; to improve it with practice; and to try to make sure that it accomplishes what it is intended to accomplish – student learning. We should also perhaps experiment with alternative styles at times.

The learning programme material

Being the main instructor of the learning programme will involve introducing the learner to the material comprising the learning task. One of the duties of the teacher is to encourage the student participants to engage directly with the subject matter for themselves. Here the triangle of learner, teacher and subject matter occurs again. In many cases, the subject matter is at first mediated through the teacher; then the teacher gradually withdraws, urging the learners to encounter the material face to face, until we have rendered ourselves to a large extent (ultimately completely) redundant to the learning process (see Figure 8.3). Unless we withdraw from this process of interaction between student participant and subject matter, learning will tend to cease when the class comes to an end or the group disperses.

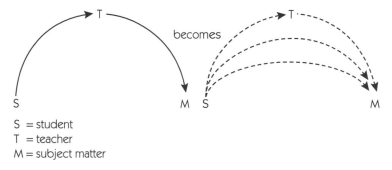

S = student
T = teacher
M = subject matter

Figure 8.3 Encouraging students to engage directly with learning material

3 . . . as group member

As teachers of adults, we are concerned with the learning needs of our student participants. Their learning styles need to be practised, their learning skills strengthened and enriched. In this process the teacher's third role, as member of the group, becomes of importance. Not only will it enable us to experience something of what the other group members will be experiencing, it will directly assist us in helping the various members to learn. The teacher can become a model of learning for the student participants. It has been said that 'the most important attribute of the teacher [is that] he [*sic*] must be a learner himself. If he has lost his capacity for learning, he is not good enough to be in the company of those who have preserved theirs' (quoted in Kidd 1973: 303). The way we ourselves learn and engage with the subject matter can be used as an illustration of the way other learners in the group can relate to the subject matter. All of us in the group, including the teacher, are learners; and we can all learn from each other how to learn.

The teacher and the class session

If we approach our learning group in this way, the meetings begin to assume a different perspective. We will become conscious that we, as teachers, do most of our learning for this programme outside of the group meetings. So that, instead of seeing our students as 'attending classes', we, and they, will see all of us as engaged in a course of study, a programme of work that will occupy a good deal of our time as long as we remain committed to it. Just as teachers of adults need to learn between class/group meetings – as they engage with the subject matter, prepare the material for the next learning step and evaluate progress made – so it is possible for them to encourage the other members of the learning group to learn in similar ways. It is odd that so many teachers of adults expect their students to learn in class only, while they themselves learn on their own. Those teachers who aim to make their students independent learners will seek ways to enable them to learn as much *between* class sessions as in the group meetings. Open and distance learning has shown some of the ways to do this effectively.

There are two possible models of the face-to-face teaching session in relation to learning. Teachers will adopt either model to suit different sets of circumstances, or indeed mix them from time to time. In one, most of the learning activity is done during the class meeting: demonstration of a new method of working, for instance, reading and discussing a text, listening to a lecture, engaging in practical exercises etc. The period between each class/meeting is spent by the learner reinforcing (by practice, reading, writing etc.) the learning done in class (Figure 8.4a). Part of each class session will then often be spent in feedback, an assessment of how much and what sort of learning has gone on since the last meeting. This is not a waste of time. Indeed, to expect all learning to be confined to those times when we are face to face will not only create dependency, it will waste all the time between each meeting available for reinforcement and run the risk of learning changes being lost.

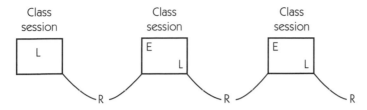

L = doing the learning exercise
R = exercises reinforcing the learning done in class
E = evaluating the reinforcement exercises

Figure 8.4a Different models of using teaching and learning time

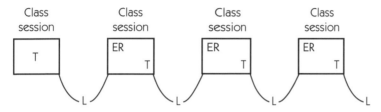

T = setting the learning task
L = learning
ER = evaluation and reinforcement

Figure 8.4b Different models of using teaching and learning time

The alternative model moves the main learning process out of the class session to the period between each meeting. A task is thus set during the class, to be completed before the next session. In this case, the next meeting will be spent partly assessing and evaluating how well the task has been performed and the material learned, and partly setting another task (or an adaptation of the same task if it has been inadequately learned). Most of the new learning will take place outside the class/group meeting (Figure 8.4b).

Using the space between meetings for learning will not occur automatically. As long as we concentrate on the teacher teaching, we shall think of the learning programme session in isolation from the rest of the student-learners' lives; we shall believe that all learning goes on during the face-to-face encounter. Even when we reorientate ourselves and think more in terms of the students' learning as an ongoing process, continuing even when we are not present, there will be obstacles in the way of using to the best effect the time between each session. Many adult student participants tend to see the encounter between teacher and learner as the essential focus for learning. We need therefore to take conscious steps to ensure that continued learning occurs outside of the group meetings and to evaluate what learning is taking place.

4 . . . as 'audience'

The fourth main aspect of our task as teacher is that of evaluator. By creating the learning tasks and calling for them to be performed before us for our comments and evaluation we remove ourselves to some extent from the group. We become the criteria by which our student participants' learning efforts are judged. In this respect, we are the expert, not just the instructor but the assessor of the learning which our students have done. In this again the teacher will share the activity with the student participants so that they may become critically self-reflective on their own learning. But in the end, the students have put themselves into a situation where they call for feedback from us as teachers. This is discussed at greater length in Chapter 11.

The learners and the teacher: horizontal learning

At this point, the greatest change of role comes about in both teacher and learner. In order to learn, the student participant needs to become for a time a teacher. The learner presents the newly acquired skill or newly learned material to the teacher, who in turn adopts the role of listener/learner. Adult (lifelong) education has been described as an activity in which all the participants 'alternate between the roles of student, teacher and person' (Thompson 1980: 67). Every adult learner needs to come to teach in some way or other. The teachers watch, listen, read and evaluate as they assess the student participants' work, just as the learner demonstrates, talks, writes and displays the new learning in other ways. The teacher-learner exchange of roles is the single most effective method of learning. (Formal institutions have long recognised this when they prescribe the writing of essays as a tool of learning, though there are many better ways of the student undertaking teaching functions than writing essays, and essays are not of course appropriate for most skill-based learning programmes.)

In performing this role of evaluator, the teacher comes to make critical judgements about the work of the student participants. So it is essential that we come to know ourselves, become aware of those biases that influence the judgements we make. Such preferences include those between male and female, between white and black, between old and young, between professional and working class, between the law-abiding and the law-breaking, between the known and the unknown. We all possess them, and they affect all we do and think. We should try to be open with ourselves about such preferences.

Resistance to change

The teacher makes demands on the student participants as learners. We set tasks and call for them to be performed under our critical eye, until the stage has been reached when the subject matter makes its own demands on the learners. There will be times when we are faced with a measure of resistance on the part of some of the student participants. There will be several reasons for this:

- Some of the participants do not in fact want to change. They come to our learning programmes for many purposes (sometimes even believing that they want to learn), among which socioemotional needs may be strongest – and these reasons often militate against change. Others may be there for career-related reasons rather than out of a desire for learning. They want to acquire the accolades that go with the completion of the programme of study but they do not want to learn, to change. Most groups of adult learners contain some members like this.
- Sometimes the roles played by the student participants establish their status in the group, and abandonment of those roles may be seen as damaging. Several adults find engaging in group learning exercises embarrassing; they see such activities as damaging the picture they believe others have of them.
- Learning changes can be, as we have suggested, uncomfortable and even painful to make, the more so as the adult grows into a concept of self-maturity. To admit to learning needs is in itself challenging to some adults, while others resist the effort needed to change their views and attitudes.
- Perhaps most frequently, many student-learners will object to the teacher who abandons what they see as the traditional role of instructor and expert, especially the teacher who on occasion admits ignorance. Some students may become anxious when a teacher engages in participatory activities: they want authoritative guidance or reassurance, and even discipline from a 'superior' person. Many groups will go to considerable lengths to keep the teacher as teacher and the learners as learners.

Fight or flight
When faced with a request to engage in some learning activity, group resistance can take one of two main forms of reaction: fight or flight. In 'fight', open resistance ('We don't want to') is on the whole less common than the question, 'Why should we?' This is often not so much a genuine enquiry, an expression indicating that the participants are unconvinced of the necessity of the particular learning task, as a statement meaning – 'We won't' (although many adult students are too polite to say so). 'Flight' may be expressed in the form: 'We will, but later'; 'It's a good idea but we can't do it because/until . . .'; 'We must find the proper material (or do this or that)

before we can begin.' An alternative form of flight is compensation, the substitution of some other task for that proposed.

We should recognise these tactics for what they are. One effective way of dealing with them is to help the group to become aware of them as avoidance techniques, as resistance to engaging in learning activities.

Expectations of the teacher

Most members of adult learning groups of all kinds expect the teacher to occupy the teaching role and the student participants to occupy the learning roles all the time. They see the teacher as both *an* authority (a specialist in the subject) and *in* authority (in command of the class/group). Many teachers see themselves in this way too; they collaborate with the pressures of the student participants. They feel safer being in charge of the whole process. They are often anxious about letting the student participants loose to experiment and learn by doing on their own – fearful that the learners will 'get it wrong'. They feel that they are not fulfilling their responsibilities as teachers, not fulfilling their students' expectations of them, even not 'earning their money'.

Just as the student roles are expressed non-verbally as well as verbally, so too are those of the anxious teacher. How often do we stand up before the class unnecessarily, rising to point out something to the rest of the group or to use the flipchart, especially when pressed with a question to which we are unsure of the answer? Standing above our students reasserts our authority both to them and to ourselves, like preaching from a pulpit, 'six feet above contradiction'. In non-verbal ways like this, we buttress our position when we feel challenged. We should try to become aware not just of how the roles of the learners are expressed but also of how we express the position we wish to occupy in the group.

This position is compounded of many different roles. The students call upon us to express many of these in the course of our encounter with them. Particularly, many group members expect the teacher to be a performer, what Richard Hoggart (in Rogers 1969) has called 'a Pied Piper of Hamelin', leading our flock by our playing to a dreamland of success. Some students consciously exert pressure to keep a teacher in this performing role: 'I could listen to you all day'. And some teachers respond to this demand willingly, adding one more role to the many they are already playing: 'Even more than most teaching, adult education invites its tutors to a range of attractive . . . forms of role-playing'.

Some of these roles contradict each other. The list in the following exercise, selected from the descriptions compiled by different groups of teachers over the years, indicates some of these roles; you may wish to add to it from your own experience. It is no wonder that at the end of a discussion of these roles one teacher in the tutor-training group exclaimed; 'We have just described God!'

Activity

List some of the roles that teachers adopt in relation to their student participants. You may find it helpful to write notes against each of them to say how you expect the teacher to behave in these circumstances. Some examples are given below.

Expert: a resource, a source of knowledge

Provider:

Explainer: demonstrator

Discipliner:

Organiser:

Instructor:

Motivator:

Protector:

Chairman: arbiter

Examiner: evaluator

Counsellor:

Others:

Expected to provide instant answers to all queries

Gives access to resources

Especially against a disruptive group member

Assessor of the work done, the one who maintains standards, checks work etc.

The one who will help, advise, guide, reassure, support, encourage the individual learner

---

Conclusion

This last remark provokes a few final comments about the role of the teacher.

Expect a life of isolation. As teacher, it will rarely be possible for you to join the group fully. You will always have one foot outside the group, however much you join in. You will nearly always be the 'audience' before whom the participants will practise their newly acquired learning and who will be expected to evaluate and judge their performance. The teacher is 'in' but not always 'of' the group.

Clearly a thorough knowledge of one's subject is essential for teaching adults. Teaching adults is not low-level work, as many in other areas of education have suggested, for the learners frequently push the teacher by their questions to the very limits of the subject. The teacher of adults needs to be fully acquainted with all aspects of the subject, for unlike the university lecturer we cannot always choose what we teach about; the learners often determine that.

Equally, the teacher of adults must be prepared on occasion to say, 'I don't know'. We will usually have some idea of how to find out. It is very rare that an adult group will respect any teacher the less for admitting gaps in their knowledge. They are themselves aware that the amount that is not known is far greater than what is known, and they will rarely expect the teacher to be an expert across the whole of any field.

Expect on occasion to feel threatened by the students. Some of them know more about parts of the subject matter than their teacher. Some possess many of the social skills which the teacher may wish they possessed. In such circumstances, there is a danger of the teacher falling back onto authority – the claim to leadership which the role of teaching endows. The teacher of adults needs to allow and indeed encourage the group to be student-led without feeling that their role has been usurped.

This suggests that social skills may be more important in selecting teachers of adults than subject specialism. It is not always the best policy to get the most up-to-date expert or series of experts to talk to a group of adult learners. Continuity of contact may be more important to allow for growth over a period of time rather than a series of individual teaching sessions by specialists.

If our task as teachers of adults is so demanding, it follows that we should seek out all the help we can get. Most teachers of adults work in isolation from each other, and we rarely spend enough time searching for the resources available in the community to assist us in the task. We need support, and it is up to us to find it. Our employing agency, if we have one, should help; but if not, there *are* other teachers of adults in our neighbourhood.

We must not become too self-conscious about our roles, our methods and our relationships. It is useful now and again to check how we and the group are performing, and every so often something will pull us up and make us realise the nature of the group reactions. But provided we are sensitive to what is happening, we can let things flow naturally, helping just a little here and there to direct the current towards the goals.

In view of the superhuman range of expectations that both we and the group hold of the teacher's role, we must not expect 100 per cent success. Most of our teaching sessions will have at least one blatant error, sometimes many more. The task of being a teacher needs to be learned, and that takes time.

Further reading

Apps, J. (1985) *Improving Practice in Continuing Education*. San Francisco: Jossey Bass.

Ostervan, K. and Kottkamp, R. (1993) *Reflective Practice for Educators*. London: Sage.

Ramsden, P. (1992) *Learning to Teach in Higher Education*. London: Routledge.

Rogers, A. (1991) *Teaching Adults in Extension*. Reading: Education for Development.

Rogers, J. (1984) *Adults in Education*. London: BBC Publications.

Schön, D.A. (1995) *Educating the Reflective Practitioner*. San Francisco: Jossey Bass.

Verduin, J.R. (1983) *Adults Teaching Adults: Principles and Strategies*. Mansfield: University Associates.

Chapter 9

TEACHING: CONTENT AND METHODS

How shall we do it . . . ?

This chapter argues that the learning content we choose and the teaching-learning methods we use in the process of making learning conscious are inextricably linked. Here again we can build on the methods of acquisition learning which our student-learners already employ.

We have seen that, in order to build on the natural learning process – acquisition learning which is based on social interaction – we can utilise the learning group and the various roles within it. Equally, in order to ensure that each of the student participants in our groups can learn in their own way, using their own learning practices and styles and at their own pace, we can use a varied range of teaching-learning methods that will involve the student participants in their own programme of work. It is the purpose of this chapter to explore this second avenue.

Curriculum

Methods and content together make up the curriculum, and a word on curriculum is thus necessary. There is relatively little material on curriculum in adult or lifelong education, and what there is tends to focus on the subject areas felt to be most appropriate to adult participants rather than on curriculum as a whole. Griffin's pioneering study (1983) concentrates on socio-philosophical concepts of the adult curriculum, and on the whole neglects more practical aspects. Most work on curriculum has been done in relation to schools. It is therefore necessary to adapt what is known about curriculum in schools.

Curriculum is often seen as a body of knowledge, the content of education to which the students need to be exposed. But curriculum is much wider than a list of subjects to be studied; it is not only what you say but how you say it! One view of curriculum is that it is all the planned experiences to which the learner may be exposed in order to achieve the learning goals, 'all the planned conditions and events to which the pupil is exposed for the purpose of promoting learning plus the framework of theory which gives these conditions and events a certain coherence' (Travers 1964: 42). The word 'curriculum' itself comes from a Latin word meaning 'racecourse', and this is a powerful reminder that what we are talking about here are the activities which the students will undertake to achieve their own learning goals rather than a programme of action which the teacher will fulfil.

Five elements have been seen as making up the curriculum:

Philosophical framework

Part of the curriculum which the learners learn consists of those attitudes which underlie all of our teaching. Woodwork may be seen as a series of techniques or as part of a concern for good design and good living; family planning may be taught on its own, in isolation from all other subjects, or as part of a holistic approach to personal growth, family development and human sexuality. Sociology may be taught in higher education as an academic study or as a practical exploration of personal experiences. Natural history may be taught as a leisure pursuit or as part of socially concerned issues. In every case, the difference will show in the way the subject is taught. This philosophical framework relates to those overall goals discussed on page 147. In particular, it will reflect our assumptions as to whether the education we are engaged in is designed to reproduce or transform existing social systems, whether it is aimed to lead to conformity or to liberation (see pp. 56–7).

Context

The learners will also learn much from the way in which the learning programme is organised. There are two main aspects to this:

- The *setting* – the room, the furniture, the lighting and heating, the levels of noise and other distractions in the immediate learning environment. The amount of attention the teacher gives to these factors forms part of the curriculum experience. But it goes further: the institutional setting and even the building within which the learning programme is located, whether formal or non-formal, the location of the course, the social and academic environment in which it is set, whether it is close to or distant from the learner's base, whether the student participant can reach the centre easily or only with difficulty – all of these are part of the learning experience and will teach the learners much. They will not always, of course, be under the control of the teacher of adults, but the teacher needs to assess such features and take them into account when planning the teaching-learning experience.

- The *climate* – the atmosphere created in the class session by two sets of relationships: those between teacher and learners and those between learner and learner. The climate, as we have seen, may be warm, informal and open or it may be cold, formal and closed (see pp. 194–5). In adult learning programmes particularly, the climate will reflect how seriously the organisers and teachers take the intentions of the learners, what importance they attach to the expectations and hopes of the student participants. In particular, it will reveal how much the different expectations of the student-learners about the formal or non-formal nature of learning and of the particular learning programme (see Chapter 1) have been taken into consideration by the teacher.

The most important factor in creating the climate in any programme of adult and continuing education is the staffing of the learning programme. A series of lectures given by different experts may tend not only to create problems for the students in relating both to the teachers and also to the subject matter (problems of overlap or gaps or contradictions between the material of different lectures, or establishing the relationships between the different material in each lecture), but it will also arouse a number of questions about the nature of knowledge itself and the relationship of the student-learners to knowledge. Are they all expected, for example, to know everything that each of their different lecturers know? If not, which parts are important and which not?

This raises the questions: to whom does knowledge belong – to the expert or the learner? Whose knowledge counts? Can the learner ever become an expert, and how? More continuity of teacher-learner contact will reveal a care to help the learner to learn. It will indicate that learning is in many cases a continuous process, to be pursued consecutively, not a spasmodic series of inputs; that learning goes on all the time, not just in the lectures.

Again, frequent and arbitrary changes of timetable to suit the demands of the organisers and/or teacher will teach the learners the level of importance which the agent attaches to the programme – and the learners may begin not to take the learning programme seriously themselves. A commitment to honour the contract to learn, clear indicators that the learners come first in every case, will form part of the learning experiences of the course. These will teach the learners much that is not discussed formally as part of the learning programme. They will form the 'hidden curriculum', the learning by subconscious acquisition that goes on inside every formalised learning programme.

Content

The subject matter to be covered clearly forms part of the curriculum. There are many different aspects to this area of our discussion. Apart from the amount of subject matter to be covered, there is the *sequence* in which it is handled, and the *conditions* attached to the learning. These are matters where formalised learning brings special insights to the teaching-learning process, for there is in acquisition learning little of sequencing and of conditions attached to the learning other than are required within the task to be performed. The sequence is planned to facilitate learning; if a change is introduced because a particular teacher or resource is not available, the participants may learn that the order in which the material is pursued does not matter much. And the level of performance, the speed at which the task should be completed, the fluency of the use of the material, all form part of the curriculum. What is required of the learner is as much part of the learning experience as the subject matter itself and needs to be made explicit.

The content of a learning programme is often set out in a syllabus. But syllabuses normally omit to say much about the conditions attached to the learning. And they rarely indicate in any detail the teaching-learning *materials* which may be used. Here we can go to acquisition learning for some guidance. In acquisition learning, the materials for learning are what comes to hand, what is needed to achieve the task. They are directly relevant and usable materials, 'real' in the sense that they relate to the daily life task on which the learner is engaged, not 'special' in the sense of being created specifically to promote learning. As well as specially prepared materials which involve sequencing and the conditions for the learning, we also need in our teaching of adults to use materials which are immediately relevant to the student learners, materials which they choose and provide. This calls for great innovativeness on the part of the teacher of adults.

On the other hand, a syllabus will frequently include elements of *methods* as well as subject matter. A management course syllabus may include not just topics such as 'personnel recruitment; selection procedures; career development; staff training; promotion criteria' etc., but also activities such as 'workshops; syndicate work; group discussion with report back to plenary session'. Many course outlines for adults in higher and further education now indicate the kind of in-class and out-of-class activities which the tutors expect of the students.

Events

The activities which the teacher plans and the learners experience, and the sequence in which they occur, are all part of the curriculum. The planned lectures, talks, discussions, small group work, reading, written exercises, student presentations; the materials used, visual and audio aids, handouts, reading lists and texts; the educational technology used with varying levels of competence – all these and many other elements help to create the curriculum, the programme which the student-learners are expected to follow. Some events of course occur which are not planned: the interruption of a learning programme because of the absence of a lecturer; the interruption of a session by an organiser or supervisor to make an announcement; or even in some cases the weather – all form part of the learning experiences of the student participants. Such unplanned events will either contribute to or distract from the learning, and one of the traits of an effective teacher is the ability to use such happenings as they occur to help forward the learning process, to direct even distractions towards the learners' goals.

Processes of evaluation

Among the experiences of the learners are those planned processes of evaluation – examinations and tests; assignments and other activities for feedback; criticism and assessment; ways in which the learners can express their satisfactions and so on (see Chapter 11). These too form part of the curriculum.

All these five elements contribute to that sequence of experiences and the philosophy which embraces them which together go to make up the learning course. It is the curriculum that brings the content and methods of our learning programmes close together.

Content and methods

The link between the methods and the content of the teaching-learning encounter thus depends upon the approach which we as teachers adopt. An emphasis on content, a set amount of matter that must be covered, to a large extent prescribes the methods to be used in the class/group. It will normally lead to a concentration on presentation methods of some sort. On the other hand, a concentration on the processes of learning will tend to mean that more time will be spent on the varied student-learners and their needs; relatively less of the content will be dealt with, and it will normally be used as an example of how the rest of the material may be handled by the learners on their own. The emphasis will thus vary according to whether the approach to learning is teacher-centred or learner-centred. This distinction corresponds to what Bruner (1966) describes as the *expository* approach to teaching-learning, in which 'the decisions concerning the mode and pace and style of exposition are principally determined by the teacher as expositor, the student as the listener', and the *hypothetical* approach, in which 'the teacher and the student are in a more co-operative position . . . The student is not a bench listener but is taking part in the formulation and at times may play the principal role . . . [through] acts of discovery'.

Others have made a distinction between decontextualised learning (the material being mastered is generalised) and contextualised learning (the material is drawn from, related and adapted to the experience of the different student-learners in the group). Contextualising the learning will not only affect the material chosen for study but also the teaching-learning methods used.

There is on the whole a close correlation between these two sets of approaches. A content-/subject-based decontextualised approach tends to be teacher-centred, to emphasise the teacher's presentation methods, the sort of activity the teacher engages in in the group; whereas a process-/methods-based contextualised approach will be more learner-oriented, more concerned with what the student participants do than with what the teacher does. But this is not necessarily the case, and a matrix (Figure 9.1) would seem to be a better model. (It may be helpful for you to locate your own learning programme on this matrix.)

Most of us need to adopt varied approaches. Sometimes our work will need to be teacher-centred, sometimes learner-centred; sometimes it will be concerned with subject matter, sometimes with process. Both Bruner's expository and hypothetical approaches will be called upon at different times. Exposition is a valid tool of the teaching-learning situation, a necessary part of the process – it is one of the basic skills the teacher needs. Despite the protests of some adult educators, much learning by adults consists of the acquisition of new knowledge. The student participants need to inform themselves, to learn new processes, to obtain new information and understanding from outside of themselves. They do not possess all the knowledge they need. They can of course do this in a variety of ways, and presentation is a valid and widely used method of teaching. Nevertheless, in order to promote independence of learning, the student participants need to engage in acts of discovery for themselves. The decision as to the balance between presentation and discovery learning to be adopted will to a large extent be determined by our attitudes towards the balance between content and methods in our teaching programmes and by the learning styles of the participants.

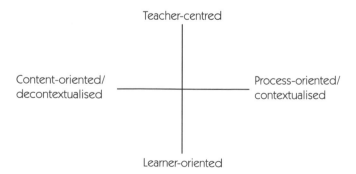

Figure 9.1 Matrix of methods/content in the adult learning process

Content

There are two parts to our discussion of the acquisition of new knowledge: the amount of new knowledge needed to complete the learning task, and the ways that students can acquire this new knowledge.

Amount

The amount of knowledge required for any specified learning task is almost always decided by the teacher. The evidence suggests that teachers in life-long education (as in other parts of the educational world) regularly over-estimate the amount of such input. Many teachers try to insist on what they see as a complete coverage of a topic. There are, it is true, some pro-grammes where the amount of new knowledge is *under*estimated: 'Learn this skill and don't bother with the theory' is sometimes the approach. But there are signs that many adults wish to learn something of the background to the particular process they are engaged in learning, some framework of understanding within which to locate the new material meaningfully. On the whole, however, most programmes are over- rather than underloaded. Perhaps the reason for this is that teachers tend to take themselves and their own range of knowledge as the norm for their students. They often deter-mine the amount of knowledge needed for the completion of the task by what they themselves know rather than by what the learners need to know. They judge the speed at which the student participants will be able to move by how quickly they themselves can learn. They assess the learners' ability to cope with new knowledge by their own ability, and they frequently choose the processes of learning by taking the way they learned in the past as the norm. None of this may be correct.

The result can be undue pressure on the student-learner. The teachers set the pace of learning by judging the amount of material they feel they need to 'cover' against the time they have at their disposal, not by the abilities and commitments of the student-learners. Teachers of adults often think that the time allotted to them amounts to more learning time than is in fact the case. But seen against competing pressures on the learners, the time available is not great, especially when a significant number of adult learners may have been away from formal learning for some consider-able period. Acquiring skills and understanding takes time; and adults need to relate their new knowledge and understanding (present experience) to past experience, which also takes time. We may underestimate this and press on, bound by our material and the time available for the learning programme.

On the other hand, as teachers we need to recognise that we ourselves experience internal pressures. We have been asked to teach a subject for which we may possess considerable enthusiasm. We have in our minds the amount of material we think the learners *ought* to cover. There is a compulsion on us to round off our subject matter, to bring the episode of learning to a satisfying conclusion. We may feel unresolved, incomplete, if only part of this matter is dealt with, if the material is 'broken off' before its 'natural end', if the syllabus is not finished.

This compulsion may encourage us to employ formal modes of presentation (lectures and the like). It is not inevitable that a concern for the comprehensive nature of the content of the learning programme and expository methods should go together. It is possible to combine a realistic assessment of the amount of new knowledge needed with formal methods of instruction, just as one can choose an excess of material to be covered while trying to use participatory methods.

But on the whole the pressure of trying to cover a good deal of subject matter in a limited time leads to a concentration by teachers on their own presentation of the material to more or less passive students, and teachers tend to resist efforts to pursue anything other than the main line of the learning process. How many groups have heard a teacher say, 'I can't deal with that point now; I must get on'? Yet there is no reason why the teacher 'must get on'; it is the learners who must 'get on'. It is likely that the majority of adult learning programmes now have externally set syllabuses to be covered and examinations to be passed, though there are still a number which are relatively free in what is taught and learned, which set out to 'explore' jointly (learners and teacher) some field or other. But in both, it is more important that our student participants learn than that we teachers complete for our own satisfaction the whole of the content. Many of the student participants will expect us to cover the ground, to deal with most of the important topics of the subject matter, whether it be skills-related or knowledge-based. But if covering the whole of the material means going so fast that the learner cannot learn deeply enough, with understanding and the ability to use the new learning, then the learning programme is not effective. What is the point in the teacher completing the syllabus if the learner does not really learn?

In most cases, such pressure is not only harmful, it is unnecessary. The main aim of our work is to create more effective learners, people who will carry on their own learning when our learning programme is over. They do not need to learn everything from us. A view claiming that complete coverage of the subject matter is desirable in a learning group is based on the assumption that the learners cannot be trusted with their own learning, that they can learn only when a teacher is present, that if they don't learn it now they never will.

It is far better to help the students learn how to learn more effectively by concentrating on part of the syllabus and to let them do the rest for themselves than to try to teach them everything. A course on 'keep fit' does not need to cover all aspects of the subject; as new fashions of exercise, new understandings of health and new equipment continue to become available, the range of learning is constantly widening and the learners will need to cope with these for themselves. Similarly, an English or European history course that sets out to cover the entire range from the Romans through medieval and early modern to the twentieth century will make unrealistic demands on both teacher and student participants. To concentrate instead on part of this field, however much it may offend the susceptibilities of academic authorities, may well provide the students with both a greater sense of satisfaction (intrinsic motivation) which will lead to a desire to pursue the learning further, and at the same time an acquaintance with the methods of continued learning to enable them to do so. By examining one or two shorter periods in depth, the learners will learn more of how to study history than a teacher-presented overview will teach them. I am reminded of a former colleague who said (talking of another colleague), 'He wants his students to *know* history; I want my students to *like* history'. The purpose of teaching adults is to help them to continue learning, not to teach them all they need to know.

Ways of acquiring new knowledge

The adult learner needs to acquire new knowledge: practical knowledge of processes (how to do something), factual knowledge (data) and theoretical knowledge (concepts). The teacher is there not to *impart* anything – skills, knowledge or information – to the student participants but to help the learners to acquire these for themselves. We cannot impart literacy or the skills to run a cooperative, a knowledge of politics or an understanding of healing; the learners develop these for themselves. Our task is to help and encourage them to learn.

Research and experience suggest that the more active the student-learners are, the more effective is the learning process; the more passive they are, the less deep will be the learning. Figure 9.2 indicates those processes that are seen to be most potent in achieving learning, ranked on a scale from 1 to 6. As may be seen, a high emphasis is placed on student-centred activities, especially those in which the student participant engages with the teacher and/or with the material directly.

Substantial amounts of teacher-centred activity may not advance the cause of greater student learning. The straight lecture is one of the least efficient methods of teaching. It calls for very advanced learning skills on the part of the listener (concentration over a long time, adaptation of the mental images, and the testing of the subject matter against experience *at the same time* as listening to yet further material etc.), and the rate of forgetting the subject matter is high ('What I hear, I forget; what I see, I remember; what I do, I learn'). Too often the lecturers choose their own ground to discuss rather than the concerns of the students, and there is often little opportunity

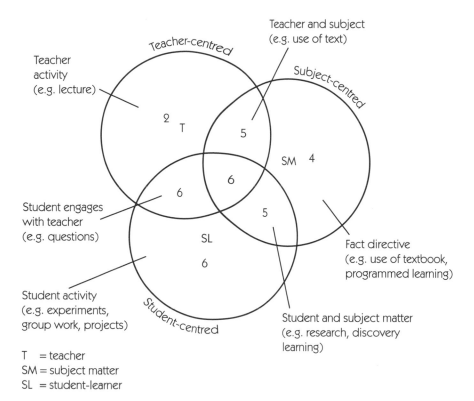

Figure 9.2 The figures indicate the relative effectiveness of these methods –
6 being high, 2 being low

for feedback or further exploration, except perhaps at the end. So the listeners
have to retain in their minds the points they wish to make or questions to
ask while still paying attention to the next points the lecturer is making.

There are occasions of course when a lecture has value – when summing
up a previous complicated discussion, for instance, or when introducing an
overview of a new area of study, or when as a part of the learning process
one might say to the other participants, 'Allow me for a time without
interruption to explore the implications of a particular argument to see
where it leads us.' But these will need to be set within some other kind of
learning context, because lectures call for special skills on the part of the
participants, and they will thus be most appropriate to limited numbers of
adult students. In every case the teacher could well ask whether there are
other, more active, more effective ways in which the student-learners could
acquire the new knowledge: by reading a text, by discussion, by discovery
methods and so on. There nearly always are better methods than direct
exposition by the teacher.

Knowledge and authority

A combination of teacher-chosen subject matter, a teacher-determined amount of knowledge and teacher-presented material can create one of the greatest obstacles to effective adult learning: authoritarianism. Authoritarianism is not confined to the teacher; it can also attach itself to other statements such as a textbook or handout. There are several reasons for avoiding excessive reliance on such statements: the adulthood of the student-learners, the fact that their well-established learning patterns are usually based on testing the validity of all statements against their experience, the fact that such statements normally lay new patterns of knowledge (authority) on top of older patterns without disturbing them. A different approach, which disturbs the existing pattern of under-standings, is needed. This calls for a range of social skills and attitudes towards the learner that the teacher of adults will come to only gradually (pp. 190–200).

Once more a balance is necessary. At times the dynamics of the situation will call for the teacher to be assertive – for instance, when constructing a learning exercise or perhaps in relation to a participant who persistently slows down the group (see pp. 228–31). The teacher will then want to be conscious of the reactions of the other participants if the work of the learning programme is being held up by one person. The sensitivity of the teacher to the needs and intentions of the participants will dictate the approach (i.e. methods and content) to be used.

The teachable moment

Teaching is not just a mechanical process and teachers are not made to a set recipe – a packet of this, a pinch of that. Each teaching-learning situation (especially with adults) is unique, calling for innovation on the part of the teacher, untried and individual responses to new circumstances, the courage and willingness to venture into new methods, to experiment, to dare. All the skills, knowledge, experience, attitudes, understanding and emotions of the teacher come to be focused onto the one moment in which the learning may be successful. Once past, the opportunity may be lost. That moment should be flexible, not set by any textbook or manual of teaching; it should be inspired. Teaching is an event, a fusion of enthusiasm, of adaptability, of reacting on the spur of the moment.

Learning too consists of the same sort of inspiration, the catching of enthusiasm. It comes from encounter, interaction – either person-to-person interaction or learner-and-material interaction. Some people have seen this engagement in terms of struggle; a learner struggles to 'master' a new skill, subject, tool or concept, and to use the new material. Others see it as a 'spark' between two poles which fires the imagination, illuminates new fields, motivates the learner, gives power and throws light on new ways of looking at reality.

Such interactive learning requires three contributions from the learners: the use of their existing experience and knowledge (it is increasingly appreciated that all forms of learning, even of young children, are dependent on what is already possessed by the learner and the way the new material engages with what is there); the exercise of their learning abilities (intelligence and learning skills); and effort (practice of the technique, reflection on the new material, collection of data, discrimination between the various elements of the learned matter). In determining the methods to be used in teaching, we should bear in mind these requirements on the part of the learners and provide them with opportunities to:

- use *their* existing experience and knowledge;
- exercise *their* learning abilities;
- practise.

Planning the schedule of learning
Does this emphasis on the practical and direct involvement of the learner with the subject matter mean that the teacher has nothing to do other than to set the tasks and watch the learners do them? Real learning can be going on in a group when everyone (especially the teacher) is silent, and perhaps we should try this more often. The existentialists have shown us that it is in silence that moments of crisis lie – moments of decision, of rearrangement, of change; and it is noteworthy that in some adult groups the student participants, rather than the teacher, try to avoid silence by any means.

But the role of the teacher is not just that of overseer and taskmaster. There are (at least) four main areas of activity in selecting the programme for learning:

- Determining *the general approach* – the goals of the learning, whether the programme will be curriculum- or process-oriented; whether the student participants are intended to learn something or to learn how to learn something (some may wish to do both at the same time). Our concern in this part of the task is with the end product: what the student-learners will have achieved by the end of the learning programme. As we have seen (Chapter 6) we cannot avoid taking up some sort of attitude towards this; it underlies everything that we and our student participants do together. We make a decision on this even when we are not conscious of doing so. It is best if such decisions are taken with the student learners and certainly they need to have been accepted by the participants; but in many cases these decisions are taken by the teachers and by the agencies/institutions in which they work in the course of planning the programme.
- Selecting *what will be learned* – choosing the material and the way it is marshalled in order for learning. The overall subject of the programme will have been agreed by all members, but the detailed content of a learning opportunity on computers, keep fit, geography, management or nutrition

will be the concern of the teacher. Again much of this can be determined in association with the student-learners, but the decision will normally rest with the teacher.

- Deciding *how much of this material can be covered* in the time available – what will most help the learning process and what can be left to a later stage; phasing and sequencing the work of the group or the individual learner. As we have seen, most of us tend to overestimate the amount that adult learners can cover. It would be better to underestimate and surprise ourselves and perhaps the learners. Interaction with the students will be necessary to ensure that an appropriate balance is maintained.

- Determining *how the student participants will engage with the material* – whether they will watch and exercise for themselves, whether they will listen, read, discuss, write, practise and so on. We will determine the steps the learners will be asked to take in order to complete the task, to learn the process or the subject matter. As far as possible, close relations with the individual members of the learning group will be needed to ensure that the tasks set and the steps taken are the most useful for learning.

The learning steps

Some writers have suggested that such learning steps will normally be cumulative and sequential, combining to make a course for the learners to engage in for themselves. They have analysed the stages by which a new skill or concept is learned. One such list is as follows:

- *Stage 1* – 'Play': this is the encounter stage, when the learners meet the new elements, gain familiarity with them, lose their fears of the field of study and begin to experiment with one element in it – perhaps playing it backwards or asking 'Does it *always* work?' etc. A good deal of time is often needed for this stage.

- *Stage 2* – 'Structured play': trial-and-error exercises are planned. The material and situations are so arranged to lead in a certain direction – i.e. to Stage 3. This stage too must not be rushed, it takes time.

- *Stage 3* – 'Grasping': the material 'falls into place'; it is related to other material, mostly by insightful learning; it 'clicks', makes sense, becomes 'real' or 'true'.

- *Stage 4* – 'Mastery': practice, not just learning but using, exploring the material or process further, discovering more relationships and properties, obtaining mastery over it. This in turn leads to an appreciation of further learning needs and intentions, new skills or concepts. The process is a dynamic and ongoing one.

Such steps call upon us to set for ourselves and for the participants clear signposts throughout the programme of learning, indicating the point reached and the relationship of what is being done to what has gone before and what will follow. This is an important task for the teacher, often overlooked.

Some student-learners may not be able to see the overall structure that we have in our minds unless we make special efforts to clarify it as we go along. An understanding of this structure of the learning process is required for effective learning to take place.

In this way the teacher sets the curriculum, the syllabus and the schedule of work for the group. This should as often as possible be done in discussion with the group, but in the end it is the teacher's responsibility. Such a task calls for a series of skills that are part of the essential equipment the teacher needs and which can be practised and learned:

- The skill of determining what is needed to achieve the goal – what basic concepts, facts and techniques are required to perform the task and how they relate to each other.
- The skill of selecting the tasks most suitable and of grading them in sequence. Again these will be related to each other, not isolated or compartmentalised. The relationship may be *vertical* (one task can be attempted only after another has been successfully mastered), *horizontal* (a parallel task at the same level of complexity) or *oblique* (a mixture of both of these). Several of these tasks will overlap with others.
- The skill of breaking down the subject matter and processes into steps for learning. For this activity we need to learn something of what goes on in the process of learning, based partly on theory and partly on experience of what works in practice.
- The skill of identifying and selecting the resources to be used – the equipment, materials, objects and texts, sequence of demonstrations, words of the teacher, discussions. We will devise some of this material for ourselves, other parts we will take from elsewhere. It is our task to choose, arrange and often present it; this is what the students will expect of us.

Methods

We have begun to see how the teacher, in selecting the content, also implicitly selects the methods of the learning group. We need now to look at this in more detail.

Most teachers underestimate the number of different teaching-learning techniques available to choose from. We often tend to be unimaginative in this part of our work. In one group of teachers, we listed 49 different teaching-learning techniques by using a brainstorming session, and that did not exhaust the possibilities. Some research suggests that when teachers feel unsure of themselves – threatened by inexperience, new material, lack of time or self-doubt – they frequently revert to using those teaching methods by which they were themselves taught; perhaps we should all watch for this and see it for what it is. We need to think about and identify different methods, to experiment with them and select those that seem to suit us and our student participants for each particular purpose. We should test whether this or that method does in fact fit the students' learning practices and, if not, choose another one. We need to practise too, until we can use them effectively. A new method may not always go well for the first few occasions it is employed. We should also try out other methods with which we are less familiar. In short, we should become 'reflective practitioners', thinking critically about our own teaching: we can learn much about teaching while we are teaching.

Activity

In the space below:

- List any teaching methods you can think of; you can add to it as time goes on and as new ideas or experiences present themselves.
- Indicate against each item whether it is *primarily* a teacher activity (T), a learner activity (L) or group activity (G).
- Mark those that are more content-oriented (C) and those that are more process-oriented (P).

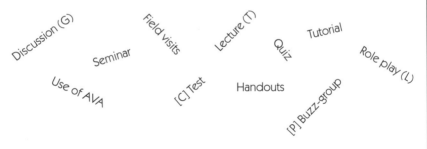

Which type of method predominates in your own teaching?

The basic range

Methods may be divided into four main categories (Rogers 1991b):

- *presentation* methods (teacher activities such as demonstration, exposition, use of whiteboard or flipchart, text or audio-visual media);
- *participatory* methods (interaction between teacher and learner, or learner and learner, such as questions, discussion, group work);

- *discovery* methods (in which the learners on their own or in groups work on tasks, exploring and discovering knowledge for themselves through practice, experiments, reading, writing).
- *evaluatory* methods (some of the techniques we adopt to evaluate the learning already done such as tests, quizzes, role play; these can be the means for further learning).

Many programmes of taught learning concentrate more on presentation methods than on the others. But acquisition learning employs the other three sets of methods, seeking out presentation methods less frequently. In acquisition learning, we use discovery, play, trial and error and role play; we discuss and ask questions; we use our learning to see if it works and test it out on other people. If the goal of our teaching is to build on acquisition learning and make it more conscious, to take it further, we need to use these other teaching-learning methods more consciously.

And not in isolation. They can be built up into a complex range of activities. Thus exploratory methods may be followed by interaction methods as the learners present the results of their exploration to the group or to the teacher for evaluation. Not all of these take place in the classroom; field visits and excursions frequently partake of all four kinds of method during the course of the programme.

The different methods can be divided in other ways. There are those, such as demonstrations, the use of texts, lectures and handouts, that are more concerned with the subject matter of the learning programme. Others, like simulation exercises and projects, are more concerned with the process of learning. Equally they may be divided into those that are primarily teacher activity, student activity or group activity.

Activity

Looking again at the learning programme you have chosen, which group of teaching-learning methods predominate in your planning?

Presentation?

Participatory?

Discovery?

Evaluatory?

The basis for selecting the methods

The determination of the approach most appropriate to the particular teaching-learning situation depends on a number of factors – for example, the area(s) of learning involved: whether it is *primarily* skills, knowledge, understanding or attitudes; the need to get the learner actively engaged in the process of learning; the learning styles of the student participants – what they prefer and what they are able to do; the demands of the subject itself; the availability of resources. Decisions on all these matters can often be taken jointly by teacher and learners, not by the teacher alone.

If, then, our classes and groups are really to promote learning, four things seem to be necessary, as Dewey (1933) pointed out:

- An *experience* on the part of the learner. The learning group is itself an experience that ought to be maximised: 'All genuine education comes about through experience'.
- A *climate* in which the learners play their part in structuring the learning process, where there is 'a concern for the development of persons . . . [where] the growth of people has precedence over the accomplishment of things'.
- *Continuity* of encounter. The process of learning builds on what is already there. The present experience of the learning group needs to be related in the learner's mind to past experience; the latter can be used by the teacher, not left passive: 'Continuity of experience means that every experience both takes up something from those which have gone before and modifies in some way the quality of those which come after'.
- *Interaction* between the learner and the new material, either through the teacher, or directly by practice; interaction between what is outside and what is inside the learner.

Student engagement

Many adult students seem to expect and even prefer teacher-centred and content-oriented methods. Some studies have suggested that for goal-oriented programmes (e.g. directed towards an examination), where the learners feel the speed of learning is more important than the depth of learning and thus a leisurely pace cannot be afforded, the students achieved more of their intentions in a teacher-centred environment. Even outside these contexts, it is often urged that active learning methods are slow, that the material can be dealt with more quickly if the teacher instructs and expounds and the learners watch or listen. This is true. Much more ground can be 'covered' by expository methods than by participatory methods. But 'covering the ground' is not the purpose of the exercise; the goal is learning. The learners may listen but in listening they may not learn what the teacher intends.

It is argued that such varied methods are not appropriate to some subjects or in some contexts. For example, in examination-led programmes which are increasingly dominating the lifelong education scene, it is suggested that active methods are inappropriate because they are too time-consuming. Equally, some teachers of adults find it difficult to accept interactive methods. How can they be applied, for instance, to music appreciation which tends to involve listening to recordings often over long periods? But a little imagination will quickly suggest a variety of methods, all appropriate to the subject matter, apart from 'discussion' – so ubiquitous in adult learning programmes. Other tutors have encouraged their student participants write their own programme notes, record-sleeve introductions or reviews of particular recordings, or to present to other group members in a structured way a concert programme – why one piece of music 'goes' or does not 'go' with another. The student participants can in fact do most if not all of the tasks that we as teachers reserve for ourselves.

It is not however just a case of the teacher devising situations in which the learners can use their new learning. Rather, it is a question of approaching the learners in a new way. Too often we treat the student participants as if they are totally incompetent or ignorant and have to be taught everything (see p. 61). As with other self-fulfilling prophecies, many of the students will therefore cast themselves in the role of ignoramuses – 'you must teach us everything' (see p. 76). It will be hard for the teacher to encourage these persons to *learn by doing*, by reflecting critically on what they already know and what they can already do, when they wish instead to *learn by preparing for doing*, when they seek to learn what they think they do not know or cannot do.

Nor can we encourage such student engagement during those periods *between* each group meeting or class session while at the same time treating the learners as passive listeners *during* the class meeting (see p. 199). The way we treat the student participants in class and the methods of learning we select for them to use at other times should be consistent in approach. Student activity begins in class.

Critical teaching and learning

The learning cycle (see Chapter 4) can be adapted to provide a framework for teaching (Figure 9.3). A major concern of adult learning programmes is with the promotion of critical reflection on experience followed by action (see pp. 107–10). In this process it may be helpful to remind ourselves:

- that the learners need to experience the material directly for themselves. If the material is embodied in the teacher alone, this may make for dependency. The material needs to be separated from the means of conveyance, be that teacher, film or book. This can be done by using more than one conveyance for the same material (which incidentally reinforces the teaching-learning material), by helping the student-learners to draw on their own experience, or by creating opportunities for the participants to have a new direct experience of the subject matter.

- that the student learners' activities should be *productive* – mastering processes, answering questions as actively as possible; not just watching or

Figure 9.3 Applying the learning cycle to teaching adults

listening but doing, reading, writing, talking etc. Only if the learners are engaged in activities which they see as meaningful and relevant will they learn and change. New skills will thus be grasped, new knowledge be acquired permanently, new understandings and concepts be formed.

- that the student participants need to become more conscious that *learning is the task* they are engaged in. They need to continue to learn how to learn, with encouragement. They should spend the maximum amount of time on this process.
- that the student participants should come to realise that learning is *not a matter of rote memorising* of processes and facts but a complicated matter of asking and answering questions, finding solutions, practising skills, spotting relationships and linkages, constructing explanations and making 'maps' in the mind. They also need to realise that this is done by producing their own work or written or spoken words, both for an immediate check by themselves and for a more considered check by others. This is the 'questioning, thinking and testing' of which Handy spoke (see p. 114).

Such considerations as these help us to choose the most appropriate methods of learning – not just a demonstration (of computer program writing, say) by an expert but a fumbling practice by the learner, followed by an evaluation by the learner, by the teacher and even on occasion by other student participants as well; not just a lecture (on psychology, say) but a series of carefully constructed observational analyses and role plays; not just a slide show (on architecture) but the development of a new sense of awareness by looking at buildings in the neighbourhood; not just reading a text but the construction of an argument on the basis of the material contained in it.

Teaching

The function of the teacher of adults is thus wider than just that of a demonstrator, lecturer or presenter of information. Rather, the teacher constructs a sequence of learning activities for the student participants to engage in. But this does not mean that the traditional instructional activities are inappropriate to a teacher; we need both types of skill.

What, then, makes a good teacher of adults? A number of different skills and attitudes appear to be necessary:

First, a series of *attitudes towards the student-learners* – concern, sensitivity and support; attitudes of flexibility and innovativeness; a willingness to experiment, to adapt the material to meet the specific needs of the learning group, not just be stuck with one set of teaching-learning methods and content – and *towards the subject matter*, an enthusiasm for the material and its philosophy.

Second, *a clear understanding of the philosophy of adult teaching*. The effectiveness of what we do depends to a very large extent on the clarity with which we hold the logic frame of our activity. We need to know and understand the concepts of adult learning and adult teaching. The aim of our work is to help make learning conscious.

Third, we need to develop *the skills of teaching*:

- *Planning skills* – selection of teaching-learning strategies and the effective use of learning resources.
- *Communication skills* – the development of means of communication and a sensitivity to how effective these are, an awareness of when (for example) the wrong message may have been received from the presentation. It is surprising how few teachers can place themselves in the position of the receiver of their messages, how often they use vocabulary, concepts and sentence construction outside the field of experience of some of the participants, how often they present written forms of language rather than spoken when expounding to the student-learners.
- *Caring-guidance skills* – counselling the participants, adjusting the learning tasks to the needs, intentions and capabilities of the individual learner.
- *Evaluation skills* – identifying the goals, monitoring progress and evaluating the usefulness of the learning process, presenting such evaluations to the participants.
- *Subject skills* – competencies in the subject matter of the learning programme, and continuing learning in this area.

But above all, we need to possess a measure of *self-confidence and self-respect* based on a belief in our own competence – a feeling that will quickly communicate itself to the student-learners. Adult participants will come to respect us as teachers and accept willingly the learning tasks we set for them in so far as we display confidence in ourselves and trust in them. This respect comes about only when we respect ourselves.

Working at teaching

We must not become too confident, however, nor confident without the skills and attitudes to go with that confidence. It has been said that in lifelong education, as elsewhere in the educational world, there are no bad students; that if there is a failure to learn, or if attendance falls off, this is because the teacher has not prepared an adequate programme of learning or adopted appropriate teaching-learning methods. This may not always be true, but we must not expect our task to be an easy one. It is difficult, lengthy and at times tedious. We may have to prepare our own teaching material, adapted to the needs and intentions of the particular group of adult learners we are helping, which may be equivalent to writing and experimenting with a good-sized textbook with exercises. Even when we are able to use material prepared by others, we still need to fit it in with each situation, with each student group, and this too can be a time-consuming process. As teachers of adults, we cannot rush into teaching without preparation, relying on our experience and expertise to help us flannel our way through. Preparation and choice between alternatives lie at the heart of the process.

Much of our learning how to teach adults is acquisition (task-related) learning. Part of the aim of this book is to help you to become more conscious of this process. We need as teachers to continue to learn in many ways – by personal study, by experimenting and evaluating our experiments and by meeting with others. Through networking with other teachers of adults we can form or join communities of practice; we can learn from and with our peers in a 'zone of proximal development'. The task of learning to teach is never finished.

Activity

At this point in my tutor training programmes, I usually ask the participants to draft for themselves, individually or in small groups, an action plan for their own continued learning. It is a useful exercise to do.

Note: Facing some problems in an adult learning group[1]

We are all faced with many problems in the course of our teaching of adults, and with experience we learn how to solve most of them. The main point is to be sensitive to the existence of a problem. Once we are aware of this, the task of solution often becomes less difficult. Some people have this sensitivity from the start; others have to learn it the hard way. It would be a good thing, as a first step, if we can *decide where we stand on this issue of sensitivity*, whether we think we are or are not aware of how our group members are reacting to our teaching. But even if we are among those to whom such awareness comes easily, it will still be helpful for us to *arrange as many and as varied channels of feedback* as we can, so that we can keep ourselves informed of how well our student participants are doing and how they feel about aspects of the work.

---

1 This note has been adapted from a paper prepared by Dr Sam Lilley of the University of Nottingham for use in traditional adult education classes consisting mainly of discussion and included in that university's training packs for part-time tutors. However, it may be useful in other contexts including more formal courses for adults in educational institutions.

A few of the more common situations that can arise are listed here, and some of the ways of dealing with them are suggested. The solution to any problem that works well on one occasion may not work equally well another time; each situation in adult education is unique. Thus the suggestions listed here are not meant to be prescriptive. In most cases there are several possible ways of coping with a problem, which need to be tested out at our discretion so that eventually we can evolve our own ways of meeting such situations.

The primary attribute of the teacher of adults, above all, is *tact*. What is stated here briefly and on occasion baldly could be disastrous unless the execution of it fits into the normal pattern of our relationships with our students. An artificial reaction based on a set of instructions in a teaching manual, bringing with it an abrupt change of classroom climate, could be ruinous for the work of the group. We thus need to choose a tactic that suits our own teaching style and adapt it; we must take our time over it.

Problems involving individual student participants

Persistent talkers

It is important not to let them wreck the group. Their behaviour can generate considerable anger among the other members, and this will rebound onto us as teachers unless we are seen to take some steps to limit their impact on the group.

To begin with, a gentle approach may succeed: 'Let's hear what the others have to say first.' If that doesn't work, they may have to be taken on one side and spoken to, either by ourselves or by one of the more respected participants.

If gentle tactics fail, slowly increasing firmness may be necessary. Take advice before going too far along this route. 'You really must give the others a fair chance' can lead on to a firm indication that, by monopolising the discussion, the over-talker is spoiling the enjoyment of everyone else. (We must not forget, however, that they may have a following in the group.) Such remarks could first be made privately, but after a time the group will expect us as teacher and group leader to adopt a firm line in public. We risk losing a group member, but this is usually a smaller risk than we think; and in any case ruining a learning group is worse than losing one member.

The monomaniac
The person who raises essentially the same issue in every session is fortunately relatively rare. A simple statement that they have already mentioned the point in question and an appeal to stop is worth trying but unlikely to succeed. Fairly harsh measures may become necessary at an earlier stage than with the persistent talker. We can try to pre-empt the particular

contribution: when setting out the work to be done, we might end with the words that 'So-and-so will no doubt say that . . .', summarising their point in perhaps a quarter of the time they would take. We could even involve the person directly – 'That's how you would put it, isn't it?' – but allow them little or no time to develop the discussion by bringing in the rest of the group. One can go further and prime other members of the group to speak up: 'We've heard that often enough; let's talk of something else.' Sometimes we can even develop our own contract with a monomaniac – give them a set time to present their views on condition that they agree not to raise the point again. But they may not keep the bargain, and a firmer line may be necessary in the end.

The quiet participant

A reticent member may refuse to be drawn into any discussion or group activity. This needs great care and tact, for the causes of the reticence are rarely clear. Unlike the cases above, the loss of a shy person as a result of tactlessly applied pressure would deny the whole purpose of the adult group.

We could perhaps try to persuade the member to talk outside of the group session – before the meeting starts, after it ends or during refreshments – to ourselves or to another participant. It may be possible to find out some opinions they hold, some skill or experience they possess; we can then try to guide the work of the group into these fields so that eventually they can fittingly (but never easily) make some contribution. Even then the hoped-for participation may not be forthcoming, and we may have to put words into their mouth: 'I was impressed with what so-and-so was saying to me . . .' We could then repeat the point, perhaps not quite accurately or with doubt expressed about some aspect of it; this may at last provoke an interjection. And once the ice is broken . . .

An alternative is to increase the contribution such members can make to the group by getting them to prepare a particular piece of work. It may then turn out that at some point this person is the only one with the relevant skill or knowledge to help forward the group's work. In this case, still using caution so that they do not feel too exposed, we can ask them directly to join in. It is useful to keep an eye on them (but not too obviously) as the programme continues; a frown or raised eyebrow, a drawn breath or a change in posture may indicate the one moment in the session (even perhaps in the whole course) when something is ready to burst out. We need then to abandon all else to make this happen if the student is to be freed to become a full participant.

Sometimes the use of sub-groups will help such a student to participate. But some group members are so reticent that even the most experienced teacher is unable to extract a contribution from them during the whole programme. Because of this, we can never be sure that any progress is being made at all. Yet the person may still benefit from the course. Active participation by all the members is a desirable goal of all learning situations, but ideals are never fully attained. Silence is not a sin.

More serious is the case of a whole group of reticent members, who may even sit together in silent sympathy. They may think of themselves as less skilful, less knowledgeable or slower thinkers than the others. Equally it could be our own fault for concentrating our attention on a few more congenial learners. Such a group needs careful attention, as we shall see.

The alternative expert
One member may continually remind the group that they are more knowledgeable than the teacher in some part of the subject. We are often asked by our student participants to teach on the limits of our subject; indeed, on occasion we are challenged on aspects of the subject about which we know little or nothing. In these circumstances, a person who asserts publicly that they know a good deal about some part of the subject can be looked upon by us and/or the rest of the group as an alternative expert.

This person is exceptional only in degree. Every group member knows something relevant to the subject that the teacher doesn't know, and they must all be given the opportunity to teach the others what they know. It is not always easy to discover what that something is, but if we can find it, every student participant can have their own teaching moment.

But for this particular person, the expert, there is usually no such problem. They often parade their special knowledge at every possible moment, perhaps with a display of more or less deference to our role as teacher. They may even deny our right to teach. We could find this threatening. We need to accept the situation – indeed, we can make them feel welcome, for they can be valuable teaching assistance. They almost certainly respect our general position, our expertise or experience, or they would stop coming to the group. In return we need to respect their expertise and involve them from time to time in the work of the group as teacher of either the whole or part of the group. Maybe they will show themselves knowledgeable but unskilled in teaching adults, in which case we can help them in this respect. In doing so, we too will learn about teaching adults. Watching others teaching, and talking to them about their teaching, is an instructive experience.

It may be that the alternative expert comes to the group simply because it provides them with an easy platform to demonstrate their knowledge and skills. They are less concerned with the rest of the members learning something than with showing off. It is not easy to cope with this, for these people tend to be thick-skinned. One possible strategy is to formalise the situation as they would wish it to be for a short time. We could give them the opportunity to take over from us formally for a while. They may then learn that their knowledge, although deep, is too limited to sustain them over a lengthy period face to face with the student participants. It may be that the rest of the group will indicate their preference for us as teacher. Equally, they may not!

Problems concerning the working group

The mixed group

This group contains members of varied abilities and/or experience and/or knowledge. Most adult learning groups will comprise a wide range in terms of age, existing knowledge, experience and willingness to learn from that experience, skills, attitudes and learning abilities. We may in time come to regard the mixed-ability situation as an advantage, a widening of the teaching opportunities open to us. But for the moment:

1 We do not need to feel that we have ourselves to do all the work of teaching. On carefully chosen occasions, we can ask those who know most or have more verbal facility to explain a point to the ones who know less about the subject or are slower thinkers. We may be surprised how much the 'learned' will expose their own weaknesses – and set about remedying them; equally how much the less experienced members can flourish. The group will become rather more united as time goes on.

2 On the other hand, we could teach a sub-group of the class. No group objects to a teacher who spends time now and again on an elementary explanation of some process or concept for those who need it, or another two or three minutes making a special point that only the most knowledgeable or skilled appreciate. It is surprising what can be done for the more advanced members of the group by means of a few well-chosen asides.

3 We may be able to satisfy the demands (or some of them) of the more advanced and well informed at some occasion outside of the group meeting. It is often possible to ask those who require some special 'bridging' provision to come a few minutes early or to stay behind for a short while.

4 Dividing the group into smaller groups in order to give each of them the attention they need – provided the other members are engaged in meaningful tasks, either as individuals or in their own small group – is a useful strategy that paradoxically makes the entire group cohere more strongly. The use of sub-groups to maximise learning is a key element in the teacher's armoury. There are many kinds of sub-group, selected on different criteria: by ability (though the dangers of 'streaming' remain as true in adult education as in schooling), or mixed-ability groups working on different or the same assigned exercises. Sub-groups throw up their own structures, and we can help or hinder this by choosing or not choosing a leader/chairperson who may or may not be the same as the *rapporteur* (if one is needed). We need to experiment with various forms of sub-grouping.

5 Perhaps the most rewarding, but the most difficult, procedure is to adopt an unorthodox and original approach to the topic, to use materials that the knowledgeable have never seen before and that keep both beginner and more advanced interested. This requires a lot of time and resources, and it may be that the full-time adult teacher will be able to work out such approaches more fully than the part-time teacher. It would be useful for us to keep in touch with other subject specialists we may know; they will probably have teaching material and/or methods that are new to us, which they may be only too glad to share.

6 The class/group meetings are not the only times available for learning to take place. The use of differential tasks (not the same work set for all participants like school homework) to be done individually between sessions helps to overcome the problems of disparate learning groups. We need to structure these carefully and be prepared to give time to discussing this work with the participants.

In the end, however, all the members of the group start at different places and, using skills and aptitudes that vary markedly, end up at different places. Our objective is not to make all the learners alike, not to bring them all up to the same 'high' standard but to enable them to get the best out of themselves, each in their own way.

The duologue

A group may degenerate into a dialogue between the teacher and one member (or a very few). The danger is greatest when a participant has presented some piece of finished work for us or the group as a whole to evaluate. One possible answer is to get the fellow members to do their evaluation before we take part. But the teacher and the individual participant may be the only people present who have adequate knowledge of the subject under review, and it is natural for us to address our comments entirely to this one participant, which reinforces the exclusiveness of the situation. We need to remember that others are present also, to embrace them with our looks, to keep our eyes open for some slight change of expression or posture that will reveal the time when we can invite someone else to join in. Sometimes direct questions can be thrown out to the other members: 'What do you think about that?'

The mêlée

On occasion two or three topics get mixed up. This arises (particularly in discussion groups) largely because members of the group, instead of listening to and addressing their attention to what has gone before, are anxious to deliver themselves of what they have prepared, while other group members may continue to concentrate on earlier subjects. We cannot afford to let this go on too long; the intermingling of different material causes confusion and mis-learning. We may have to turn martinet for a short period and insist that the issues be sorted out so that each can be dealt with separately. To prevent people thinking that they are being cheated of what is their concern, we can make a list (perhaps on the blackboard, flipchart or overhead projector for all to see) of the different topics to be covered and tick them off one by one. The chances are that the subjects turn out to have more in common with each other than appeared at first sight.

The irrelevant topic

A question may come up at the wrong time. We may be in the middle of a carefully prepared demonstration or presentation, intended to develop a clear logical sequence, when suddenly a participant pops in with a question or comment that may divert attention away from the main point. Or it may be a question we intended to raise rather later on. Do we answer now or ask the participant to wait?

The act of teaching adults involves continual judgements on matters like this. Sometimes we get it right and sometimes wrong. We have to think on our feet.

The matter is relatively simple if the question reveals ignorance of something essential for the success of the demonstration or presentation; we should deal with that issue before going any further. We may feel inclined to do the same, even if the question is a hindrance to the group session, if the comment or question comes from one of the more retiring members who rarely makes a contribution. Sometimes the interruption will have less of an effect on our carefully prepared material than we think; at least there may be several strings to our answer that can lead back to the main topic.

On the other hand, we need not be too hesitant about asking members to wait until later for us to deal with their point. We can briefly explain at what stage in the session the matter will be handled and ask that it be postponed until then. Making a note of the matter or doing something to convince the questioner that the issue will not be evaded is useful. Many students have had experience of education that is designed to avoid answering difficult questions and they may expect the same of us. We must be sure to deal with the matter in the end, perhaps with some recognition of the value of the participant having raised it at all.

The missing group

Sometimes only two people turn up – it happens to most of us occasionally. The first thing to do is to try to avoid it by persuading all members to indicate when they cannot be present. But it will still happen in groups of adult learners; bad weather, illness or a popular local event can interrupt even the most loyal attendance.

It may be possible to deal with some discrete topic that is not essential to the main line of the course that the two or three who are gathered together find useful and rewarding for their efforts but those who are absent will either not miss or can catch up on quickly. This is especially important if there is a high degree of continuity in the group's work and to have a vital chunk of material missed by many of the learners would be harmful. One useful activity is to spend part of the time getting to know the participants better – their interests, experiences, abilities and intentions. We may learn a lot about how the course is going on these occasions.

The missing problem
It is impossible to compile a complete catalogue of problems faced in teaching in adult education. New ones are always appearing and even the most experienced teacher never learns how to solve all of them. So we need not be discouraged. But some of the comments here may help us to identify such problems and to worry out some home-made solutions to them. In many cases it will be useful, both for our own sake as teachers as for our students' sake, to find another teacher (or a supervisor/provider/organiser), or someone else to swap experiences and advice. It always helps to talk things over.

Further reading

Belbin, R.M. (1980) *The Discovery Method in Training*. Sheffield: Manpower Services Commission.
Bligh, D.R. (1972) *What's the Use of Lectures?* Harmondsworth: Penguin.
Daines, J., Daines, C. and Graham, B. (1993) *Adult Learning, Adult Teaching*, 3rd edn. Nottingham: University of Nottingham.
Galbraith, M.W. (ed.) (1991) *Adult Learning Methods: A Guide for Effective Instruction*. Malabar, FL: Krieger.
Griffin, C. (1983) *Curriculum Theory in Adult and Continuing Education*. Beckenham: Croom Helm.
Rogers, A. (1991b) *Teaching Methods in Extension*. Reading: Education for Development.
Rogers, J. (1984) *Adults in Education*. London: BBC Publications.
Stephens, M.D. and Roderick, G.W. (1971) *Teaching Techniques in Adult Education*. Newton Abbot: David & Charles.

PAUSE FOR MORE THOUGHT

In the first part of this book we looked at the nature of learning. We saw it as a natural and largely subconscious process (like breathing), using 'acquisition learning' processes, or what I called 'task-conscious learning' because the learners are not conscious of learning but only of a task they wish to fulfil. We saw that taught learning (education) uses 'formalised learning', a different process which I called 'learning-conscious learning' because the task of which the learners are conscious is learning. I suggested that our teaching of adults should build on both processes, making the task-conscious learning more learning-conscious and building a task into the learning-conscious learning.

We also identified two major problems for the teacher of adults:

- the wide range of experience, learning abilities, styles and intentions that the members of the learning group possess;
- the tension between the need to define learning objectives clearly in order to achieve learning on the one hand, and the desire to be open to, respect and encourage the autonomy of the mature adult on the other.

In the second part of the book we saw that there are at least three ways in which these problems may be addressed:

- by negotiating the goals and objectives with the participants as far as possible;
- by the use of the learning group;
- by the use of a wide range of varied and active teaching-learning methods and materials.

The remaining chapters are devoted to making our work of teaching adults more effective – making their learning more conscious, overcoming obstacles to learning, testing the value of our work and encouraging the student-learners to take more and more control over their own learning processes.

Chapter 10

BLOCKS TO LEARNING

What is stopping us . . . ?

This chapter examines some of the barriers to learning and suggests that, although some of these may spring from both pre-existing knowledge and psychological factors, others come from the process of making learning conscious. They do not exist in the same way in the natural (acquisition) learning process. We may be creating barriers for our participants.

Identifying the problem

At different times, everyone who has taught adults has come across the person who seems unable to learn something they say that they wish to learn. A serious block appears to exist. We have all experienced this in ourselves as well, a failure to comprehend or master some aspect of the subject under consideration.

This chapter sets out to discuss the nature of these blocks to learning. Two introductory points are needed. First, all we can try to do here is to assess what appears to be happening and, if possible, why. What is not always so easy to see is how to cope with each situation as it arises.

The second point is that when we as teachers of adults come across these blocks, we will lack firm evidence for an analysis of the situation under review. We will be trying to draw a picture of what is 'really' happening rather than what the student participant *says* is happening. On occasion, the two may be the same. But more often, even when the learners are able to describe why they find themselves unable to learn something (and that is on the whole rare), they may be unwilling to give the reason for this problem.

One way of bridging this gap is for us to use our own experience to describe and explain the situation. This is a useful tool, provided we recognise the limitations of this process. Those who teach adults are likely to be people who have been successful in their approach to the subject, not a failure. We are therefore unlikely to understand fully the problems that some of the learners will feel. Nevertheless, it is necessary for us to draw upon our own insights in this field; and throughout this chapter, as elsewhere in the book, you will find the material of greater value when you test it against your own experience. To be an effective teacher of adults, we must learn to know ourselves.

It is important for us to remember that we are discussing here the blocks to *learning*. Patricia Cross in her study of *Adults as Learners* (1981) identified three main sets of barriers which adults face: barriers which arise from the *situation* in which they find themselves; barriers which spring from the *learning programmes* themselves; and barriers which lie within the learners themselves, the *attitudes* which the adults may possess towards themselves or the programme. She was talking about 'barriers to participation' in planned learning activities rather than barriers to learning once one is participating in adult learning programmes. Although her three categories can be applied to the blocks to learning, the primary focus to our discussion of barriers to learning will be the personality barriers which prevent some adult student participants – people who attend classes regularly and who want to learn – from learning. What is it that is stopping them from learning effectively within our programmes?

The scope of the problem

Blocks to learning exist, and there are many reasons for them, the most important of which are personality factors. At one end is the 'I-don't-want-to-learn-this-thing' participant – not the wholly unmotivated but those who find the difficulties of some particular part of the learning programme so great that they withdraw from learning. At the other end is the learner who tries most anxiously to grasp a particular process or idea but just cannot make it fit, remember it or understand how the various pieces of the subject go together. For the first, self-perception prevents the development of new skills or the assimilation and creation of new knowledge; they think that the problem lies with themselves. For the second, something perceived to be within the subject matter itself or the way the new material relates to existing patterns of knowledge gets in the way.

There are other reasons for the failure to learn, and we can discuss these briefly first. Some blocks to learning new skills and new concepts arise from *physical changes*: for example, declining dexterity or failing eyesight or hearing account for many futile learning experiments. More important and frequent are those immediate, and on occasion temporary, *situational* causes: physical or contextual factors such as hunger, poor health, tiredness or other preoccupations (money, family needs, work, shopping etc.)

which may weigh on the minds of the learners. How many adult classes have been ruined for the teacher or the student participants because one of them has just recalled some errand left unfulfilled, some commitment uncompleted and their mind is engaged in concocting excuses with which to meet the offended party? Other situational factors more specifically related to our *programmes* include the room being too hot or too cold, too bright or too dark, overcrowded, smoky or poorly equipped (for instance, with uncomfortable seating), or where there are too many distractions that prevent concentration. There are also those blocks that spring from bad relations between the teacher and the learner or between learner and learner, or from the teacher's failure to communicate properly with the learner.

All of these, although not unimportant or rare, may be relatively easily remedied, once identified. The evidence is that these physical and contextual factors are hindrances rather than blocks. They seldom operate on their own but rather provide material for the other mechanisms to work on. Distractions alone rarely form a block to learning but come into play when other blocks begin to exert themselves. They are used by the learner to prevent learning, rather than preventing learning by themselves.

This is not of course to say that these situational barriers to learning are not significant. They are. It is most important that we recognise that our adult participants are part of a particular sociocultural context, and that their knowledge and values are rooted in and are continually being created by them in interaction with their environment. They are not psychological isolates divorced from a specific context; they are social beings. And this context will be at one and the same time a help and a hindrance. It will often provide the cause of the learning intention, but it will also provide many barriers to learning changes. It is from this context that our student participants will bring to the purposeful learning episode which we are building for and with them the knowledge and experience which they have accumulated over many years.

Hindrances which arise from this context will thus reinforce personality blocks, those blocks to learning that exist for the alert motivated student participant even in a context conducive to learning. Although these all spring from psychological and emotional factors, it is still useful to distinguish between those more concerned with pre-existent knowledge and those arising from personality factors. Learning is not simply a matter of reason; it also involves the emotions and the physical well-being of the learner.

Activity

Before we go further, try to identify two 'blockages' that you have experienced, either as teacher or as learner. Among mine, for instance, are learning to draw and learning what goes on under the bonnet of a car; I *know* I can't learn either.

Blocks	*Column 1*	*Column 2*
1		
2		

In relation to the blocks you have identified above, can you determine whether they arise more from pre-existing knowledge or from self-perception factors (put your answer in Column 1)?

Pre-existing knowledge

We have seen that adult student participants know a good deal about what they are studying, often more than they think they know (see p. 61). Students in a learning programme on medieval English history frequently assert that they know nothing about the subject, but it is not very difficult to elicit from them a series of names such as Robin Hood and Sherwood Forest, the Black Prince, Wat Tyler, Chaucer and Wycliffe, the Black Death, as well as the clear markers of Domesday Book, the Crusades and the Wars of the Roses. Most of them will have visited a medieval parish church, if not a castle or monastery. Any view of medieval history that omits to deal with these, to make sense of them in an overall context, may prove unsatisfying to the participants. Indeed, these topics provided by the group members can become hooks onto which most aspects of the course of study can be hung. The learners can see that they have helped to construct the syllabus. The same is true of woodworking, keep fit, management courses, academic subjects and literacy classes. The learners will already have some knowledge and experience, direct or indirect, of these fields of study, much of it obtained through acquisition learning from their socio-cultural context.

Adult student participants have already invested emotional capital in acquiring this knowledge and experience. They will expend much more in defending the integrity of this knowledge, so new learning changes will sometimes be strenuously resisted. Thus a blockage arises from the *emotional investment in knowledge* that we make. We all learn from some 'significant other', some outside authority such as a person or a book etc. Any challenge to this learned material implies either a challenge to our significant other (it may be mother, father, teacher or some other respected authority), or a challenge to our self-judgement (we *chose* to rely on that person, book, magazine or newspaper; it seemed reasonable to us at the time), or to both. Two reactions may then be created. In the first, by the use of 'withdrawal mechanisms' the challenged learners will seek to defend their knowledge. In the second, through the employment of 'ego-defence mechanisms' the learners will seek to defend their self-image. We will discuss both of these in a moment.

A second cause of such blockages is existing *prejudices*. These may be defined as strongly held beliefs, perhaps based in part on knowledge, that we are reluctant to examine in detail. Often this is because we suspect that they are not firmly founded. It may also be that the fear of others prevents us from exposing prejudices to analysis, for we may be forced to abandon stances we have taken up in public. Prejudices are one form of what is called 'over-certainty', a state that results in stereotyped reactions. Racial, religious or ideological hostilities are perhaps the most conspicuous forms of prejudices; sexual, social or cultural preferences perhaps the most insidious.

A third cause of such blockages arises in those who are *habit-bound*. They have traditional patterns of thinking or ways of doing things, not merely from their search for security but also from an undue reverence for the past. Similarly, some people's *conformity needs* are very strong. Such people cling to existing ways and understandings as long as they perceive them to be the ways and views of the majority. Once more, emotional investments lie at the base of these reactions.

All these factors lead some of our student participants to resist learning changes. They cling to pre-existent knowledge and attitudes and they find it difficult to assimilate new material, to make it harmonise with what is already there. So they adopt mechanisms, most commonly of withdrawal, in an attempt to preserve what they already possess.

Withdrawal mechanisms

There are many ways of withdrawing from a situation. The most obvious (not necessarily the most common) is physical withdrawal; the student participant stops coming to the group. More common are the following:

- *Compartmentalism* – the learners keep their knowledge in separate boxes; they create distinct patterns that don't touch each other but are drawn upon in different circumstances. This is a particular favourite of people who have been exposed for a long time to a formal educational system with its separate 'schools' of history, geography, maths etc.; but others too engage in it.

- *Authority-ism* – the quotation of and excessive reverence for authorities. Some learners fall back on books (the *Encyclopaedia Britannica* syndrome) and just seeing something in print leads them to conclude that 'It must be true'. New knowledge is challenged if it lacks such authority. Others cite trusted people as the ultimate source of wisdom: 'If they say so, we can believe it'.
- *Reality-evasion* – i.e. daydreaming and lack of attention. This is more likely to be a withdrawal mechanism than anything else. This can be tested, for the withdrawal mechanism is highly selective in its attention and perception. The student participants will notice everything that supports their existing patterns and just not hear whatever contradicts them.

Perceptive teachers will come to recognise other withdrawal mechanisms. Teachers are also selective in what they notice. We ourselves often ignore those things that contradict the views we hold about our adult students as well-meaning, highly motivated and intelligent friends – or alternatively as dull, reluctant learners. We should constantly examine ourselves to see what we are perceiving and what we are missing.

Unlearning

To grapple with this problem of the pre-existent knowledge, habits or attitudes of our student participants, we need to explore the notion of unlearning. It is sometimes said that for adults the process of unlearning is as important as the process of learning; that all participants in adult learning activities have much to unlearn as well as new material to learn. It is not possible for us to know in the case of every individual learner precisely where the new material conflicts with pre-existing patterns, but an awareness of the reactions of the learners to such situations reveals much to the sensitive teacher.

The new material, to be properly learned, must enmesh with the older knowledge and not be left lying 'on top of' the existing patterns, leaving them unchanged. This may mean not merely an exploration of the pre-existing knowledge itself but also of the way it was acquired. This is particularly important when dealing with the many long-standing myths with which all subjects, both skill-oriented and understanding-oriented, abound. Authoritative denials of traditional practices or other knowledge will be weighed against existing beliefs in which considerable emotional investment may have been made.

Unlearning: an illustration

In any church training course which involves the narratives of the Christian Nativity, we will run up against the traditional stories of those who came to bring gifts to the infant. The existing information held by most of the student participants (i.e. that there were 'three kings') will be seen to be 'incorrect'. We can pursue a number of strategies:

- We can *tell* the learners that they were not kings and that there were probably not three of them. Such a statement will be assessed and may even be accepted out of respect for our expertise, but it will lie uneasily on top of the earlier acquired knowledge because it has not challenged the source of that information. Within three or four minutes the participants will be talking of 'three kings' again.
- We can *show* them the narrative accounts in the New Testament that speak of 'certain wise men' (soothsayers or fortune tellers), not 'three' and not 'kings'. Such a reference will give cause for more serious reflection, and some will be convinced. Nevertheless, most of the student participants will within a relatively short time be talking once more in terms of 'three' and 'kings'. We will not have challenged the weight of tradition and the emotional atmosphere of childhood, families, Christmas festivities and the constant reinforcement by Christmas cards, carols and the like, all of which have created an attachment to the idea of three kings.
- The only successful way to bring about the new learning will be through a process of *unlearning*. This will involve seeing how the two ideas ('three' and 'kings') arose in the first place – how the statement in the Psalms that 'kings from the East shall bring gifts' was quoted in the primitive Christian Church; how the early representations of the magi in pictures and mosaics with tall headdresses were taken by later interpreters to indicate royal imagery; how the fact that there were three gifts led to an assumption that there were three travellers etc. The students will thus understand the processes involved in the transformation of these stories, and their traditionally held views will become readjusted. They will see the constant reinforcement of incorrect knowledge for what it is, and when they themselves join again in references to 'three kings' they will hold a part of themselves back with an inner assertion that now they know better. Only as the learner comes to see *how* the description of the visitors in these narratives was altered will there be a major change in knowledge and attitudes. The story will be seen to be what it is: a later myth making an important theological statement, rather than historical truth.

The above case study is a trivial example, not one to be pressed too hard. It is not perhaps important to bring about this particular item of unlearning, any more than the correction of the traditional tales of Robin Hood and the Sheriff of Nottingham may be important. But each of us at some stage will run across an area where an unlearning process will be necessary – where some traditional but ineffective or harmful process, skill or knowledge needs to be corrected. It is not enough to make authoritative statements of facts or to give orders, for neither will overcome the weight of tradition combined with the practice of contemporaries. Rather, the process is in most cases much the same as above. The most unsatisfactory and impermanent method of dealing with such views is one of authority, laying new knowledge on top of the older learning without disturbing it or relating the new to the old. A better way is to examine the basis of the old (incorrect or undesired) knowledge and the newer (desired) knowledge; but this too will lead to conflict, setting authority against authority. The most effective unlearning process is not straight contradiction but the lengthier activity of helping the learner to examine how the incorrect pattern came about and has been reinforced through long acceptance and use. Unlearning is a difficult and lengthy process, but an essential part of teaching adults.

Self-perception factors

Sometimes there is no great range of existing knowledge to impede new learning, but still an inability or a refusal to learn exists. In these cases, another set of factors comes into play: emotional manifestations of negative self-concepts, some of them enduring (in which case they may be seen as long-term personality traits), others situationally controlled (which we may term emotional variables). The most important and the most common of these, especially for adults, is *anxiety*.

Anxiety

Anxiety is a characteristic of many adult learners. Most teachers of adults will face it in their student participants at some stage. It is a diverse phenomenon. It seems to consist of two main elements:

- a fear of externally imposed requirements that are seen as a threat – the difficulty of the subject matter itself;
- worries about the self, the capacity to cope; issues of self-esteem, an awareness of the process of ageing, of physical tiredness and declining powers of memory and concentration, or a negative self-image, promoting too high a sense of need.

We must be careful of attributing such attitudes to all student participants in adult groups. But they do exist. A too low assessment of one's abilities, judgements and resources in comparison with one's peers, or a lack of trust in oneself may be elements in anxiety-creation. A sense that to admit need at all means that one is less than adult, or that by becoming a student-learner one is rejecting the company of adults, even denying one's adult role (based on the view that 'education' is for children, a process of initiation) can play a part in creating over-anxiety. On the whole, these persons see the cause of their 'failure' as themselves: 'Far from regarding themselves as casualties of an inadequate and ramshackle system, they see themselves as educational failures' (J. Rogers 1977: 50). Thus for some, adult education is seen to be for failures, those who did poorly at school or who never took advantage of the initial education system and who must return to a system built on pupilage and dependency, opposed to adulthood and responsibility.

Such anxiety is not confined to 'second-chance' adult learners. It can exist in many other forms of adult learning, in both the formal and the non-formal sectors. Teachers selected to engage in learning programmes on educational management, hospital administrators required to learn new skills or new approaches to their task, community workers coming to grips with new social trends, adults entering full-time certificated courses and so on – all of these can experience a concern as to whether they can cope with what is required of them: 'I opted to go on a special course for chief executives. The publicity emphasized that it would be very stretching – it was being run by a university business school. I know it was silly, but I felt that there was a severe risk of being out of my depth' (quoted in J. Rogers 2001: 8–9).

Anxiety may not take the extreme form of over-anxiety as described above, but it may well be present in some form. In many cases, anxiety becomes highest at times of evaluation: tests or examinations, submitting work to the judgement of the teacher or other members of the group. At such times, consciousness of what is perceived as the lack of educational skills is at its greatest: 'I can do this task but not that one'; 'I can discuss but I can't write'. Uncertainty about the standards to be used for assessing work done will add to such anxiety. For those who see education as instrumental in achieving a set goal beyond the learning itself, there will be pressure against 'wasting time'.

What seems to be happening is that the change from a task-focused learning situation (using acquisition learning which does not generate anxiety) to a learning-focused situation (with all that conscious learning implies in contemporary constructions) is creating the anxiety. It is the idea of 'learning' that is making these student participants worry about whether they can cope or not.

Over-anxious adult learners tend not to trust themselves and thus turn to authority for guidance. As we have noticed, we can welcome anxiety as useful for motivation for certain tasks (see p. 78), especially for those calling for persistence of application and the less difficult kinds of 'reception' learning. Anxiety can *help* performance, especially in a task where traditional answers pay off; after all, the anxiety in most cases could not have been too strong or the adult would never have come to the learning group. On the other hand, anxiety tends to interfere with and inhibit original thought. It can impede even the mastery of new motor skills. Anxiety tends often to be higher when the learner is faced with intellectual or creative exercises, lower when faced with physical tasks. Tasks requiring some degree of personal judgement are thus harder for the over-anxious student participant than tasks demanding conformity to rules. Anxiety inhibits complex learning tasks that are more dependent on improvised skills than on persistence.

Such anxiety may be expressed in a number of ways. Sometimes there are physical reactions – sweating, shaking and other signs of distress. More usually it will be confined to inner emotions which the learner seeks to hide. The individual, like the group, will take refuge in 'fight' or 'flight': attempts to avoid the testing situation by either absenting themselves physically (non-attendance) or mentally (daydreaming), or refusing to join in (see pp. 201–2, 255).

What can we do about it?

Because there are so many different causes of anxiety, there are no simple answers. It may be tackled by trying to reduce the anxiety itself or by trying to reduce opposition to the learning tasks.

Some strategies will help. Perhaps we can cultivate an atmosphere in which the fact that one dares even to the point of looking foolish becomes acceptable. The use of the group is helpful here. On the other hand, sarcasm and ridicule will be counter-productive: 'The adult tutor is there not to correct what the student says, because this denies his [sic] previous experience, views and beliefs, but to build up ways in which the students can evaluate their own opinions against those of the teacher and the rest of the group' (J. Rogers 1977: 39–40). This is as true of skill-based learning programmes as it is of information-processing courses. The learners need to be encouraged to experiment with new techniques and to evaluate the older practices against the new. Criticism, poor evaluations, signs of disapproval (the so-called 'chain-anxiety-producing sequence') will increase anxiety.

We can do more than just try to prevent the anxiety from growing. By managing the learning situation, we can help to reduce anxiety. The learning tasks can be broken up into smaller units to build up a sense of achievement. Carefully tailored rewards and reinforcements will be needed. The use of sub-groups may help, especially if the anxiety includes fear of failing before other members of the learning group. Something of the fear-inducing 'novelty' of the new learning can be lessened, although some sense of novelty is often needed to key the learner up, to create expectations and awareness. The pace of work should be monitored and adjusted if necessary.

Above all, we should seek to build up a sense of confidence in the learner. Student participants who see in the teacher a sense of confidence and an encouragement to confidence, and who thus come to trust the teacher, in time also come to accept the teacher's assessment of their own ability to learn. If we believe that our student-learners with our help *can* cope with learning tasks put clearly before them, and if we command their respect, most of the participants will come themselves to believe that they too can cope. It takes time but it can be done.

Positive aspects of anxiety

It sometimes gets overlooked that a certain amount of anxiety is desirable, for it will often motivate the learner. A series of graphs that appear in a number of books on education and learning illustrates this point. Figure 10.1a shows that maximum learning is achieved by a steady but relatively slow arousal of interest until high motivation is attained; but excessive arousal so as to create too much anxiety will prevent learning.

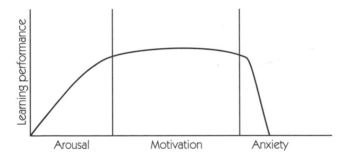

Figure 10.1a

Figure 10.1b suggests that too-quick arousal can achieve high performance in the short term, but the subject will be underlearned and performance

Figure 10.1b

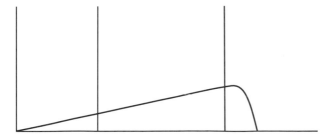

Figure 10.1c

will soon fall off. It will prove impossible to maintain the level of interest and therefore the level of performance.

On the other hand, Fig. 10.1c indicates that failure to arouse a student's interest will result in the material apparently never being learned properly.

In all three cases, once arousal has passed through the motivated stage to the stage of excessive anxiety, learning falls off sharply and a block to learning occurs at this point.

Sources of emotional difficulty

Emotional blocks other than anxiety may present themselves. The *fear of failing*, in the eyes of the group or the teacher (either as friend or as authority figure), or indeed in one's own eyes, causing possible pain or shame, is one of these. The pictures we have created of ourselves and of others spring in large part from our personal experiences, and these may exert real pressure on us: 'We were told we were going to have a free discussion and that we were all going to be expected to speak. That was all right for those who'd been at school more recently than me, but I'd been a mere housewife only a week before, and I made up my mind on the spot that wild horses wouldn't drag any discussion out of me. I *knew* I'd say something silly' (quoted in J. Rogers 1977: 34).

Such an individual will refuse to take risks. This is particularly characteristic of people who preserve a 'stiff upper lip', who consistently undervalue or hide feelings and who use their emotional energies to hold back spontaneous reaction.

Another such block may arise from a *reluctance to join in the methods of learning*. This may be due to an unwillingness to 'play' on the part of someone who is too serious, too academic in their approach, who fears to seem foolish. Activities such as buzz-groups and role plays are below their dignity; they are not willing to play around with problems or with concepts, to imagine, to experiment with the unusual. Or it may spring from an 'impoverished fantasy life'. Such an individual asserts that the world of the senses is the real world; fantasies or play are unreal. They won't pretend, won't say, 'What if . . . ?' They cannot work out the implications of a hypothesis because they are wondering all the time whether the hypothesis is true or not.

On the other hand, student participants who refuse to engage in the methods of learning may be running away from what they are sure will be inevitable frustration. Their thresholds are too low. They give up quickly in the face of obstacles. They try as hard as they can to avoid pain, discomfort or uncertainty. They will not practise or memorise, asserting that they know it will not be worth the effort.

A third and frequent personality block comes from the individual taking too low a view of themselves; their *'self-horizon' is too narrow*: 'I can't do it, I know I can't'. These people suffer from resource myopia, the failure to see resources to help them, either in their environment or in themselves; they undervalue both, especially themselves. Sometimes this may be due to sensory dullness. The would-be learners make only partial contact with themselves and with their environment. The result is that their capacity and desire to explore the world become atrophied.

A further block can be seen in those who *fear the ambiguous*. These people avoid situations that lack clarity or where the probability of success is unknown. They will not 'try this' to see if it works, for they are convinced that, even if it does work, the reasons for success will remain unknown. They overemphasise the unknown against the known, and so they won't set out to explore any part of the unknown.

Similar to these individuals are those who *fear disorder*, who dislike confusion and complexity, who have an excessive need for balance, order and symmetry. We all like to know where we are in any subject, to have signposts; but with these people it goes further than this. Their fear often leads to over-polarisation into opposites. They see everything in terms of black and white, good and evil. They thus fail to integrate the best from both sides of an argument. Role play for such student participants could become dangerous, for they may identify too closely with the case they are presenting.

Some student participants *fear to seem to influence others*. They don't want to appear too pushy or aggressive, and thus they hesitate to identify with new points of view.

There are other blocks to learning, but those listed above are probably the most common. Some of them can lead to other forms of blockage. Anxiety or too narrow a self-horizon can result in a failure to make any effort (most of us have met the student participant who sits on the edge of the group looking on with admiration as the other members master step after step of the subject), or conversely in trying to push too hard. In the latter case, the learner makes a more or less desperate attempt to keep up, to arrive at a solution. They become unwilling to let things 'incubate' or happen naturally. Too much effort sometimes springs from the same cause as too little effort.

There is a danger of exaggeration here. With all these various types of blockage present in every group of adult learners, and since we all to some extent share these characteristics, it may be wondered how any learning is done at all. But a good deal of learning does take place. The reason for itemising these blocks is not to deter the teacher but to remind ourselves that, when we meet a block to learning, it may well be caused by one of these factors.

Ego-defence mechanisms

Faced with a challenging situation like a lifelong education group, student participants with one of the above characteristics tend to employ a range of defence mechanisms to preserve their self-image. Such ego-defence mechanisms may be defined as unwitting devices, unconscious distortions, subterfuges or self-deceptions that we all practise to some extent to maintain our conscious psychological equilibrium, to avoid mental pain, to keep up appearances to ourselves as well as to others when threatened by frustration, conflict or painful emotion.

There are a large number of such mechanisms. Some are aggressive in nature, others involve compromise or substitution. What follows is a brief annotated list intended for the teacher who wants to know what is going on in the group. Those who wish to learn more about the subject can turn to the standard works on psychology.

- *Fantasy* – not just random idling or daydreaming but escape from the situation in imagination even though physically the person remains present. In fantasy the participant gains alternative satisfaction; they fulfil themselves in imagination.
- *Compensation* – the group member turns to alternative activities (such as bizarre behaviour or costume) to make up for real or imagined inadequacies. If this leads to perpetual evasion of present problems and responsibilities, it will be over-compensation.
- *Identification* with others – the vicarious achievement of goals. This often happens in an adult learning group. One participant will join with another more successful one and bask in the reflection of the latter's glory though making no effort themselves. Sometimes identification can be with an imaginary 'hero' but normally it is with a real character, whether acquainted or not.
- *Projection* onto others of our own impulses and traits – we observe them in others or we attribute them to others. This usually takes the form of criticism; we blame others for the faults that lie in us. Most adult groups which engage in participatory learning methods end up having a scapegoat. Sometimes it is possible to imagine that others are more critical than in fact they are. Those who adopt this mechanism are often on the

defensive against imaginary criticisms, noticing slights and innuendoes, and hence constantly taking offence.

- *Rationalisation* – the spontaneous giving of 'good' reasons. We find arguments to justify what we want to do or believe and even convince ourselves that these are the 'real' motives behind our actions or beliefs.
- *Repression* – selective forgetting according to the level of interest or displeasure associated with the technique or idea. Here again is a mental device that may prevent learning.
- *Sublimation* – a form of release, the diversion of frustrated energies into other (normal) channels of activity. In this, it differs from compensation. For an adult student participant, it may take the form of being particularly helpful in the group, performing certain chores and so on, in an attempt to avoid the more distasteful (i.e. active learning) work of the programme.

There are others. *Displacement* is a process by which frustration or some other such emotion is turned away from the object that caused it and is vented on someone else. Supervisors reprimanded by their superiors have been known to 'take it out' on the people under their control; these in turn may express anger towards their families or other groups. Some teachers may vent the irritation caused by their student groups on others close to them, while others bring outside frustrations into the learning group. *Negativism* sees every request as a threat that will ultimately lead to trouble and blame, and thus sees the appropriate response as 'No'. It is an extreme form of an uncooperative attitude designed to avoid difficulties. *Reaction formation* is another mechanism by which we concentrate on the opposite of what we really want to do but are rather ashamed that we want to do it.

We are likely to meet most of these ego-defence mechanisms at some stage or other. If you look again at your own blockages (see p. 239), you will probably be able to determine what withdrawal and/or defence mechanisms are employed in each case. In my own case (drawing and car repair) there is withdrawal; probably I set my horizons too low for both skills (I have been told so by colleagues who teach these subjects to adults; a certain art teacher still insists that *anyone* can learn to draw). In the case of the car I employ displacement, turning my frustration at my own failure and helplessness against the garage or the AA or anyone else in sight when the car won't work and I can't do a thing about it. Still I refuse to learn!

It is easier to describe 'blocks to learning' than to know what to do about them. Knowing what is happening is usually more than half the battle, and lines of approach may suggest themselves. But it is not always easy, when faced with student participants who persistently fail to learn, especially when this distresses them, to identify which of the many causes underlie the failure and precisely why the learners are seeking to defend themselves. It must be left to the individual judgement of each teacher in each setting to determine what to do about it. As with so much in lifelong education, there are no answers for universal application by all teachers, just a series of options to choose from, alternatives to try out.

Activity

In relation to the blocks you identified in the activity on page 239, can you identify any of the strategies which you have adopted (Column 2)?

Learning attitudes

The introduction of learning changes into the area of attitudes is perhaps the most difficult task that faces the teacher of adults. In an oral rehydration therapy project in India, it was possible to teach mothers in certain villages that children plagued with diarrhoea should not be starved, the traditional remedy, as they would suffer from dehydration and die, but instead should be fed with the rehydration mixture of water, sugar and salt. The knowledge and skill levels were quite adequate for the change to take place. But it was not so easy to persuade them to follow this in practice. It went against their family and community traditions, what they had learned from the past and what others around them were doing and expected all members of the village to do. There was a block to learning new attitudes, not new knowledge. The experience over many years of Alcoholics Anonymous, anti-smoking campaigns and drug programmes have demonstrated that it is not lack of knowledge which inhibits effective behavioural learning but inadequately learned attitudes.

Modifications of attitude are the hardest change of all. The following suggestions may point to some strategies:

• Identify as clearly as possible precisely what the attitude is that is preventing learning changes and what are the most important pressures against making such changes, not just what the student-learner says they are.
• An adequate basis of new or revised knowledge is necessary for any attitudinal change. Later threats to the new attitudes will be resisted in proportion as the new knowledge is firmly based and internalised.
• The amount of change called for should not be so great that the learner rejects it outright as calling for too radical a reappraisal of thinking and behaving. It should build on existing life patterns, not oppose them. (But equally it should not be presented as insignificant or trivial; no effort to change will then be made.)

- The learners should be left to draw their own conclusions from the material learned in this context, not exhorted to change their attitudes and practice.
- The new material should come from a source regarded as trustworthy and attractive (this will reflect on the teacher). The main mode of learning is what is often called 'human modelling'.
- The use of a learning group to create a climate in which such changes can be brought about is often effective. A public display of new attitudes helps to promote more permanent changes. It is largely a matter of commitment to new ways of thinking and behaving, and commitment to a group can assist in this.
- Role play, through which the participants play out the parts of those who hold the new desired attitudes and perhaps also those who hold in an extreme form the undesired negative attitude, can also be useful, though it needs to be used with great care.

Each teacher of adults needs to face every situation as a unique event, requiring a new assessment and perhaps new methods. What will work with one group may not work with another.

Most of these blocks seem to come from the way the learners are constructing themselves as students. They spring from their conception of what is involved in 'learning'. They do not exist when these same persons engage in acquisition learning, for their attention there is concentrated on the task they intend to perform. It is up to us as teachers to help the participants to reconstruct their perceptions of what it means to be a student so as to reduce these blocks.

Conclusion

I have suggested that many student participants put a good deal of emotional investment into defending their existing patterns of knowledge, attitudes and behaviour. In addition, adult learners have built up a self-perception which they will often be reluctant to change. Attempts to build up new patterns, to encourage changes in their self-perception, may result in strong emotional reactions. The teacher must therefore tread carefully.

I have also suggested that all our student participants are part of a specific sociocultural context. They are not psychological isolates but have created and are constantly recreating themselves in interaction with that context. We need to help them to identify and to build upon the motivators and resources, and the support networks and mechanisms in that environment, just as we need with them to identify the demotivators and to take action to weaken their effect (see pp. 99–100).

Further reading

Alexander, C. and Langer, E. (eds) (1990) *Higher Stages of Human Development: Perspectives on Human Growth*. Oxford: Oxford University Press.

Birren, J.E. and Schaie, K.W. (eds) (1990) *Handbook of the Psychology of Aging*, 3rd edn. San Diego, CA: Academic Press.

Gibbs, G., Morgan, A. and Taylor, E. (1982) Why students don't learn, *Institutional Research Review*, 1(10).

Gross, R.D. (1987) *Psychology: The Science of Mind and Behaviour*. London: Hodder & Stoughton.

Storant, M. and van den Bos, G.R. (eds) (1989) *The Adult Years: Continuity and Change*. Washington, DC: American Psychological Association.

Tennant, M. (1988) *Psychology and Adult Learning*. London: Routledge.

Chapter 11

EVALUATION

How can we tell . . . ?

The criteria used in natural acquisition learning are different from those in formalised learning. The evaluation of task-conscious learning is based on the performance of that task (does it work?). In taught learning, where the task is learning, the criteria tends to be: has it been learned? This chapter argues that it is necessary to use both kinds of evaluation when evaluating our teaching of adults.

The need for evaluation

Like earlier sections of this book, this chapter is intended to raise questions rather than to propose firm answers. The approach to evaluation here is a practical one; the intention is to make conscious what most of us do subconsciously much of the time as part of the process of teaching. It is often assumed that the need for and the means of evaluation are self-evident, but if this were so, teachers would be better at doing it and would be able to see themselves doing it, more often and more effectively. Evaluation is one of the more difficult skills required of the teacher, and we need to work at it consciously. There are different possible strategies involved, and our task is to choose between them, to decide for ourselves our own preferred way of working.

Along with this there will go a willingness to change what we (and our student participants) are doing. There is no point in evaluating the teaching-learning situation if we are unwilling to change course. Evaluation will be effective only if we are prepared to alter or even scrap our existing programme when we detect something wrong, and if necessary begin again.

A distinction also needs to be drawn between evaluation and assessment. One possible definition suggests that *assessment* is the collection of data on which we base our evaluation. It is descriptive and objective; if anyone else were to do it using the same criteria, they would come up with much the same findings. *Evaluation* on the other hand is a process of making personalised judgements – decisions about achievements, about expectations, not just the effectiveness but also the *value* of what we are doing. It involves notions of worth, of 'good' and 'bad' teaching and learning and outcomes of learning programmes. It is based on our own ideology.

Evaluation in acquisition and formalised learning

There are few areas where the difference between task-conscious learning (acquisition) and learning-conscious learning (formalised learning) can be seen so clearly as in evaluation: the former evaluates whether the learner performs the task while the latter evaluates whether learning has been achieved, not whether it is being used.

If what we are doing, teaching adults, is helping them to learn more effectively, which involves building upon the natural task-conscious learning process and making this process more learning-conscious, then we need to look at evaluation in the natural learning process. Evaluation in acquisition learning is inherent within the whole process, not separate from and after learning. Indeed, it is through constant evaluation that we learn. It is therefore frequent, running throughout the whole process of learning. Evaluation in task-conscious learning is not a clear-cut process, not linear from simple to complex, but messy, using any criteria to hand, but always related to the performance of the task rather than to some external standard. Like acquisition learning, it is a largely subconscious process, or at least consciously related to the task rather than to the learning. Much of it is self-judged, relying on a sense that the newly learned material 'fits', 'rings true' or 'works'. In this, the learner uses a number of different sources for evaluation and a range of different criteria, both chosen by the learner. The outcomes of the learning will express themselves in multiple ways, not just one set of performance indicators for all the varied student-learners.

Formalised learning, even in lifelong learning programmes, denies almost all of this. On the whole, education views evaluation as an external process using criteria chosen by the teacher-agent, undertaken at a time chosen by the learning programme rather than by the learner. And it relates to the learning: it asks 'Has the material been learned?', not 'Does the material work?' Teachers of adults are part of this formalised educational culture, and have learned attitudes towards and processes of evaluation from that context. Of all aspects of formalised learning, much attention has been given to evaluation, and its use and formats justified. We need to look at these justifications and processes in some detail.

Why evaluate?

Evaluation in education is important for at least three reasons:

- To improve our performance as teachers. Questions of quality, of accountability, of protecting our 'customers', of being effective, are important not just for the providers and organisers but also for our student participants and for ourselves. We need to judge what we are doing and ask whether we are doing it well, in order to do it well.

- To plan new strategies, make choices and establish priorities; to determine where we are in the teaching-learning process at present and what to do next; to identify helps and hindrances and decide what to do about them.
- To learn: to assess how much progress has been made, in which direction and how much farther there is to go. Evaluation is an essential part of learning.

Evaluation has been divided by many writers into two main kinds: *formative* – the ongoing evaluation that is inherent in the learning process itself and which leads to learning changes; and *summative* – evaluation that takes place at different times, particularly at the end of the programme of learning, to see how far we have got. But these are not in fact two distinct processes. If a summative evaluation undertaken at the end of a course (a teacher's report, for instance) is used to plan new programmes and new approaches, then it becomes formative. It is the way evaluation is used that distinguishes it. If it looks only backwards and reviews what has been done, it is summative; if in addition it looks forward to, and influences, new procedures it is formative. The latter is more productive; evaluation judgements should lead to change. But there is also a time for the former, especially when issues of accountability come to the fore.

There are other distinctions – between formal/public and informal/private evaluations, between case-specific and generalised, between descriptive and judgemental and between holistic and analytical. Evaluation can take many forms according to who it is done by and who it is done for.

Who evaluates?

A similar distinction can be drawn between *external* and occasional evaluation, practised by the organiser of the programme or some inspector or external validating body, and *internal*, more regular evaluation, practised by the teacher in the course of the teaching programme.

The *organiser* and/or those to whom they are accountable (governments, funders, clients etc.) will be assessing how far the programme objectives are being met. Are we getting in our groups the right kind of student-learners, the ones the programme is primarily intended for, those we feel to be in most need? Are they learning the right things? Are the courses meeting their needs and intentions? Are the programmes on offer reflecting the selectivity-, competitiveness- and competency-based criteria of the existing educational system, or are they offering a different (non-selective, non-competitive and effort-based) ethos? In addition, the providers' concern will be with matters of quality control. They need to determine whether the resources they have at their disposal are being used most effectively and, in certain circumstances, to establish priorities. To do all this, they will need criteria to determine whether some courses are better than others and to plan accordingly.

The *teachers* also evaluate their work but they will have different questions to ask. They are concerned with whether they are being effective as teachers; whether the objectives they have set are the right ones and at the right level, as well as whether they are being met. They will be assessing progress, and the match between intentions (objectives) and outcomes (the results of the teaching-learning process). They will be seeking to measure change, appraise efforts and identify new needs, strengths and weaknesses. They will wish to learn whether the short-term goals and the tasks they have laid before the learning group have been achieved and whether they are of the kind that will contribute towards the desired longer-term learning changes. They need to test whether the learners are ready to move on to the next stage or not. They will want to see clearly the *intended* programme of learning, the *implemented* programme (which may be different from what was intended for various reasons) and whether that again differs from the *received* programme.

Both organiser and teacher, then, evaluate for much the same reason: for their own learning and to plan changes. But teachers also build evaluation into the teaching-learning process for the learners' sake. They use evaluation for motivation. What is more, an ongoing programme of evaluation is a necessary part of the learning process itself and becomes part of the work of the whole group.

So thirdly, the *learners* themselves also evaluate in the course of learning. Evaluation is an essential tool for developing new skills, knowledge and understanding. As we have seen, the learners are well accustomed and indeed expert in evaluating their own learning episodes. Hitting a ball against a line on a wall in a tennis practice session brings about no learning changes by itself (though it may strengthen the muscles). What is needed is a series of judgements: 'That was too high'; modification; 'That was too low'; modification; 'That was about right'; repetition; 'That was good'; once more; and so on. Without such an evaluative process, learning changes would not be made. Trial-and-error learning in particular is based on evaluation, but most other kinds of learning methods rely on this process for effective changes.

The learners then engage in formative evaluation in order to learn. They will also pursue summative self-evaluation for motivation: assessing their own progress and performance, determining how far they have progressed and whether it is in the 'right' direction (participant evaluation will include some judgement about the 'relevance' of the learning programme to their own purposes), thus diminishing or rekindling their enthusiasm for the learning goals in the light of their achievements (what is called *ipsative evaluation*).

It is likely – though not inevitable – that the evaluation by the teacher and by the outside body (usually the organiser) will not be the same, for their objectives differ to a certain degree. It is also likely – and almost certainly undesirable – that the evaluation by the teacher and by the learner will be different. A hierarchy of evaluation thus emerges and should perhaps be developed more consciously: the organisers and inspectors (where they exist) should encourage the teachers to evaluate, and they in their turn should encourage the student-learners to engage in evaluation. Since evaluation is largely a skill, the teachers need to help the participants to learn how to evaluate; they should demonstrate the process. Evaluation is one of those exercises that need to be practised jointly between teacher and student participant rather than be taught by exhortation.

This of course involves negotiation between the teacher of adults and their students. Just as agreement is needed to establish learning goals, so too negotiation will be needed to determine the criteria to establish whether those goals have been met or not.

Evaluate what?

The most common approach to evaluation in taught learning programmes suggests that we need to look at three areas: *outcomes* (intended and unintended), *structures* and *processes*. But the last two are assessed by whether they contribute to the intended outcomes; there are no independent criteria for judging structures or processes.

Some approaches adopt tools of evaluation, such as the appropriately named SWOT approach: to assess the *strengths* and the *weaknesses* of the programme or class; to assess the *opportunities* which it opens and which may or may not have been taken up; and to assess the *threats* (or obstacles) which will hamper the effectiveness of the programme and which need to be addressed if the goals of the programme are to be achieved. This approach has specific advantages in that it encourages us to look beyond the normal assessment of outcomes and achievements to explore other possibilities and the risks faced in the programme.

In evaluating our adult teaching activities, there is one overriding concern – whether the learners are learning or not. That must be the eventual standard by which our programmes need to be judged. In order to assess this, we may look at three main elements: goals set, the structure and processes of teaching and learning, and the learning and other outcomes, including student attainments.

Goals and objectives

The learning objectives need to be submitted to evaluation not just in terms of how far they are being met, but also (and perhaps more importantly) in terms of whether they are the 'right' goals.

We need to identify how far the intentions of the programme of learning are clear in our minds and in the minds of the student-learners before we submit them to some form of judgement. The definition of the goals (see Chapter 6) will need to be very clear if we are to engage in meaningful evaluation.

Perhaps we take for granted that the goals of our courses – to learn a craft or other skill, to study literature and so on – are the right ones, self-justifying. But these assumptions need to be examined in some depth. Are they in fact the most appropriate goals for this particular set of learners? What criteria shall we use to assess this? Is the learning primarily concerned with personal growth, or with socialisation and/or social change, or with vocational advancement? Whose goals are they – ours or those of the student participants? Are they open or closed goals? (see pp. 162–5). For example, in a literacy learning programme, is the goal to help the participants to *develop* literacy skills or is it to promote the *use* of literacy in real life (which is quite a different matter)? To assess the former, we shall need tests at the end of the learning programme. To assess the latter, we shall need to engage in follow-up procedures some time after the end of the learning programme to see if and how the new learning is being used. The same is true of management training programmes – it can be argued that helping the participants to learn managerial skills and attitudes which they do not implement will not bring about the goal achievement intended. This is part of the difference between task-conscious learning (in which case we will draw our criteria from the performance of the task) and learning-conscious learning (in which case we will use criteria related to learning).

We shall also need to assess how far these goals and objectives, these intentions of both the teachers and the student-learners are being achieved – whether the programme of learning is proving effective. Throughout, we need to ask whether the participants are learning in a particular area, even when this learning is seen as a means of achieving some goal that lies beyond the learning. Whether the goal is to pass an examination or to create a work of art for oneself, the means to the satisfactory attainment of these goals is student learning, and it is this which needs to be assessed.

The teaching and learning processes

The entire process by which the teacher creates the learning opportunity (planning skills as well as powers of exposition) needs to be evaluated. The way the programme has been set and is resourced, the climate created, the methods and materials used will all need to be analysed and valued. Once again the main concern is with the learner rather than the teacher; the purpose of effective teaching is student learning. The question is less whether we are teaching well than whether the student is well motivated and enabled to learn. There is not much point, as I have remarked before, in the teacher engaging in a range of 'teaching' activities if the learner isn't learning. Regular ongoing evaluation of our own teaching thus includes the process of feedback.

Student-learner attainments and other outcomes

At the heart of the evaluation process, then, lies the question of student learning. How much and what are they learning? What form of learning are they engaged in: is it product or process, to handle tools or to produce a table to a set standard (see p. 163)? What is the quality and level of their learning? How well is the material learned? Have their skills of learning increased during the programme? These and many other similar questions occur in the process of thinking about the evaluation of student learning.

One of the issues here lies with the concept of progress in learning. If ignorance is seen to be deprivation, then progress will be seen in terms of acquisition – of new skills, knowledge, understanding and attitudes. 'Progress' is usually viewed as advancement along a straight line of development. But there is not always a straight line of progress in learning. Learning, as we have seen, can be a messy business.

An essential part of this evaluation will be concerned with the attitudinal development of the student participants – with how much additional confidence, how much increased motivation have arisen from the teaching-learning programme. This aspect is often omitted from evaluation processes, which concentrate more on 'value-added outcomes' – on increased knowledge and more highly developed skills. But the assurance and enhanced self-image of the students, their willingness to continue to study, their increased interest are all outcomes which need to be evaluated.

Finally we will need to look for the unexpected outcomes, the impact of our teaching-learning programmes. There will be many of these, and not all of them will be life-enhancing for the student participants, although many will (I once asked a group of students for those 'other outcomes' and one person told me that she got married!). Some of this unexpected outcome evaluation may have to be done some time after the course has finished – what is sometimes called *post hoc* or postscript evaluation. Experience indicates that at times, whereas the learning objectives of a programme may have been achieved, the longer-term impact of the programme could be negative (Rogers 1992: 216–25).

Evaluation methods

Student learning, then, is the main focus of our process of evaluation. But there is no single right way of evaluating this; we have to decide for ourselves how to do it. Obviously we need to ask a series of questions, and determining what some of these should be is relatively simple. It is more difficult to come to some agreement on the criteria by which to judge the answers.

Activity

Before starting this section, look at the course which you are taking as your case study (p. 8) and try to determine how it is or will be evaluated – what indicators are being sought? I suggest that you write them down:

It is perhaps in the area of evaluation that the recent changes in adult lifelong learning programmes has been felt most keenly. More and more adults are being subsumed into formal learning programmes inside educational institutions (although battles are being fought in an attempt to hold onto some of the ways by which both the curriculum and the methods of assessment can be contextualised rather than decontextualised, determined by the adult student participants rather than by the institution). The result is that more and more adults are being assessed and their learning evaluated by formal procedures.

Examinations

Despite the hesitations of many of those who teach adults, examinations are now being used with the majority of adult learners to evaluate their learning. The variety of so-called 'objective testing' (usually subject-based) is also increasing. Coursework (assignments serving both as part of the learning process and also as a form of assessment) is very normal now, not only in distance learning programmes but also in many face-to-face adult learning programmes. End of course assessments, for adults as well as younger age students, now range from the very formal (standardised testing) to the very informal: written examinations (unseen, open-book, pre-set or home-based), tests, essays (whether structured or subjective – i.e. devoted to whatever the learner wishes to write about), practicals, observation of exercises, oral tests, questions, discussion, projects and so on. Some are group-based, more are individual. They attempt to test the competencies attained, and their effect on the learning process is usually short term.

The problems of marking examinations, of norm and criterion referencing (i.e. whether each exam is to be marked against a 'normal' distribution pattern of success and failure, say 5 per cent top grade, 20 per cent second, 50 per cent third etc.; or against an objective standard of competence that is supposed to exist somewhere outside of the examiner), and of whether the learners are thinking for themselves are well known. Their accompaniments – the prejudices of the examiners in relation to particular learners, the problem of extrinsic rewards rather than intrinsic motivation, the increase in competitiveness and selectivity, enhanced feelings of anxiety, failure and injustice, the distortion of the curriculum and of the pace of learning, the fact that many exams are set and marked by people unknown to the learners so that the aim comes to be to defeat the examiner by guesswork rather than to learn – are again well known. They have led to a widespread concern to seek ways to replace élitist and selective examinations with other forms of evaluation; to replace prizes with goals that all may achieve (the distinction which we noticed on p. 4 between the athletics match and the marathon). Some modern approaches to evaluation are seeking ways of helping student participants to assess their own learning progress through self- and peer assessment. This chimes in well with acquisition learning, for self-assessment is the primary mode of evaluation in the natural learning process, with self-initiated peer evaluation also a feature.

Nevertheless, we should not dismiss such formal methods of evaluation entirely, for they can be formative as well as summative in their nature. Internal tests may be as much a means of new learning as of assessment. Sometimes they are intended to be solely summative, leading to the determination of attainment levels and on occasion to the award of certificates of competency. There is clearly a place (and a good deal of demand) for these in some adult teaching programmes, but a number of factors limit their usefulness:

- The problem of how to evaluate *progress* made as distinct from *levels of attainment*. Some student learners, starting from a base lower than that of others in their group, make more rapid progress but remain well behind the attainment levels of the rest. The wider range of the participants in adult learning programmes makes this issue more acute, especially in institution-bound education. The way to reward such effort and advances while retaining the prescribed or desired attainment levels is problematic.
- Adult learners not only start at very different points; they also choose different goals for themselves. The ends and intentions of adult learners are not always homogeneous.
- There are no age-related criteria for adult learners as have been agreed for many younger people.

Other criteria however are still being used to evaluate some adult teaching programmes, and it is worth listing these in order to indicate that there are other ways of assessing adult learning than the ubiquitous formal assignments and examinations.

Satisfaction indicators

There is still some reliance on student satisfaction indicators such as:

- *indicated demand* – requests from prospective student participants, individually or through organisations, on which the programme is built and which are taken to indicate that it must be meeting needs;
- *effective demand* – the numbers of student-learners attracted to particular classes (the size of the group is sometimes taken as a means of assessing the value of a course);
- *follow-on* – whether an extension of the learning situation is requested and taken up (a course is deemed successful if the learners request more of the same);
- *follow-up* – whether the learners continue to study on their own or pass into new programmes, whether they practise their new skills, read more etc.;
- *attendance figures* – in terms of both regularity of attendance and low numbers of drop-outs;
- *verbal or written comments by the student participants* – both approval and complaints, indicating the learners' sense of success or dissatisfaction. End-of-course student evaluation schedules are being increasingly used.

Teachers frequently use such popularity or satisfaction indicators to help evaluate their work. Such criteria are closer to those used in our personalised learning episodes; we judge if we have succeeded by a sense of satisfaction that 'it works' or 'it feels good'. But it is not always clear that these truly signal that effective learning is taking place.

Contextual preconditions

Quality assurance is now a keyword in much education which involves adult student learners. Among the factors that contribute towards the effectiveness of the learning process are those relating to the context within which the teaching takes place. These too are the concern of evaluation by both organiser and teacher. Since part of the task of evaluation is the identification of the good and bad influences that affect the impact of our teaching, we need to consider carefully the *setting* (the room, furniture, temperature, lighting, teaching aids) to see whether it is conducive to the participants' learning and to remedy any hindrances it contains. Some evaluators have looked to the *emotional climate* and *management controls*, both of the institution within which the course is set and of the learning group itself (see pp. 192–5) for their indicators. These do not necessarily reveal whether learning is taking place, but they do contribute to the criteria by which we can assess teaching-learning effectiveness. For example, there is little hope of creating effective learning changes in the direction of greater self-confidence and self-determination if the whole ethos of the institution is opposed to this or if the class denies the learner any opportunity to exercise such qualities. Overt and covert pressures for or against the goals are important elements in the process of teaching adults, and need evaluation.

Criteria from teaching

Other criteria are being used, both by organisers and others concerned with the quality of the programmes provided and by teachers concerned about the effectiveness of their work. Some of these are based on what happens during the teaching-learning experience. Such evaluation sometimes consists of a description of what is going on, moment by moment – an analysis in terms of learning events. Some attempts have gone further, trying to identify those processes that need to be reinforced and those needing to be corrected or nullified. Thus:

- Some have recorded the number of *learning events* taking place and what kind they are. (One such scheme divides these events into acts of memorisation, acts of divergent and convergent thinking and acts of evaluative thinking.) Others have concentrated on the logic of teaching and of the language used in teaching; episodes have been listed such as defining, reporting and designating. However, these techniques are more readily practised by others than by the teachers themselves; you cannot easily use them on your own group except by watching yourself teach with the use of a video recorder. (It is well worth doing this, if you can get hold of the equipment; but if not, you can visit other classes and see other teachers at work, and in this case it is valuable to have in mind what you are looking for.)
- Another analysis lists the number and kinds of *transactions* between teacher and learner, and between learner and learner that take place during any teaching session. The participation of the student-learner in the work (activities) of the group is seen as one indicator that learning is taking place. If the teacher talks for a long time, only one kind of transaction is taking place; questions on the other hand comprise more transactions. The most frequently cited analysis of these transactions is that by Flanders (1970) which records events every few seconds, but once again teachers usually need to rely on what they can deduce from their own teaching, and sophisticated techniques are probably not appropriate.
- Others have concentrated on *types of teaching-learning method* used in the class and the involvement of the student participants in their own learning. The use of 'approved' methods such as demonstration or

discussion is frequently felt to lead inevitably to learning. But it is not always easy to see how the teacher can judge, at the end of each such occasion, how much and what kind of learning has taken place by the use of these methods. A substantial amount of subjective impression will add itself to our evaluation; we will *feel* good about the teaching session. But a reliance on particular teaching methods will not always lead to learning and may introduce an element of artificiality into the experience.

One part of this analysis of classroom activities relates to our *performance* as teacher, centred upon our subject expertise and skills of presentation and communication. Evidence of preparation, both of the subject matter and of the modes of teaching; awareness of the student-learners; the clarity with which the goals of learning are defined; the structure of the learning programme – its level, pace of learning, relevance to the learner and to the task in hand; the clear signposting of each step of the learning process; the number and nature of the teaching-learning materials used – all these are capable of assessment. Our personal style of teaching (self-projection, confidence, voice level, powers of organisation, the rapport built up with the learners, the development of interaction and feedback), the methods used, the involvement of the learners in the processes and the creation of feedback and evaluation procedures can all be recorded on a positive-negative scale. Positive recordings are those which it is believed will produce an occasion conducive to learning. This is perhaps as far as we can go along this line of enquiry.

The range and nature of *student activity* can also be recorded as part of the evaluative process. The nature of the group, the kinds of interaction between members, the range of expectations and intentions they declare and the clarity of their goals, the kind of work they do in each session and between sessions, the questions they ask (as signs that they are grappling with the new material), the involvement of the learners in evaluating themselves – positive recordings in each of these areas are thought to be indicators that learning is taking place. At each stage, judgements need to be made: for example, as to whether the activity in which the participant is engaged really aims 'at the *improvement* and development of knowledge, understanding and skill and not merely at its exercise' (NICCE 1980: 10). In the end a description of the programme of work is not in itself an adequate means of assessing effectiveness, but a programme in which the learners are active is more likely to lead to learning changes than one in which they are passive recipients of information and instruction.

Performance testing

Involvement by the learners in the learning activities does not always reveal the *kind* of learning taking place, even if it can be relied upon to indicate that some form of learning changes are taking place. We noted in Chapter 6 the difference between private (inner) learning and the behavioural expressions of that learning (the 'public' effects of our teaching), and the debate as to whether all 'private' outcomes can and should express themselves in behavioural (performance) terms. Behavioural changes and performance targets are easier to assess than inner changes in understanding, values and attitudes, and this fact will influence the procedures of assessment and evaluation we adopt. Part of the process of evaluation is to interpret behavioural patterns and to look for a range of performance indicators in order to see how the more private learning changes are expressed.

When devising ways of assessing the kinds of learning which are occurring in their classrooms, teachers of adults need to identify or create certain student activities (e.g. making something, writing or speaking) which in themselves express the desired learning, in order to assess whether progress is being made and what kind of learning changes are being achieved. But once again we need to remind ourselves of a number of caveats:

- these situations will be real ones – there is little point in asking adult student-learners to engage in artificial activities that they will never engage in again once the course is over;
- the primary purpose is to evaluate the hidden depths (expressive objectives) that lie beneath these competency-based activities;
- outside influences may hinder or prevent the exercise of the desired function – activities (including words) do not always reflect inner learning changes or their nature, but they may be at times the only way we can evaluate the learning changes of others.

For it remains a fact that the most frequent means of assessment and evaluation in adult education is the quality of an end product, be it a piece of writing, the ability to engage in a series of exercises, a fabricated article or role-play exercise, completed to the satisfaction of the teacher who is for this purpose the assessor. These, as we have seen, are not to be judged solely on their own but according to certain criteria attached to the performance of behavioural objectives: the level, the purpose for which it is being done, the conditions under which the actions are being performed, and so on (see pp. 157–8). Any evaluation will need to include some clarification of these conditions as well as a definition of the activity itself (see Figure 11.1).

Post-hoc *evaluation*

The only fully satisfactory mode of assessment as to whether the learners are learning the 'right' things (i.e. the pre-agreed outcomes) and at the right level is the performance of the student participants *after* the end of each stage of the learning programme. Do they act in such a way as to reveal increased confidence, in whatever field of learning they are engaged in? Do

Objectives • their nature • the clarity with which they are perceived
Context • the milieu/setting • the climate
Teacher • subject competency • performance as teacher • materials used
Student learners • activities in group • activities as individual learners
Level of performance • the finished product
Unexpected outcome • positive • negative
Indicators of satisfaction • whether goals have been/are being attained
Assessment of success or failure • and reasons

Figure 11.1 An evaluation schedule: suggested headings
(Try this out on the course you listed above, page 8)

they exercise new or enhanced skills better and/or more often? Do they reveal new understandings and new knowledge in what they say and do? Are they continuing to learn in directions of their own choice? Do they show signs of being satisfied with their own performance in their chosen field or of striving towards further improvement? The ultimate evaluation of the success or failure of our teaching will be seen in the *exercise* by the participants of new skills, knowledge and understandings and of new attitudes towards themselves and the world around them.

Such *post-hoc* evaluation is not easy, especially as most teachers of adults lose contact with their student participants soon after the end of the course or programme. The possibility of delayed learning (we know that it takes time for feelings, creative approaches and understandings to emerge) means that we can never be sure, in the case of seeming failures, that our work will not eventually bear fruit. Nor can we be sure that the learning of those with whom we seem to have been most successful will be permanent.

'. . . making the important measurable'

Here we come to the heart of what is perhaps the most important issue in the evaluation of lifelong learning at the moment. In place of uniform pre-set learning objectives which are expected to reveal themselves in precisely the same way for all the student-learners, lifelong educators are aware that the way each of the learners plans to use their learning will vary. There will be multiple outcomes of the new learning. One way in which this issue has been expressed is in the statement that traditional educational evaluation 'makes the measurable important'; i.e. what can be measured (by tests and examinations etc.) comes to dominate the teaching-learning programme, and this becomes the goal of the programme, valued above all the other outcomes. Today however educators in lifelong learning are seeking for ways to 'make the important measurable'; i.e. to find techniques by which the many different ways in which adult learners will express their new learning can be measured and converted into statistical form on a comparative basis.

The problem is that such multiple expressions of new learning inevitably raise issues of value judgements on the part of the evaluators. Let me give one example. In a recent adult literacy programme, a *post-hoc* evaluation found that the women were using their newly developed literacy skills for reading fashion magazines and writing Christmas cards rather than 'for new learning' (for health, or family welfare etc.). The evaluator would clearly rather have seen the women conforming to her own standards of 'development', indeed to the stated goals of the programme itself (Stromquist 1997: 151). But it is inevitable with adult participants who each have their own agenda that they will express their learning in quite different ways. The problem is how to make each of the many varied ways in which the new learning will be used assessable and measurable.

Criteria and the participants

So how far can and should the participants be involved in establishing the criteria for the evaluation? If they have their own agendas, their own purposes in coming to our learning programmes, should we not evaluate the success of the programme by how far these goals have been met rather than by whether the goals of the programme itself have been met? And is it not likely that the student participants will only determine in what ways they wish to use the new learning *after* they have engaged with the learning programme itself? For example, one student in a photography for pleasure class determined almost at the end of the class to set up a small business for wedding photographs; this was not his intention at the start of the programme, but it was a clear *outcome of* the programme. This is a good example of the final criteria of the evaluation of learning: 'the event by which we recognise [learning] as having occurred is the expression of a preference, an act of choice' on the part of the student participants.

The evaluator of lifelong learning thus needs to determine:

• whether the criteria being used will be closed (i.e. uniform and pre-set) or open (i.e. allowing for multiple expressions);
• whether the criteria being used will be external (imposed on the programme) or internal (negotiated with the participants).

A useful matrix of these issues has been produced which will cause many of us to think more deeply about our evaluation (see Figure 11.2).

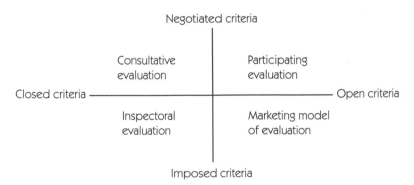

Figure 11.2 Matrix of evaluation (based on Thomas 1987: 386)

Activity

See if you can determine where the evaluation of your case study fits into the matrix shown in Figure 11.2, if at all.

The implication of this current emphasis on *post-hoc* evaluation will be that our evaluation will always be tentative; we can never know for sure. The student participants may have learned enough to get a certificate or a degree, they may have learned something about managing a business; but whether they have really learned anything which will change their practices and in which directions will often remain unclear.

Some teachers of adults will find this unsatisfactory, but we will often have to be content to cast our bread upon the waters in the expectation that it will (may?) return to us after many days. Perhaps the most rewarding aspect of the evaluation of adult learning are those signs of satisfaction that so many adults reveal in their relations with their teachers. The student participants are after all the best judges of whether they are getting what they feel they need, for this is how they evaluate their own acquisition learning. We ourselves need to see our evaluation as 'an extension into the everyday work of educators of those continuous appraisals of conditions and events on the basis of which humans act and interrelate' (Adelman and Alexander 1983).

Further reading

Andrews, G.J. (ed.) (1991) *Practical Handbook for Assessing Learning Outcomes in Continuing Education and Training*. Washington, DC: International Association for Continuing Education and Training.

Easton, P.A. (1996) *Sharpening the Tools: Improving Evaluation in Adult and Nonformal Education*. Hamburg: UNESCO Institute of Education.

Guba, E. and Lincoln, E.S. (1981) *Effective Evaluation*. San Francisco: Jossey Bass.

Rowntree, D. (1987) *Assessing Students*. London: Kogan Page.

Ruddock, R. (1981) *Evaluation: A Consideration of Principles and Methods*. Manchester: Manchester University Press.

Thomas, H. (1986) Perspectives on evaluation, in M. Hughes, P. Robbins and H. Thomas (eds) *Managing Education: The System and the Institution*, pp. 373–93. London: Cassell.

Chapter 12

PARTICIPATION

Can we all join in . . . ?

Adults are natural learners; they learn in a self-directed way. They are accustomed to determine for themselves what they want to learn, when and how, and to decide when they have achieved their own goals. This chapter argues that in our teaching of adults we should as far as possible build on this experience rather than deny it. But it points out that many adults, coming into educational encounters, expect to abandon this self-determination in their desire for learning assistance. This tension faces all of us who teach adults.

Participation is a word and a concept which has many different interpretations and values attached to it. It is not my purpose here to unravel all of these, for there are many detailed works on participation. Rather, I shall pick out three which have direct implications for our work as teachers of adults:

- participation as active involvement in the learning process;
- participation as control over the teaching-learning process;
- participation as presence in the teaching-learning process.

Participation as involvement in the process (active learning)

Learning is an active process

We have seen that acquisition learning (which is the main way we all learn naturally) is active learning, initiated and controlled by the learner. This implies that, for learning in our taught learning programmes to be effective, the student participants in our groups need to be active, fully involved in the learning activities. Although the teacher 'teaches' (whatever that may mean), it is the learners who do the learning. It has been said that for teachers to say that 'we taught but the students didn't learn' is as ridiculous as saying, 'I sold him a car but he didn't buy it'. Teaching adults is a matter of setting up a programme of activities, study and practice, and encouraging and enabling the student participants to engage in it. They run the length of the 'course', they do the work and arrive at the goals. The teacher cannot make the learning changes; only the learners can do this.

It is surprising how often we forget this simple truth, how often teachers concentrate on what *they* are doing rather than on what the student participants are doing, how often we think that learning is dependent for its effectiveness on our teaching activities (the way we present knowledge or processes, our skills of communication, our demonstrations and visual aids and so on). Naturally, any book that deals with teaching adults runs the danger of compounding this error by concentrating upon the activities of the teacher rather than on those of the student-learners. So right at the end, especially when we have just been considering evaluation, a task most teachers see as theirs alone, it is necessary to spell out once more that learning is a natural and essential human activity, undertaken via a more or less subconscious process we have called acquisition learning in a human context (see pp. 125–30). Within the more formalised learning programmes which are implicit in our task of 'teaching adults' we need to build on this active learning process. Learning is what the learners do, even in 'taught learning' programmes.

This is important for a number of reasons. First for motivation. Students need to feel that they have accomplished something regularly in order to build up and maintain a sense of success. Summative activities, assessments as to how much has been completed, how far the learners feel that they have got and how much further they feel they need to go to approach the goal, are essential for keeping going at the learning tasks. Secondly, for learning itself – the introduction, acceptance and internalising of the learning changes. Formative activities, their own assessments as to whether they see themselves as being on the right lines, trying out whether this is or is not a useful way of going about it, reflecting critically if these are the right processes for themselves or not – all of these activities and judgements are involved in the process of learning itself.

Learning is lifelong

There is a further reason why the student-learners should be active, and that is the need to encourage them to continue purposeful and structured learning once our particular programme is over. As we have seen, planned and purposeful learning continues throughout life in the form of learning episodes (see pp. 120–5). It is a necessary part of life itself, not just a preparation. We need to continue to learn because we cannot learn at the start all that we shall need during our uncertain path through life. Not only is there not enough time, but also many things will be unforeseen. In any case, many things will not make sense until we are actively engaged with them. To give an example: alternative therapies are now a regular part of many medical practices but many GPs who find themselves faced with this subject have had to learn about these from scratch. Their initial training made no contribution to their understanding in this area. Even if the subject had been included in the curriculum of their medical training programmes, it would not have made as much sense or been treated with the same regard as it is now that these doctors are faced with the question in real life. The same is true in other fields. It is also true of teaching adults; we need to learn how to do it while we do it. However much training we may have received in advance, however many books we read about it, it will not make sense until it is put into practice for real.

Such continued learning will come upon all of us at the most unexpected moments in our lives. As we have seen (see p. 46), we shall find ourselves learning as our occupations change, as we enter new social roles and relationships or reinterpret existing ones, and as we enter new phases of self-development, develop new interests or discover new talents within ourselves.

In some parts of Western societies, it is agreed that the ultimate objective of all this learning is enhanced adulthood – i.e. the drive towards greater maturity and self-development, the search for meaning and a fuller sense of perspective and the impulse towards increased autonomy: responsibility for ourselves and perhaps for others. In this sense, the final aim of learning is liberation, self-determination, freedom, individuation, although increasingly today other perspectives may put the well-being of (economic) society before private gains as the main outcome of lifelong learning. Other cultures see the main purpose of continued learning throughout life as greater and greater consolidation within communities of interest, finding self-fulfilment in the welfare of the group.

Most adult learners engage in our programmes as part of their ongoing life-related learning activities. This means that the way we conduct our adult learning should contribute towards the goal of their learning, whether that be self-fulfilment, social commitment or occupational advancement. Our aim is to enable the learners to achieve *their own* goals. For some, this will be to enhance their own adulthood, to maximise the range of choices before them, to increase their control over aspects of their own lives, environment and their own learning. For others, it will be to improve their occupational prospects or to fulfil their social goals.

Teaching for freedom

It has been argued in this book that the most effective means of helping adults to learn is to understand and then build our teaching-learning programmes upon these natural lifelong learning episodes, their formats and their processes. The taught learning opportunities we create for the student-learners should *utilise* these more structured natural learning episodes rather than contradict them: make them more conscious, enhance their processes, make them more efficient.

Such an approach will give us not only the goals of our teaching of adults but also our subject matter and our methods. Both the selection of the content of our programmes and the methods we use should foster the adulthood of the learners, however that is constructed. Thus, in Western societies which value an autonomous understanding of adulthood, our work with adult learners will seek to assist the full development of the learners as individuals, foster the growth of wider and more balanced perspectives and provide opportunities for the exercise of autonomy. All such education needs to contribute to continued learning and strengthen the independent learning habits of the participants.

This means breaking the traditional dependency lying beneath so much current education: 'To build a safe atmosphere where people can trust one another across divisive social differences, we must begin to name the inequalities in the classroom and devise ground rules for communication' (Campbell and Burnaby 2001: 3). Anything we do that leads to the student-learners becoming dependent upon ourselves or others as teachers will be denying their adulthood. We teachers must work to make ourselves redundant in the process of creating self-directed, self-managing and discriminating learners. This can be achieved only through active learning methods in our adult learning groups.

The dangers of directive participation

There is however a dilemma here – what if our student participants do not wish to join in the activities we have so carefully planned for them? Many adult learning programmes have failed because the teachers have employed what can be called 'directive participation': marching to another's drum. They tell the students that they *will* engage in this or that active learning process when the student participants do not wish to join in ice-breakers or role plays or simulation games. What if they do not wish to exercise responsibility for their own learning?

We have noted above a view which suggests that there are two main modes of learning: acquisition and formalised learning (see pp. 125–30). The participatory approach to teaching-learning is more closely akin to the acquisition mode in which the self-directed learner chooses to engage directly in learning through self-selected activities, games and exploration. But many adults do not expect their taught learning to be like this. They expect and indeed wish for it to be more formal (see p. 139), for the teacher to 'teach' and for themselves to be more or less passive recipients of wisdom. To employ participatory approaches when the students want formality; to employ discussion when the students feel they need guidance from an expert leading to a page of notes; to try to share power when the students want hierarchy; to ask the students to tell the teacher when the students want the teacher to tell them – all of these would be to court disaster.

For some student participants, then, participation in almost any sense can be seen as a threat. As a tutor has written:

Some of my learners come from such chaotic backgrounds and families that they actually welcome and thrive in a structured, formal learning environment . . . I'm finding that the majority of my students don't function well in [a participatory] environment . . . many need more structure and expectations from me in order to feel 'committed' and to persevere . . . I'm beginning to feel that I need to model and help them practice the skills of meeting expectations, showing perseverance, facing problems and finding (not always pleasant) solutions etc. Perhaps some people who come from abusive or controlling situations need lessons on *how* to develop these autonomous skills. I no longer think I can just expect those skills and attitudes to spring forth when I provide a safe environment.

(Personal communication)

I believe that it is important that we 'start where the students are' and not expect them to join us on our own starting line. It is important that we help the students to learn in whatever way they wish, even if that is formal and we wish to be nonformal. Experience suggests in any case that after some time during which they have been treated not as peers but as pupils and more or less ignorant learners, they will themselves begin to challenge, to ask questions, to indicate points at which the things they are learning do not correspond with their own experience. Most adults test what they are learning against their own accumulated experience, they assess whether 'it rings true'. When they begin to feel that it does not is the moment when they start to become critically reflective of the learning programme, when they begin to engage actively rather than passively with the learning process. Teaching adults is not always a matter which can be rushed; it will often take a lot of time.

Sharing, not serving

Does this mean that the teacher of adults is simply a facilitator of someone else's learning? I want to suggest that, if we reject 'the arrogance of the learned', the 'deficit and input' model of learning, we must equally avoid the opposite extreme, what may be called the 'pooling of ignorance', the rejection of the help of any teacher, the refusal to admit that the experience of the qualified teacher has worth. Some new insights, some introduction to the processes of finding out, some available new experience for the learners to search and select is necessary to achieve effective learning programmes. Just as adult students have much to bring to the teaching-learning programme, so too adult teachers have valuable experience, insights, knowledge and skills; just as the teacher needs to take the student seriously, so too the students need to take the agendas and experience of the teacher seriously.

Any process of teaching adults that introduces divisions and despises the views and activities of others is unacceptable. Teachers must not only be able to admit that they have much to learn from their students, they must seek to strengthen rather than weaken the different elements brought into the learning situation by all the participants. It is a process of sharing, of valuing each other, of increasing diversity, of 'celebrating the other'.

Participation as increasing control over the process

The ownership of the learning programme

Participation as involvement in does not imply any real control over the processes used. But adult learners are more likely to learn effectively if they have become involved in the creation of the teaching-learning programme; if they feel that (in part at least) they 'own' it: 'Learning will be enhanced as control over and responsibility for learning is concentrated in the hands of the learners, or at least shared between learners and resource people' (Campbell and Burnaby 2001: 318). They need to participate in determining what they should be able to do and what they should know about:

> It is now coming to be widely accepted that the best and most secure learning occurs when students are centrally involved in controlling, directing and monitoring their own learning progress, in ways and according to particular modes of proceeding that they select for themselves, in accordance with their own characteristic mode of cognitive operation and their awareness of how best to proceed in mastering new concepts, information and skills.
>
> (Aspin *et al.* 2001: 21)

As Albert Mansbridge put it long ago (1920): 'The initiative must lie with the students. They must say how, why, what or when they wish to study'.

Adult student-learners can join in the planning of the learning programme, helping to determine the stages of learning, the steps by which the skills and knowledge are developed – areas that most teachers guard carefully to themselves. They can contribute to setting the goals, for they have their own intentions in joining our learning groups, and it is best, if we wish to encourage autonomy and independence, to start from these intentions rather than to impose our own. Student-learners can help in constructing the learning schedule, the methods/content part of the learning programme, the sequence of events and activities, for they all have their own skills of learning. They can also share in the process of evaluation; they will often watch more closely than the teacher what is happening in the group. Adult learners *can* contribute to all parts of the teaching-learning process.

Activity

In the learning programme you have chosen as a case study (p. 8), what parts of the decision-making process have the student-learners participated in?

Learning for freedom

All this implies that education, especially the education of adults, consists of 'two-way learning'. Teaching seen as 'informing' will be one-way and dependency-creating; it will not be liberating education. Clearly some information-gathering is necessary as part of the learning process, but the new knowledge does not need to be provided by the teacher alone. Compared with 'informing', training in the skills of locating and mastering knowledge for themselves can make the learners free to exercise their newly-won learning as and when they wish. But training on its own can also be binding, especially when it sets out to demonstrate the 'right' way to do something without considering that there are likely to be circumstances in which the 'right' way might well be wrong! It is not enough to teach people how to do something or other without encouraging them to consider the social and political factors involved in this activity and the structures of society that control access to these resources. Only by undertaking this wider task of helping the students to consider critically the power implications of what they are studying will the participants be able to grow towards a freer way of life.

How do we do this? It is easier said than done. We can talk about 'teaching on equal terms', and we can see how it applies in some contexts. Social action groups that choose their own leader, women's studies circles and community development programmes will be able to operate on such a basis more easily than will dressmaking, advanced engineering courses or computing classes (although management training programmes have followed this route for a long time). But even in these contexts it is not always plain sailing, for 'voices are never equal, even in a democracy', and participation can 'increase the learners' sense of powerlessness because they do not speak the language of the educators' (Campbell and Burnaby 2001: 223, 229).

New relationships

We each need to explore these attitudes and the changed relationships between learner, teacher and subject matter for ourselves. Perhaps the key, when we have come to put the student-learner first rather than the teacher, is the need to listen more and to talk less. This book is, as we saw early on, not a good example of what I mean. It is by nature one-way, though I have tried to encourage you to use your experience on the material it contains and to test the views it expresses for yourself. Throughout, I have sought to promote the development of a listening society rather than the talking (or even shouting) society in which so many of us live. The maintenance of pluralism rather than uniformity, the valuing of the experience, knowledge and insights of others, and the search to strengthen these rather than weaken them, are, it seems to me, basic to all approaches to teaching adults, if we truly respect their adulthood. Participatory education 'will act as a catalyst to begin addressing the power dynamics outside of the educational environment' as well as within it (Campbell and Burnaby 2001: 3).

Such insights have led providers and teachers of adults to experiment with different forms of learning groups for adults. Some of these are very exciting – experiential learning programmes, confidence-building, self-exploration, self-programming groups such as those with unemployed workers, immigrant women, local community groups, shelter residents, parents' groups and young men who have been prevented from benefiting from traditional education (see e.g. *Adults Learning* 2001). Many other types of participants, such as weight-watchers, Alcoholics Anonymous, group therapy and self-awareness programmes, writing circles, social action groups (especially local community and residents' groups engaged in self-directed conservation and environmental enhancement activities), and quality circles have emerged from such concerns. The variety of groups is great and the range of activities wide. Even in more traditional programmes, whether based in the community or in an educational institution, where the presence of a recognised teacher figure is accepted, experiments with different forms of learner involvement in all the stages of constructing the activities have been conducted. Deciding what shall be learned, how it will be studied and what shall be done with the learning changes at the end of the programme are all matters for the group and not for the teacher alone.

The learners and knowledge

But it can go further than this. Adult learners can create knowledge. This truth has come to be recognised in some forms of teaching adults that have sprung up: self-learning groups, community action, research study groups and project study groups which publish their findings (A. Rogers 1977, 1995; Thornton and Stephens 1977). The archaeology group that under supervision explores an area and excavates new sites; the natural history members who record the flora and fauna or survey the geology of a region; the residents' group that investigates the schooling, housing or development needs of its own community; the village community that conducts its own needs survey; the literature course that engages in creative writing – all of these create knowledge. Many of them seek to give that new knowledge back to the community from whence it came, through exhibitions, publications, radio programmes, videos and films, websites and other media. In the process, new insights into the varied kinds of knowing have been produced and a new relationship between learner and knowledge has come about (Unwin 1994).

It is important for us as teachers of adults to appreciate this. Knowledge is not the preserve of the few, the educated, to be doled out in small parcels to our student participants so that they in their turn can become 'experts'. It is something all of us can share in creating and discovering, and disseminate to others; something which we will all view from our own particular perspective.

The teacher and knowledge

This calls for a radical change in the role of the teacher. Teachers and organisers nearly always do too much for their students; they work too much on their own. They exclude (often without realising it) the student-learners from many parts of the task. It is the teacher and/or the provider who determines the length of the learning programme, the subject and the content matter. It is the teacher who selects the goals, the pace of learning, the level of the learning programme. It is the teacher who chooses the materials, the methods and who evaluates the results.

All of this is done naturally, for it springs from a deep-rooted set of attitudes towards the learners. Some of us tend to see the learners as deprived of skills and knowledge, in which case those who possess the ability and the knowledge should give it; the learners need 'input'. Some of us also tend to believe that the student-learners are not capable of taking control of their own learning, that they cannot act on their own; they need to learn first before they can participate. There is a sense of the superiority of the teacher arising from the traditional world of education, a world that sees being 'learned' as the desired goal of all education, a state of attainment that the student-learner might, by great effort, ultimately reach. There is often in this attitude a view of education as a one-way process, the transfer of knowledge and expertise, the imparting of some good. Education (teaching) has become separated from life, from the kind of learning we use in our own natural learning episodes. Formalised learning has become separated from acquisition learning.

A reappraisal of the roles of both teacher and learners will affect all parts of the teaching-learning encounter. If the teacher abandons the attitude of 'I know and I'll tell you' and instead says 'I'll help you to work it out', the whole curriculum will change. If the teacher abandons the attitude of 'I'll communicate with you' and instead says 'I'll help you to engage in a series of learning activities', the whole body of teaching methods will change.

Such a reorientation of the relationships between teacher, student-learner and subject matter will seek to cast aside attitudes based on 'the arrogance of the learned'. There will be no more room for saying 'I know what you should learn'. We will move away from a view of education based on a hierarchy of knowledge: there will be no more placing of theoretical knowledge higher than practical or experiential knowledge. Such attitudes demean experience and lay unhealthy stress on accumulated practice or book knowledge. A view of teaching based on acquisition learning as well as on formalised learning will give value to all views (not just those of the academic), will see the application as well as the general principle, and will admit on occasion that 'I don't know' or 'I don't see it like that'.

Participation as presence in teaching-learning programmes

Those outside and those inside?

Perhaps this leads to the view that teaching adults is not a process of instructing others but of enabling them to get a voice; not a process of bringing them 'into society' (our society) from a position of exclusion through our learning programmes but of helping them to play a fuller and more equal part in the society of which they are already full members. We hear much today of 'social inclusion', especially in educational matters – a concept which is frequently used without deconstructing it to see precisely what it means and what attitudes it reveals (or hides). For example, in a country where those who are functionally non-literate form nearly 70 per cent of the total population, a view of literacy that speaks of 'bringing the illiterates into society' treats the majority as inferior and will hardly lead to active learning. The same goes for other social and cultural contexts where those who have been defined by the dominant groups as 'excluded' may not be majorities but minorities.

For, the so-called excluded are already part of our society, and it can be argued that our task is to help them to lead a fuller life of their own, not necessarily to join *our* life pattern. It may well be to encourage and enable them to share in the work of controlling what is already their society. As we have seen (p. 3), much adult education is aimed at helping some to escape from the slums rather than helping those who live in the slums to change the slums.

If we see our work as part of this process, if we seek to share with equals rather than to instruct our inferiors or to persuade the excluded to become included into a core which they did not help to create, to help those who live in the slum to change the slum and improve their way of life in their own way, then we will be concerned about those who are *not* in our learning groups as much as with those who are. If we teach gardening, it will concern us that there are some who have gardens who apparently do not wish to learn more about this aspect of life; it will also be important to us to consider why some people have no gardens at all. If we teach health studies, we shall be concerned that those who are not in reach of our programmes have opportunities for their needs to be met as well. If we teach adults in university degree courses, we will have some concern for those who wish to participate but are prevented from participating in such programmes.

The teacher and the outside world

The question of participation is not just a matter of what the student-learners in our classes and learning groups do in the process of learning. It is not just a matter of persuading the students to share in the planning and evaluation of the programme. It is also about encouraging others to take advantage of the learning opportunities on offer. This will lead us to experiment with new formats of learning groups, with new timings, with new approaches to the subject matter that will be more appropriate to different groups of learners, with restructuring our contents and methods to try to overcome the barriers that still exist in all societies.

There are two parts to this. On the one hand there is the provision of programmes to meet the needs of existing and new participants. In the course of this, we will become more aware of the barriers we ourselves put up to full participation – not only to those not in our learning groups but also to those who are – and seek to reduce them. We can play our part in increasing provision, creating new learning opportunities to meet the needs of those who do not attend. (Archbishop William Temple is reputed to have said that the Christian Church is an organisation that exists for the sake of those who are *not* its members; teachers of adults will often share much of the same concern.)

On the other hand, increased provision does not always lead to greatly increased participation. The barriers of attitudes (the 'it's-not-for-me' syndrome) remain among many potential participants. And formal education remains the bastion of privilege:

> A participatory model [of learning] is welcome in few workplace settings. Practitioners are often only able to weave it in, intermittently, with more traditional approaches. But this is true outside of workplace education as well, even though the language of 'empowerment' and 'student directedness' is everywhere. Adult education is generally oriented to preparing people to uncritically participate in current work, school, and political systems. Many argue this is what adults say they want. Participatory education will continue to ask deeper questions to find out if this is *all* they want.
>
> (Campbell and Burnaby 2001: 194)

It is up to us as privileged people who are also teachers to address ourselves to the problem of working to overcome any sense of exclusion that we have created in many of our fellow human beings. Then we shall be truly concerned for participation.

The invisible teacher of adults

Participation in our dealings with our adult student-learners will involve us in working with them to adopt an appropriate range of teaching-learning activities – not just the ones *we* feel they should do to be active, but the ones which fit *their* own perception of what it means to be a student.

Participation will also mean working with our student-learners, sharing all our hopes and plans with them just as they share their hopes and plans with us. In addition, it will mean not just concern about those who are not in our programmes but taking what steps we can to ensure that the doors are at least open.

It is unlikely that we shall be hymned for all this. For if we really help our student participants to become more conscious and more effective learners on their own, we shall have made ourselves redundant. Hanging on the wall of a small hut in one of the crowded suburbs of Madras, the offices of the Committee for Development Research and Action, are the following verses which have been attributed to many different persons, which say it all:

> Go to the people
> Live among them
> Learn from them
> Love them
> Start with what they know
> Build on what they have
>
> But of the best leaders [read: teachers]
> When their task is accomplished
> Their work is done
> The people all remark
> 'We have done it ourselves'.

Further reading

Campbell, P. and Burnaby, B. (2001) *Participatory Practices in Adult Education.* London: Erlbaum.
Imel Susan (1999) *How Emancipatory is Adult Learning? Myths and Realities.* Columbus, OH: ERIC.

Lovett, T. (1982) *Adult Education, Community Development and the Working Class.* Nottingham: University of Nottingham.

Rogers, J. (1976) *Right to Learn: The Case for Adult Equality.* London: Arrow.

Thompson, J.L. (ed.) (1980) *Adult Education for a Change.* London: Hutchinson.

Unwin, P. (1994) *Group Research Projects in Adult Education.* Sheffield: University of Sheffield.

Walters, S. (1996) *Gender in Popular Education.* London: Zed.

CONCLUSION: THE LEARNING AND TEACHING OF ADULTS

This book about teaching adults is concerned with two main themes. First, all of us, both teachers of adults and our student participants, construct ourselves and our learning programmes. We construct:

- the role of being an adult;
- education (formalised learning);
- the role of being a 'student-learner' and the role of being a 'teacher';
- the contract to learn between the teacher and the student participants.

These constructs are built on our diverse prior experience and on our socio-cultural context. Over the years, we and they have learned (mostly subconsciously but sometimes more formally) how to be an adult, a student and a teacher of adults. We do not always agree on what these roles should be, but in every case we construct such roles for ourselves and for others.

Secondly, there are different kinds of learning. Apart from incidental learning, we have seen two main kinds: the natural learning process which (like breathing) all persons engage in all the time, which we have called 'acquisition learning'; and the more planned and purposeful formalised learning. Acquisition learning is not just for very young children but continues throughout life, mainly in the fields of acculturation. It is largely subconscious, or rather is 'task-conscious' – the learning takes place within and relates to some lifeworld task. It is highly contextualised, limited to the specific task of which it forms a part. Formalised learning on the other hand is conscious learning. It includes decontextualised generalisations, basic principles which enable knowledge to be used in more than one context. The task here is learning for some future activity rather than for a more immediate one.

Acquisition learning takes place within and is derived from our immediate sociocultural context. It helps us to become inducted into a particular culture or set of practices. Although critical reflection is a normal part of acquisition learning, on its own it will not normally help the learner to become critically reflective. Only if the learner is engaged with a community of practice of critical reflectors will acquisition learning help them to become critically reflective on experience. This is the key role of formalised learning – to help the adult learner to move beyond the limits of acquisition learning.

This book suggests that when we help adults to learn, we will be most effective if we can bring together both acquisition learning and formalised learning, for they both have much to offer. This will mean:

- making acquisition learning (which is largely subconscious or at least conscious of the task rather than the learning) more learning-conscious and critically reflective;
- making formalised learning (which is largely decontextualised, based on general rules and theories) more contextualised, more task-conscious.

The aim of teaching adults is to do both – to explore consciously how general rules can be applied to particular situations (and indeed, how they may have to be broken by specific contexts). Teaching adults in this way is to engage in a dialectic of contextualised and decontextualised learning. Neither is more important than the other; they need to be brought together.

Teaching adults, then, is helping our student participants to become more conscious of how they learn, of what they know and do not know, what they can do and what they cannot do. This book itself is part of that process. We will have learned much about teaching adults subconsciously through acquisition learning. The aim of this book is to help the user to make their own learning about teaching adults more conscious; to help you to reflect critically on your perceptions of yourself as adult and as teacher, on your roles and practices. It seeks to explore generalities but at the same time to help you to relate these generalities to your own specific situations.

This book is not the end of the process. For some, it may be only a beginning. The real learning starts when we act, when we practise and reflect critically on that practice; when we become conscious of how much you and I have learned about teaching through acquisition processes, and plan to make that learning more conscious by using it in real situations and reflecting critically on that use. That is the task before us now.

BIBLIOGRAPHY

ACACE (1979) *Towards Continuing Education.* Leicester: ACACE.

Ackoff, R.L. (1978) *The Art of Problem-Solving.* New York: Wiley.

Adelman, C. and Alexander, R. (1983) Evaluation, validation and accountability, in O. Boyd-Barrett *et al.* (1983) *Approaches to Post-School Management.* London: Harper & Row.

Adults Learning (2001) 13(1). Leicester: NIACE.

Alexander, C. and Langer, E. (eds) (1990) *Higher Stages of Human Development: Perspectives on Human Growth.* Oxford: Oxford University Press.

Alexander, Sir William (1975) *Adult Education and the Challenge of Change.* Edinburgh: Scottish Education Department.

Andrews, G.J. (ed.) (1991) *Practical Handbook for Assessing Learning Outcomes in Continuing Education and Training.* Washington, DC: International Association for Continuing Education and Training (IACET).

Apps, J.W. (1985) *Improving Practice in Continuing Education.* San Francisco: Jossey Bass.

Aspin, D., Chapman, J., Hatton, M. and Sawano, Y. (eds) (2001) *International Handbook of Lifelong Learning.* London: Kluwer.

Ball, C. (1991) *Learning Pays: the Role of Post-compulsory Education and Training.* London: Royal Society of Arts.

Banbury, J. and Carter, G. (1982) *Teaching Groups: a Basic Education Handbook.* London: Adult Literacy and Basic Skills Unit.

Barr, J. (1999) *Liberating Knowledge: Research, Feminism and Adult Education.* Leicester: NIACE.

Barron, R.S., Kerr, N.L. and Miller, N. (1992) *Group Process, Group Decision, Group Action.* Buckingham: Open University Press.

Belbin, R.M. (1980) *The Discovery Method in Training.* Sheffield: Manpower Services Commission.

Belenky, M., Clinchy, B.M., Goldberger, N.R. and Tarule, J.M. (1986) *Women's Ways of Knowing: The Development of Self, Voice and Mind.* New York: Basic Books.

Berne, E. (1970) *Games People Play.* Harmondsworth: Penguin.

Birren, J.E. and Schaie, K.W. (eds) (1990) *Handbook of the Psychology of Aging,* 3rd edn. San Diego, CA: Academic Press.

Bligh, D.R. (1972) *What's the Use of Lectures?* Harmondsworth: Penguin.

Bloom, B.S. (1965) *Taxonomy of Educational Objectives*. London: Longman.

Blumberg, A. and Gloembiewski, R.T. (1976) *Learning and Change in Groups*. Harmondsworth: Penguin.

Boshier, R. (1989) Participant motivation, in C. Titmus (ed.) *Lifelong Education for Adults: An International Handbook*. Oxford: Pergamon.

Boud, D. and Miller, N. (1996) *Working with Experience: Animating Learning*. London: Routledge.

Boud, D., Keogh, R. and Walker, D. (eds) (1985) *Reflection: Turning Experience into Learning*. London: Kogan Page.

Brookfield, S. (1983) *Adult Learners, Adult Education and the Community*. Milton Keynes: Open University Press.

Brookfield, S.D. (ed.) (1985) *Self-Directed Learning: From Theory to Practice*. San Francisco: Jossey Bass.

Brookfield, S.D. (1986) *Understanding and Facilitating Adult Learning*. Milton Keynes: Open University Press.

Brookfield, S.D. (2000) Adult cognition as a dimension of lifelong learning, in J. Field and M. Leicester, (eds) *Lifelong Learning: Education Across the Lifespan*, pp. 89–101. London: Taylor & Francis.

Brundage, D. and Mackeracher, D. (1980) *Adult Learning Principles and their Application to Program Planning*. Toronto: OISE.

Bruner, J.S. (1966) *Toward a Theory of Instruction*. Cambridge, MA: Harvard University Press.

Bruner, J.S. (1983) *In Search of Mind: Essays in Autobiography*. New York: Harper & Row.

Cairns, T. (2001) Acquiring basic skills as part of everyday life, *Adults Learning*, 13(3): 20–2.

Campbell, P. and Burnaby, B. (2001) *Participatory Practices in Adult Education*. London: Erlbaum.

Carr, W. and Kemmis, S. (1983) *Becoming Critical: Education, Knowledge and Action Research*. Victoria, Australia: Deakin University.

Cattell, R.B. (1987) *Intelligence: Its Structure, Growth and Action*. Amsterdam: North-Holland.

Cenoz, J. and Genesee, F. (eds) (1998) *Beyond Bilingualism: Multilingualism and Multilingual Education*. Clevedon: Multilingual Matters.

Charnley, A.H. and Jones, H.A. (1979) *Concept of Success in Adult Literacy*. Cambridge: Huntington.

Chickering, A.W. (ed.) (1981) *The Modern American College: Responding to the New Realities of Diverse Students and a Changing Society*. San Francisco: Jossey Bass.

Christensen, R. and Hansen, A.T. (eds) (1987) *Teaching and the Case Method*. Boston, MA: Harvard Business School.

Claxton, G. (1984) *Live and Learn*. London: Harper & Row.

Coben, D. (1998) *Radical Heroes: Gramsci, Freire and the Politics of Adult Education*. New York: Garland.

Code, L. (1991) *What Can She Know? Feminist Theory and the Construction of Knowledge*. Ithaca, NY: Cornell University Press.

Coffield, F. (ed.) (2000) *The Necessity of Informal Learning*. Bristol: Policy Press.

Cranton, P. (1994) *Understanding and Promoting Transformative Learning*. San Francisco: Jossey Bass.

Cross, K.P. (1981) *Adults as Learners: Increasing Participation and Facilitating Learning*. San Francisco: Jossey Bass.

Daines J., Daines, C. and Graham, B. (1993) *Adult Learning, Adult Teaching*, 3rd edn. Nottingham: Department of Adult Education, University of Nottingham.

Davies, I.K. (1971) *The Management of Learning*. London: McGraw-Hill.

Davies, I.K. (1976) *Objectives in Curriculum Design*. London: McGraw-Hill.

Davies, P. (ed.) (1995) *Adults in Higher Education: International Perspectives in Access and Participation*. London: Jessica Kingsley.

Department of Education, Ireland (1984) *Lifelong Learning: Report of the Adult Education Commission for the Republic of Ireland*. Dublin: Department of Education.

Dewey, J. (1933) *How We Think*. London: D.C. Heath.

Dewey, J. (1938) *Experience and Education*. New York: Macmillan.

Douglas, T. (1983) *Groups: Understanding People Gathered Together*. London: Tavistock.

Dudley, E. (1993) *The Critical Villager*. London: Routledge.

Easton, P. (1996) *Sharpening the Tools: Improving Evaluation in Adult and Nonformal Education*. Hamburg: UNESCO Institute of Education.

Edwards, R., Sieminski, S. and Zeldin, D. (eds) (1993) *Adult Learners, Education and Training*. London: Routledge.

Edwards, R., Hanson, A. and Raggatt, P. (eds) (1996) *Boundaries of Adult Learning*. London: Routledge.

Egan, G. (1973) *Face to Face: the Small Group Experience and Interpersonal Growth*. Montercy, CA: Brooks/Cole.

Egan, K. (1986) *Individual Development and the Curriculum*. London: Hutchinson.

Eisner, E.W. (1985) *The Art of Educational Evaluation*. London: Falmer.

Elsdon, K. (1975) *Training for Adult Education*. Nottingham: University of Nottingham.

Eraut, M. (2000) Non-formal learning, implicit learning and tacit knowledge in professional work, in F. Coffield (ed.) *The Necessity of Informal Learning*. Bristol: Policy Press.

Erikson, E. (1965) *Childhood and Society*. Harmondsworth: Penguin.

Fenwick, T.J. (2001) *Experiential Learning: A Theoretical Critique*. Columbus, OH: ERIC.

Field, J. and Leicester, M. (eds) (2000) *Lifelong Learning: Education Across the Lifespan*. London: Taylor & Francis.

Fieldhouse, R. (1996) *A History of Modern British Adult Education*. Leicester: NIACE.

Flanders, N.A. (1970) *Analyzing Teaching Behavior*. Reading, MA: Addison-Wesley.

Foley, G. (1999) *Learning in Social Action*. London: Zed.

Freire, P. (1972) *Pedagogy of the Oppressed*. Harmondsworth: Penguin.

Gagné, R.M. (1972) Domains of Learning, *Interchange*, 3(1): 1–8.

Gagné, R.M. (1975) *The Conditions of Learning*. New York: Holt, Rinehart & Winston.

Galbraith, M.W. (ed.) (1991) *Adult Learning Methods: A Guide for Effective Instruction*. Malabar, FA: Krieger.

Gardner, H. (1993) *Multiple Intelligences: The Theory in Practice*. New York: Basic Books.

Gibbs, G., Morgan, A. and Taylor, E. (1982) Why students don't learn, *Institutional Research Review*, 1(10).

Giles, K. (1981) *Personal Change in Adults*. Milton Keynes: Open University Press.

Giroux, H.A. (1983) *Theory and Resistance in Education: A Pedagogy for the Oppressed*. South Hadley, MA: Bergin & Garvey.

Griffin, C. (1987) *Adult Education as Social Policy*. London: Croom Helm.

Griffin, C. (1983) *Curriculum Theory in Adult and Continuing Education*. Beckenham: Croom Helm.

Gross, R.D. (1987) *Psychology: The Science of Mind and Behaviour*. London: Hodder & Stoughton.

Guba, E. and Lincoln, E.S. (1981) *Effective Evaluation*. San Francisco: Jossey Bass.

Habermas, J. (1978) *Knowledge and Human Interest*. London: Heinemann.

Hanson, A. (1996) The search for a separate theory of adult learning: does anyone really need andragogy? in R. Edwards, A. Hanson and P. Raggatt (eds) *Boundaries of Adult Learning*. London: Routledge.

Hare, A.P. (1976) *Handbook of Small Group Research*. Glencoe, NY: The Free Press.

Havighurst, R.J. (1952) *Development Tasks and Education*. New York: McKay.

Held, D. (1980) *Introduction to Critical Theory: From Horkheimer to Habermas*. Berkeley, CA: University of California Press.

Henriques, J. (1984) *Changing the Subject: Psychology, Social Regulation and Subjectivity*. London: Methuen.

Herzberg, F. (1972) *The Motivation to Work*. Chichester: Wiley.

Honey, P. and Mumford, A. (1992) *Manual of Learning Styles*, revised edn. London: Peter Honey.

Houle, C.O. (1961) *The Inquiring Mind: a Study of the Adult who Continues to Learn*. Madison, WI: University of Wisconsin Press.

Hudson, F. (1991) *The Adult Years*. San Francisco: Jossey Bass.

Hughes, J.A. and Graham, S.W. (1990) Adult life roles: a new approach to adult development, *Journal of Continuing Higher Education*, 38(2): 2–8.

Imel Susan (ed.) (1996) *Learning in Groups: Exploring Fundamental Principles, New Uses and Emerging Opportunities*. San Francisco: Jossey Bass.

Imel Susan (1998) *Teaching Critical Reflection: Trends and Issues Alert*. Columbus, OH: ERIC.

Imel Susan (1999) *How Emancipatory is Adult Learning? Myths and Realities*. Columbus, OH: ERIC.

ISCED (1975) *International Standard Classification of Educational Data*. Paris: UNESCO.

Jacques, D. (1991) *Learning in Groups*, 2nd edn. London: Kogan Page.

Jarvis, P. (1987) *Adult Learning in a Social Context*. London: Croom Helm.

Jarvis, P. (1995) *Adult and Continuing Education: Theory and Practice*. London: Routledge.

Jarvis, P. (ed.) (2001a) *The Age of Learning*. London: Kogan Page.

Jarvis, P. (2001b) *Learning in the Third Age*. London: Kogan Page.

Jarvis, P., Holford, J. and Griffin, C. (1998) *Theory and Practice of Learning*. London: Kogan Page.

Johnstone, J.W.C. and Rivera, R.J. (1965) *Volunteers for Learning: A Study of the Educational Pursuits of Adults*. Hawthorne, NY: Aldine Press.

Kelly, G.A. (1955) *Psychology of Personal Constructs*, vols 1 & 2. New York: McGraw-Hill.

Kidd, J.R. (1973) *How Adults Learn*. New York: Association Press.

King, P.M. and Kitchener, K.S. (1994) *Developing Reflective Judgment*. San Francisco: Jossey Bass.

Knowles, M. and Knowles, H. (1972) *Introduction to Group Dynamics*. New York: Association Press.

Knowles, M.S. (1980) *The Modern Practice of Adult Education: From Pedagogy to Andragogy*. New York: Association Press.

Knowles, M.S. (1990) *The Adult Learner: a Neglected Species*. Houston, TX: Gulf.

Knox, A.B. (1977) *Adult Development and Learning*. San Francisco: Jossey Bass.

Kolb, D.A. (1976) *Learning Style Inventory Technical Manual*. Boston, MA: McBer.

Kolb, D.A. (1984) *Experiential Learning: Experience as the Source of Learning and Development*. Englewood Cliffs, NJ: Prentice-Hall.

Krashen, S. (1982) *Principles and Practice of Second Language Acquisition*. Oxford: Pergamon.

Laing, R.D. (1972) *Knots*. Harmondsworth: Penguin.

Lave, J. and Wenger, E. (1991) *Situated Learning: Legitimate Peripheral Participation*. Cambridge: Cambridge University Press.

Leagans, P. (1971) *Behavioral Change in Agriculture*. Ithaca, NY: Cornell University Press.

LEIF (1990) Erno Lehtinen: from superficial learning to true expertise – education challenge of the future, *Life and Education in Finland*, 2(90): 14.

Lewin, K. (1935) *A Dynamic Theory of Personality*. New York: McGraw-Hill.

Lewin, K. (1947) Frontiers in group dynamics: concept, method and reality in social science, *Human Relations*, 1(2): 5–41.

Lovell, R.B. (1980) *Adult Learning*. London: Croom Helm.

Lovett, T. (1982) *Adult Education, Community Development and the Working Class*. Nottingham: University of Nottingham.

Lucas, A.M. (1983) Scientific literacy and informal learning, *Studies in Science Education*, 10: 7–36.

McClelland, D.C., Atkinson, J.W., Clark, R.A. and Lovell, E.L. (1953) *The Achievement Motive*. New York: Appleton-Century-Crofts.

McClintock, C.G. (1972) *Experimental Social Psychology*. New York: Holt, Rinehart & Winston.

McGregor, D. (1960) *The Human Side of Enterprise*. New York: McGraw-Hill.

Mager, R. (1991) *Preparing Instructional Objectives*, 2nd edn. London: Kogan Page.

Mansbridge, A. (1920) *Adventure in Working Class Education*. London: Longmans Green.

Maslow, A.H. (1968) *Towards a Psychology of Being*. New York: Van Nostrand.

Mayo, M. (1997) *Imagining Tomorrow: Adult Education for Transformation*. Leicester: NIACE.

Merriam, S. and Cafarella, R. (1999) *Learning in Adulthood*. San Francisco: Jossey Bass.

Mezirow et al. (2000) *Learning as Transformation*. San Francisco: Jossey Bass.

Mezirow, J. (1981) A critical theory of adult learning and education, *Adult Education*, 32: 3–24.

Neugarten, B.L. (1977) Personality and aging, in J.E. Birren and K.W. Schaie (eds) *Handbook of the Psychology of Aging*. New York: Van Nostrand Reinhold.

NIACE (National Institute of Adult (Continuing) Education) (1970) *Survey of Provision*. Leicester: NIACE.

NICCE (Northern Ireland Council for Continuing Education) (1980) *Continuing Education in Northern Ireland: Strategy for Development*. Belfast: NICCE.

OECD (Organization for Economic Cooperation and Development) (1977) *Learning Opportunities for Adults*. Paris: OECD.

Ostervan, K. and Kottkamp, R. (1993) *Reflective Practice for Educators*. London: Sage.

Paterson, K.W. (1979) *Values, Education and the Adult*. London: Routledge.

Paulston, R.G. (1996) *Social Cartography: Mapping Ways of Seeing Social and Educational Change*. London: Garland.

Pratt, D.D. (1991) Conceptions of the self in China and the US: contrasting foundations for adult development, *International Journal of Intercultural Relations*, 15(3): 285–310.

Rahman, Md. A. (1993) *People's Self-Development: Perspectives on Participatory Action Research*. London: Zed.

Ramsden, P. (1992) *Learning to Teach in Higher Education*. London: Routledge.

Reid, C. (1969) *Groups Alive – Church Alive: The Effective Use of Small Groups in the Local Church*. New York: Harper & Row.

Resnick, L. (1987) Learning in school and out, *Educational Researcher*, 16(9): 13–20.

Rogers, A. (ed.) (1977) *The Spirit and the Form: Essays by and in Honour of Harold Wiltshire*. Nottingham: University of Nottingham.

Rogers, A. (1980) *Knowledge and the People: the Role of the University in Adult and Continuing Education*. Londonderry: New University of Ulster.

Rogers, A. (1991a) *Teaching Adults in Extension*. Reading: Education for Development.

Rogers, A. (1991b) *Teaching Methods in Extension*. Reading: Education for Development.

Rogers, A. (1992) *Adults Learning for Development*. London: Cassell.

Rogers, A. (1993) Adult learning maps and the teaching process, *Studies in the Education of Adults*, 22(2): 199–220.

Rogers, A. (1995) Participatory research in local history, *Journal of Regional and Local Studies*, 15(1): 1–14.

Rogers, A. (1997) Learning: can we change the discourse?, *Adult Learning*, 8(5): 116–17.

Rogers, A. (forthcoming) *Nonformal Education: Flexible Schooling or Participatory Education*.

Rogers, C.R. (1974) *On Becoming a Person*. London: Constable.

Rogers, C.R. (1983) *Freedom to Learn for the 80s*. Columbus, OH: Merrill.

Rogers, J. (1969) *Teaching on Equal Terms*. London: BBC Publications.

Rogers, J. (1976) *Right to Learn: The Case for Adult Equality*. London: Arrow.

Rogers, J. (1977) *Adults Learning*. Milton Keynes: Open University Press.

Rogers, J. (1984) *Adults in Education*. London: BBC Publications.

Rogers, J. (1989) *Adults Learning*, 2nd edn. Buckingham: Open University Press.

Rogers, J. (2001) *Adults Learning*, 4th edn. Buckingham: Open University Press.

Rotter, J.B. (1982) *The Development and Applications of Social Learning Theory*. New York: Praeger.

Rowntree, D. (1987) *Assessing Students*. London: Kogan Page.

Ruddock, R. (1981) *Evaluation: A Consideration of Principles and Methods*. Manchester: Manchester University Press.

Rundle, S. and Dunn, R. (1999) *The Building Excellence Adult Learning Style Inventory*. New York: Performance Concepts International.

Ryan, A.B. (2001) *Feminist Ways of Knowing: Towards Theorising the Person for Radical Adult Education*. Leicester: NIACE.

Ryle, G. (1949) *The Concept of Mind*. London: Hutchinson.

Sallis, E. and Jones, G. (2002) *Knowledge Management in Education: Enhancing Learning and Education*. London: Kogan Page.

Schein, E.H. and Kommers, D.W. (1972) *Professional Education*. New York: McGraw-Hill.

Schön, D.A. (1983) *The Reflective Practitioner: How Professionals Think in Action*. New York: Basic Books.

Schön, D.A. (1995) *Educating the Reflective Practitioner*. San Francisco, CA: Jossey Bass.

Scribner, S. (1988) *Head and Hand: An Action Approach to Thinking*. Columbus, OH: ERIC.

Shaw, M.E. (1981) *Group Dynamics: Psychology of Small Group Behavior*. New York: McGraw-Hill.

Sheehy, G. (1976) *Passages: Predictable Crises of Adult Life*. New York: Dutton.

Sork, T.J. (ed.) (1984) *Designing and Implementing Effective Workshops*. San Francisco: Jossey Bass.

Stephens, M.D. (1990) *Adult Education*. London: Cassell.

Stephens, M.D. and Roderick, G.N. (1971) *Teaching Techniques in Adult Education*. Newton Abbot: David & Charles.

Storant, M. and van den Bos, G.R. (eds) (1989) *The Adult Years: Continuity and Change*. Washington, DC: American Psychological Association.

Stromquist, N.P. (1997) *Literacy for Citizenship*. New York: State University of New York.

Sugarman, L. (1986) *Lifespan Development: Concepts, Theories and Interventions*. New York: Methuen.

Sutherland, P. (ed.) (1997) *Adult Learning: A Reader*. London: Kogan Page.

Taylor, E.W. (1998) *Theory and Practice of Transformative Learning: A Critical Review*. Columbus, OH: ERIC.

Tennant, M. (1988) *Psychology and Adult Learning*. London: Routledge.

Thomas, H. (1987) Perspectives on evaluation, in M. Hughes, P. Robbins and H. Thomas (eds) *Managing Education: The System and the Institution*, pp. 373–93. London: Cassell.

Thompson, J.L. (ed.) (1980) *Adult Education for a Change*. London: Hutchinson.

Thornton, A. and Stephens, M.D. (1977) *The University in its Region: The Extramural Contribution*. Nottingham: University of Nottingham.

Thorpe, M., Edwards, R. and Hanson, A. (1993) *Culture and Processes of Adult Learning*. London: Routledge.

Tight, M. (ed.) (1983) *Education for Adults*, vol. 1, *Adult Learning and Education*; vol. 2, *Opportunities for Adult Education*. Beckenham: Croom Helm.

Travers, R.M.W. (1964) *Introduction to Educational Research.* New York: Macmillan.

Tuijnman, A. and van der Kamp, M. (eds) (1992) *Learning Across the Lifespan: Theories, Research, Policies.* Oxford: Pergamon.

UNESCO (United Nations Educational, Scientific, and Cultural Organization) (1975a) *ISCED: International Standard Classification of Educational Data.* Paris: UNESCO.

UNESCO (United Nations Educational, Scientific, and Cultural Organization)(1975b) *Educational Radio and Television.* Paris: UNESCO.

UNESCO (United Nations Educational, Scientific, and Cultural Organization)(1976) *Nairobi: Recommendations on the Development of Adult Education: Declaration of Nairobi Conference.* Paris: UNESCO.

Unwin, P. (1994) *Group Research Projects in Adult Education.* Sheffield: University of Sheffield.

Valsiner, J. (ed.) (1995) *Child Development in Culturally Structured Environments.* Norwood, NJ: Ablex.

Verduin, J.R. (1983) *Adults Teaching Adults: Principles and Strategies.* Mansfield: University Associates.

Verma, J. (1995) Transformation of women's social roles in India, in J. Valsiner (ed.) *Child Development in Culturally Structured Environments.* Norwood, NJ: Ablex.

Vosniadou, S. (2001) *How Children Learn.* Paris: UNESCO.

Vygotsky, L.S. (1962) *Thought and Language.* Cambridge, MA: MIT Press.

Vygotsky, L.S. (1978) *Mind in Society: The Development of Higher Psychological Processes.* Cambridge, MA: Harvard University Press.

Wallis, J. (ed.) (1996) *Liberal Adult Education: The End of an Era?* Nottingham: Continuing Education Press.

Walters, S. (1996) *Gender in Popular Education.* London: Zed.

Welton, M. (1995) *In Defense of the Lifeworld.* New York: SUNY.

Whitehead, A.N. (1959) *The Aims of Education.* New York: Macmillan.

Wood, J. (1974) *How Do You Feel?* Englewood Cliffs, NJ: Prentice-Hall.

Youngman, F. (2000) *The Political Economy of Adult Education.* London: Zed.

Zander, A. (1982) *Making Groups Effective.* San Francisco, CA: Jossey Bass.

INDEX